The Violence of Austerity

The Violence
of Austerity

Edited by
Vickie Cooper and David Whyte

PlutoPress
www.plutobooks.com

First published 2017 by Pluto Press
345 Archway Road, London N6 5AA

www.plutobooks.com

Copyright © Vickie Cooper and David Whyte 2017

The right of the individual authors to be identified as the authors of this
work has been asserted by them in accordance with the Copyright, Designs
and Patents Act 1988.

British Library Cataloguing in Publication Data
A catalogue record for this book is available from the British Library

ISBN   978 0 7453 9948 5   Paperback
ISBN   978 0 7453 3746 3   Hardback
ISBN   978 1 7868 0062 6   PDF eBook
ISBN   978 1 7868 0064 0   Kindle eBook
ISBN   978 1 7868 0063 3   EPUB eBook

This book is printed on paper suitable for recycling and made from fully
managed and sustained forest sources. Logging, pulping and manufacturing
processes are expected to conform to the environmental standards of the
country of origin.

Typeset by Stanford DTP Services, Northampton, England

Simultaneously printed in the United Kingdom and United States of America

Contents

Acknowledgements

The origins of this book are a panel discussion on the 'violence of austerity' that was part of the conference, How Violent is Britain?, hosted by the University of Liverpool and the Centre for Crime and Justice Studies in May 2014. The conference brought together many of the authors in this book. Our first debt of gratitude is to Will McMahon, co-organiser of the conference, and who has supported us throughout this project. We are also grateful to others involved in organising the conference, especially Rachel Barrett, Rebecca Roberts and Arianna Silvestri. We would like to acknowledge those who participated in the conference and the Joseph Rowntree Charitable Foundation who supported it. Thanks also to the people at Criminal Justice Matters and Open Democracy who first published some of the ideas developed in the book. The support from our friends and colleagues at the Open University Harm and Evidence Research Collaborative and the University of Liverpool at different stages in the book's development is greatly appreciated. We want to acknowledge the warmth and generosity of the people at the International Institute for the Sociology of Law (IISL), Onati – especially Ainhoa Baños-Antigua, Susana Arrese, Rakel Lizarralde, Ainhoa Markuleta and Elvira Muñoz – for their support during our visits and in the use of its remarkable library. The IISL is a special place that should be protected and treasured. We are so grateful to our friends and family for their support throughout the long process of putting this book together, and especially thank Davey Blackie and Kirstie Wallace for sharing their home comforts and allowing us to complete the project in its final stages. There are a number of people who, although their names do not appear as authors, made important contributions to the development of the book. Thanks especially go to Joe Halewood and Rory O'Neill for their unacknowledged contributions. David Castle has been a consistent source of encouragement, and a model of professionalism in seeing the project through from its beginning to the end.

In particular, we thank the contributors to this book for sharing their hugely valuable insights and experiences, and also for putting up with what must have sometimes seemed like unreasonable requests and demands from us. We hope that it has all been worth it in the end.

Introduction:
The Violence of Austerity

Vickie Cooper and David Whyte

This book is about the devastatingly violent consequences of government policy conducted in the name of 'austerity'. It is about the toll of death and illness and injury that so-called austerity policies have caused. It is about the life-shattering violence caused by decisions that are made in parliamentary chambers and government offices. This book is about the violence of politics.

One decade after the Global Financial Crisis (GFC) and seven years since the Coalition government first rolled out a suite of public sector cuts it described as austerity measures, the cuts continue to devastate communities. Despite a widely reported softening of political rhetoric, as this book goes to press in early 2017, UK Chancellor of the Exchequer, Phillip Hammond has just signalled a further deepening of the cuts in setting out his plans to implement a further 18 per cent reduction of government spending. The 'Brexit' vote to leave Europe is directly connected to ongoing austerity policies and their devastating impact on communities. The claim that we cannot afford the European Union has helped to construct a political solitude and severance from other countries that involves, first and foremost, the closing down of borders and ending of free movement (or at least the qualified right to free movement). This agenda has been amplified by the politics of austerity. Although it may come as a surprise to politicians like David Cameron and George Osborne, the chief architects of the austerity package who then conveniently resigned when people voted to leave Europe, austerity has fanned the flames of a xenophobic politics, permitting powerful elites to reconfigure political alliances and forge new ones. What we describe in this Introduction as an attempt to *permanently dissemble the protection state* has been consolidated by post-Brexit political rhetoric as we see the devastating effects of 'austerity' materialise.

The contributions gathered in this book collectively present evidence showing that people most affected by austerity cuts are not only struggling under the financial strain but are becoming ill, physically and emotionally, and many are dying. Several chapters in the book demonstrate how austerity is a significant factor in suicide and suicidal thoughts. They tell how key groups feel humiliated, ashamed, anxious, harassed, stigmatised and depressed. The chapters illustrate how austerity affects people in wholly undignified ways such as having to compete for their own jobs and having to comply with welfare conditions in ways that chip away at their self-esteem and self-worth. People have to scream, kick and shout to have their most basic needs met. Street homeless people are forced to compete for the most basic provision of support by demonstrating that they are more 'in need' than the next street homeless person. Disabled people are forced to perform degrading incapacity assessments in order to prove that they are not fit to work and are entitled to state care and protection. Young people cannot find work that lifts them out of poverty and are forced to live in hostel-type accommodation. Women who urgently need to move out of abusive relationships are forced to stay with or return to their violent partners due to lack of adequate shelter provision. The physical and emotional pains of austerity are real and the effects are violent. People are fatigued, stressed, depressed and ill.

In 2013, David Stuckler and Sanjay Basu published their ground-breaking book, *The Body Economic: Why Austerity Kills*, in which they forensically detailed the deadly impact of austerity programmes on public health across the USA and Europe. Amongst their conclusions they showed that the total number of suicides had risen by 10,000 since the beginning of the financial crash in 2007, and millions of people across both continents had lost access to basic healthcare. In a series of hugely important analyses and testimonies, other writers, including Mary O'Hara, Kerry-Anne Mendoza and Jeremy Seabrook, have detailed the human impact of austerity in the UK.[1]

The first aim of the book is to extend those analyses to show how the toll of sickness and death created by the politics of austerity has left none but the most privileged in the UK untouched. Moreover, this scale of death and illness is simply part of the price that has been paid to maintain the basic structure of social inequality, whether measured by politicians as 'collateral damage' or by economists as 'externalities' (the unmeasured impact of financial transactions on bystanders who have nothing to do with the transaction). The upshot of those externalities, this collateral damage, is that attacks on the publicly funded services that are supposed to protect people in almost all spheres of social life have produced profoundly violent outcomes. The second aim is to reveal the intimate and intricate practices that generate this violence and to reveal the ordinary ways in which the violent effects of austerity are guaranteed by a range of public and private organisations. The violence of austerity is a bureaucratised form of violence that is implemented in routine and mundane ways. It is therefore a type of violence that is very different to those events we normally consider to be 'violent': being knocked down by a car, murder, assault, torture and so forth.

The book therefore seeks to make the reader more familiar with the violent capacities of those public and private institutions that have brought turmoil to the lives of those most affected by austerity: JobCentres, The Benefits Agency, Local Authorities, housing authorities, the criminal justice system, third sector programmes, employers in the public and private sectors and debt recovery companies. The chapters demonstrate how people's everyday experiences of austerity unfold through these institutions – the assemblage of powerful organisations that make up the state. The authors of this book are concerned with understanding people's routine and everyday experiences with public and private institutions in their lives as they try to make sense of the violence that has been inflicted upon key populations.

As well as pointing the finger at political leaders responsible for designing the policies that target marginal and vulnerable populations, we focus attention on the assemblage of bureaucracies and institutions through which austerity policies are made real. Not only do institutions help to convert policies from an abstract level to a material one, they are the very sites through which highly political strategies, like austerity, are de-politicised and their harmful effect made to appear normal and mundane. The routine order and administration involved in, for example, seeking asylum or determining whether a person is legally homeless can have lasting and damaging effects whereby the failure to properly support people exacerbates and reproduces other violent circumstances in their lives. These routine administration practices are not always understood as violent; but they are.

The evidence set out in this book leaves us in little doubt that much of the mundane, everyday business of austerity policies depends almost entirely upon the detached administration of violence. Where the state once acted as a buffer against social practices that put people at risk of harm and violence and provided essential protection for vulnerable groups, the contributions to this book show how the withdrawal of state support has the most devastating of consequences for vulnerable people. One key aim of the book is to identify where this violence comes from, its source and who is conducting it. The institutional structures responsible for implementing public sector cuts resemble a complex morass of rules and policies that is impenetrable and therefore un-opposable. The various chapters identify the politicians, the public and private servants and the institutions responsible for the violence of austerity and set out, in no uncertain terms, to demonstrate how these people and organisations have harmed key marginal groups whose welfare they are ultimately responsible for.

Before turning our attention to this task, this introduction will explore in detail what is meant by 'austerity' and how it has been used to legitimise a political process that we argue has comprehensively reshaped our relationship with government and the public sector.

AUSTERITY: A THREE-PART DECEPTION[2]

Austerity is a word that is used to describe a period of fiscal discipline in which governments make significant cuts to public expenditure as a means of reducing public debt. The principle idea underpinning austerity is that governments, by cutting expenditure, will encourage more private consumption and business investment and therefore more sustainable economic growth. Austerity, then, is built on the logic of 'expansionary fiscal consolidation',[3] whereby cuts to public expenditure are preferred over maintaining public expenditure and/or implementing tax increases. According to pro-austerity economists, Alberto Alesina and Roberto Perotti:[4]

> successful adjustments are those which aggressively tackle the expenditure side, particularly those components of it which are always thought of as untouchables: 'social security and governments wages and employment'.

In this model of expansionary fiscal consolidation, 'business investment is crowded in' and 'competitiveness improves', whereas more 'politically palatable policies'[5] (such as not cutting public expenditure) are seen to jeopardise the long-term aims and results of the fiscal consolidation model.

In what follows, we will demonstrate how this model of fiscal policy is underpinned by a series of deceptions that are designed to oversimplify the rationale for austerity and mislead the general public to believing that public sector cuts will bring about economic recovery. These deceptions together have constructed a 'logic' of austerity that legitimises fiscal consolidation. In the subsections that follow, we set out three major claims that underpin this deceptive logic of austerity.

The first deception: we all played a part in the crisis

In a key speech as opposition leader in 2008, David Cameron set out his explanation of the causes of the financial crisis:

> The economic assumptions that Gordon Brown made in the last decade now lie in ruins. His assumption that a government could preserve stability while running a budget deficit in a boom ... His assumption that we could permanently spend more than our income and build an economy on debt.[6]

Thus began a consistent theme in political discourse that has endured for a decade following the GFC: that austerity can be understood as a rational response to soaring levels of both personal and public debt, which in turn have resulted from a combination of reckless government spending and debt-fuelled personal consumption.

Yes, it was the Labour government that authorised and designed the bank bailout, and this did make a major dent in the public deficit, but it does not follow that all of the problems of the 'public deficit' can be blamed on 'overspending' governments. Indeed, the idea that the deficit was caused by government overspending is not supported by hard data. The Blair and Brown Labour governments, on average, borrowed less than the Thatcher and Major Conservative governments.[7] It is therefore not credible to simplify the problem as one of recklessness of Labour governments that had 'maxed out our credit card'[8] even when we take the bank bailout into consideration.

The key problem is not that 'we maxed out our credit card' but that there was a global financial crisis we couldn't control. To accept this means accepting that the problem wasn't an internal government or 'public' failure but that it was located in the global financial system. This is not to say that governments had nothing to do with this problem. The causes of the GFC can be found in constituent elements of neoliberal capitalism that the leading governments designed and shaped. The trading activities that produced the GFC – subprime mortgage lending, hedge funding, toxic asset trading, the uncontrolled boom in financial derivatives trading, and the part that the slashing of 'red tape' played in allowing these activities to take place under the radar – all magically disappeared from major political discussions on public deficit and austerity policy-making.

Of course, locating the economic problems we face in the failure to regulate the global economy is a rather more complex and less palatable explanation than the idea that we simply 'maxed out our credit card'. In a different, yet equally easy explanation for the GFC, fingers were pointed towards some key individuals in the banking sector (in the UK, they included Fred Goodwin of the Royal Bank of Scotland and Bob Diamond of Barclays), and at some particular practices (for example, badly judged investment and lending practices, especially 'toxic' mortgage lending), but those individuals and practices were always described in pathological terms: those to blame were 'rogues' or engaged in deviant practices. Those rogue bankers were easily framed as the willing accomplices of the previous incompetent governments that recklessly 'maxed out our credit card'. As a result, the systemic or normal machinery of corporate capitalism was not subject to any meaningful scrutiny or challenge, and was left untouched and, relatively speaking, unscathed.[9]

Regardless of whoever you believe was responsible for the GFC, it is the general public who have paid the price. As politicians drafted the austerity agenda, the daily routine of the financial business sector was merely cast as a peripheral issue, not an enduring aspect of the self-destructive tendencies of capitalism. It was not seen as the responsibility of the dominant political and financial class, charged with leading our countries in the global economy. Social policy professors John Clarke and

Janet Newman refer to an 'alchemy of austerity',[10] where the problem of the financial crisis magically becomes a public sector problem. The huge sums of public money used to save the banks from liquidation following the financial crisis of 2007/08 effectively turned a private sector problem into a problem of public debt. When the global financial markets began to creak in 2007, the former New Labour government in the UK presented a bank bailout package in the form of the 'Bank Recapitalization Fund', whereby the government provided cash payments, bought shares and set up bank loans to prevent the free fall of the banking economy.[11] At its peak, the total debt owed by the banks to the UK taxpayer was £1.162 trillion.[12] And, with much of the public shareholding of the banks sold off at a loss to the taxpayer, a substantial proportion of this subsidy will never be repaid.[13] The author of *Global Slump*, David McNally, estimates that, globally, $20 trillion was handed over to the banks at the height of the financial crash.[14]

It was not long before the financial crisis quickly became 'our' problem. Governments began appealing not to the banks but to the general public to tighten their belts and pull together in order to get us through these difficult times. On first announcing his 'emergency budget' in 2010, the former UK Chancellor of the Exchequer, George Osborne, preached that although the austerity economic policies are tough, 'they are fair' and that 'everyone will share in the rewards when we succeed'.[15]

This facade of 'togetherness' has played a key part in the ideological making of austerity. Not only did it help organise consent and support but helped deflect the blame for the deficit away from the businesses and private sector, framing it as a problem of the public's making. In response to appeals to reverse or slow down the austerity measures, the government consistently blamed us, the general population, or the government elected by the general population, for not budgeting properly and not managing our finances. Pro-austerity governments have therefore perpetuated the myth that *we* created the deficit problem through our own selfish making or recklessness, that we were all to blame in going along with this 'something for nothing economics'.[16]

This deception was aimed straight at the heart of the welfare state and reignited the government's vitriolic attack on welfare recipients:

'the explosion in welfare costs contributed to the growing structural budget deficit', stressing that reckless welfare spending was a major cause of a structural budget deficit and the reason 'why there is no money left'.[17]

The government had found its scapegoats for the financial crisis.

The second deception: austerity is necessary

If the first deception has a distinctly moralising tone that pits the 'good' austerity against the 'bad' public deficit,[18] the second deception draws upon a much more practical claim: that only fiscal pain can lead to economic recovery. In other words, it is only by accepting some harsh measures that we will get the economy back on its feet: there is no choice, no alternative; *only* austerity will lead to economic recovery.

UK governments have been remarkably successful in pedalling the deception that 'catastrophe' would 'ensue if we failed to deal' with our deficit problem instantly and with an austerity model.[19] In the same budget speech quoted above, George Osborne used the collapse of the Eurozone as a warning to the British public that if we don't get our finances in order, 'there will be no growth'.

Austerity, then, had been sold to the British people as the only game in town: as a credible and necessary fiscal policy where only public sector cuts will restore economic order. This view was way out of step with the dominant view of mainstream economists. Just as there is a consensus of economists who point to internal economic causes of the GFC, there emerged a consensus of economists who appealed for a Keynesian approach that would maintain high levels of public spending to ride out the crisis.[20] But successive UK governments have rejected any such proposals that challenge the fiscal consolidation model. As an illustration of the government's dogmatic commitment to the austerity fiscal model, it is worth remembering the United Nations (UN) Housing Envoy, Raquel Rolnik's visit to the UK in 2013 to gain an understanding of the depth of the housing crisis and the impact of austerity measures. Rolnik appealed to the then Coalition government to reverse the painful impacts of austerity measures such as the bedroom tax and suggested that the government should:

[A]ssess and evaluate the impact of the welfare reform in relation to the right to adequate housing of the most vulnerable individuals and groups, in light of existing data and evidence; consider whether particular measures are having a disproportionate impact on specific groups.[21]

Rather than respond with diplomacy, the then Conservative Minister for Housing, Kris Hopkins, to whom a number of Rolnik's recommendations were directed, dismissed these comments as 'Marxist diatribe'.[22] Conservative MP, Stewart Jackson, called her a 'loopy Brazilian leftie'.[23] These responses sum up the arrogant and imperious mood of the UK political leaders and their blind commitment to the socially destructive impacts of austerity. Rather than listening to the persuasive body of mainstream opinion on how to mitigate the negative and violent effects of austerity, political leaders shut down all counter opinion and continued to push the line that austerity is a *necessary* evil.

One country that didn't follow the austerity route was Iceland. Following the financial collapse in 2008, the Icelandic government initially developed a rescue plan to bail out the banks that involved compensating shareholders and foreign investors and putting the financial burden back on to the taxpayers and national bank.[24] After several weeks of public protests, the government stepped down, the austerity package was abandoned and an alternative set of reforms were put on the table. In the end, Iceland did not bail out its banks, but allowed the losses of the financial crisis to fall more directly on to shareholders, foreign investors, bankers and the financial elite. Following two referenda in which the people rejected the International Monetary Fund's (IMF) austerity package, Iceland brought about economic stability using a model that was very different to the austerity one used in the UK and other countries. Although forced to implement some public spending cuts, Iceland managed to safeguard its welfare state, healthcare and education system and shift the burden of taxation on to the shoulders of higher income families. Providing proof that austerity is not the *only* road to economic recovery, Iceland's economy has rebounded and is now heralded as one of the first countries to surpass pre-crisis economic output.[25] To put this in perspective, Iceland went from being one of ten economies critically spiralling into financial collapse, to being an exemplary model of economic recovery – all within a decade.

It is not beyond reason that the UK could have followed a similar route to recovery. The UK's deficit is not especially large in relation to other economies. Indeed, if measured as a ratio of debt to GDP, the UK's balance sheet was in a much stronger position than Iceland's following the crash. Its debt to GDP ratio is now comparable to France, slightly higher than Germany, around half the level of Japan and substantially lower than the USA. Neither is it unusually large when placed in historical context. The UK's 2013 debt to GDP ratio has been higher in a total of 200 out of the last 250 years.[26]

Yet the UK government has failed to consider any alternative economic strategies, ridiculing anyone that dared to suggest it could. George Osborne continually warned that the UK was 'on the brink of bankruptcy' and international investors would turn away from the UK if strict fiscal measures were not implemented.[27] While Theresa May, in her first speech as prime minister, rejected austerity as a strategy, her government has continued to implement public sector cuts at exactly the same pace as the previous government. In the first Autumn statement made by Chancellor Philip Hammond in 2016, none of Osborne's planned cuts were reversed. Indeed, events in 2016 show that even after imposing such punitive public expenditure targets, the financial control and planned reduction of the deficit promised by Osborne have been placed out of reach by *global* economic forces. Towards the end of 2016 it became clear that the declining value of the pound following the Brexit vote had forced the government to abandon the same deficit reduction target that the absolute necessity of austerity narrative is based upon.

In this second great deception, then, austerity was cast as the only model that would lead us to economic recovery. It was a model that was prescribed by the same wise people in government who told us that it was the fault either of the previous government or our own reckless credit habits. The third deception is one that has come to characterise UK government talk about austerity using the familiar cliché, 'we're all in it together'.

The third deception: we're all in it together

This political trope is difficult to square with the real, lived experiences of austerity and the effects it is having on targeted groups. Austerity policies have been designed in such a way that target the most vulnerable and marginal groups in society, hitting them harder than any other income group. As former Labour Cabinet minister Michael Meacher put it:

> We were not all in it together when the burden of the cuts was split 80 per cent on reduced benefits and only 20 per cent on higher taxes, and even the higher taxes were mainly the VAT increase which impacts highly regressively on the poor. Nor is it a fair carve-up of the post-crash cake that average real wages have fallen 7 per cent while the richest 1,000 in the UK population, according to the *Sunday Times* Rich List, have doubled their wealth over this short period to more than half a trillion pounds.[28]

Austerity is a class project that disproportionately targets and affects working class households and communities and, in so doing, protects concentrations of elite wealth and power. The policies levelled at working class households have barely touched the elite. Neither have suicide rates in the political class or amongst city stockbrokers risen in the austerity period. Cuts to the National Health Service (NHS) have barely affected those who can afford private healthcare. And elderly politicians and retired bankers have not experienced record rates of morbidity (for an analysis of record mortality rates in the general population, see Chapter 2 by Danny Dorling).

Since 2003, the bottom tenth of UK household income earners have seen their income fall by 8 per cent, compared to 1 per cent for those in the top tenth.[29] This widening income gap is a combined result of an increase in living costs, a sharp decline in real wage income and withdrawal of benefit payments. Since 2003–13, domestic energy prices have increased by 150 per cent, water bills by 70 per cent and public transport by 88 per cent.[30] Between 2008 and 2013, food prices increased by 28 per cent[31] (see Chapter 9 by Ruth London on fuel poverty and Chapter 8 by Rebecca O'Connell and Laura Hamilton on food poverty).

In stark contrast, we have seen a consolidation of wealth amongst the top income earners; the UK's richest 1000 people saw their wealth increase by £138 billion between 2009 and 2013. As austerity policies were being rolled out, the Coalition government made sure that high income earners would be least affected and lowered tax rates for people earning over £150,000 from 50 per cent to 45 per cent.[32] Since 2010, low income groups have found out the hard way what fiscal consolidation entails: it consolidates the income of the rich while ensuring that the poor pay for costly, and deadly, policies. Incredibly, there are now five times as many working families in the UK living below the poverty line than there were in the 1970s.[33] As the academic Jamie Peck has pointed out, austerity is always:

> about making others pay the process of fiscal retrenchment. In the language of the Occupy movement, it is something that the 1%, who continue to accumulate wealth and power at an alarming rate, *does* to the 99%.[34]

Such is the level of cuts directed at the working class that some have argued we are witnessing a throwback to the class conservatism of the 1980s.[35] The effects of Conservative policies on working class communities in the 1980s, and the avalanche of reforms that gave way to free-market policies and post-Fordist labour relations, have ultimately resulted in the deeply entrenched and divisive class composition that we see in the UK today.[36] With a hugely expanded precarious labour force and insecure housing landscape, communities are increasingly fragmented. This fragmentation is set to magnify as austerity policies take effect in communities already beset by high unemployment and dwindling community resources.

Contrary to the ideological churn that 'work pays', people in low paid, low skilled employment have about the same chance of moving out of poverty as their unemployed neighbours. Since 2008, real wages in the UK have dropped by 10.4 per cent, compared to a 14 per cent increase in Germany and an 11 per cent increase in France. Employers are increasingly using zero-hours contracts to employ staff for less wages than permanent, secured workers. With approximately 1 million people currently employed on zero-hours contracts, such people can expect to earn 50 per cent less per hour than the average worker. Such insecure employment conditions make it difficult for people to pay for essential living expenses that underpin basic quality of life (see Chapter 6 by Emma Bond and Simon Hallsworth).[37]

These precarious living experiences are made worse by a decline in housing security and housing quality, where both middle and low income groups struggle to find basic, affordable housing that matches their wage income. Adults at the bottom end of income earnings experience poorer quality, more insecure and more expensive housing than at any other time in the history of the welfare state.[38] But the housing landscape is especially grim for people in receipt of welfare benefits who are severely disadvantaged by austerity housing policies such as the bedroom tax and the 'benefit cap'.[39] As the bedroom tax forces people to downsize, pay the rent shortfall or fall into rent arrears, the benefit cap puts families with children at the greatest risk of falling into debt, even when living in cheap, affordable housing. According to housing welfare consultant and housing activist, Joe Halewood,[40] families with children are now deemed to be a 'financial risk' by a range of housing providers because the benefit cap leaves them with little or no income to pay their rent. Thus, the likelihood that families in receipt of benefits will fall into rent arrears and that housing providers will not receive their full rent payments pushes families further down the bottom of the list of 'desirable tenants'. The extreme level of housing poverty is a direct result of austerity cuts that put families on the precipice of becoming homeless.[41]

Since 2010, the number of children defined as living in absolute poverty has risen by half a million.[42] It is projected that child poverty will worsen significantly over the coming years.[43] The impoverishment of children as a direct result of austerity is accounted for by a combination of cuts to welfare benefits, the driving down of wages and poor housing provision. Poverty and deprivation affecting families with children further increases the likelihood of child mortality and premature death (see Chapter 7 by Joanna Mack). The children of this generation coming from the poorest households will fare much worse than children of the previous generation. Current adult generations already fare worse than their parents' generation, especially in relation to housing, job security, pensions and personal debt.

Austerity has exacerbated all kinds of insecurities and uncertainties (on the effect of austerity on the peace process in Northern Ireland, see Chapter 12 by Daniel Holder) and we are already seeing the devastating effects on the mental health of the most vulnerable (see Chapter 1 by Mary O'Hara).

In this book, the reader will find some overlap between chapters where several authors refer to the same cases and discuss the same body of evidence. This is because peoples' lived experience of austerity is amplified by the following social categories: sex, ethnicity, citizenship, age, disability, family size and geographical location. Those experiences determine the extent to which individuals and families are adversely affected. For example, the homeless will certainly experience the pains of austerity in ways that do not affect housed populations (see Chapter 18 by Daniel McCulloch). Journalist Kerry-Anne Mendoza also claims that around two thirds of those affected by the introduction of the bedroom tax were disabled people, a group that has suffered particularly under austerity cuts (see Chapter 3 by John Pring).[44]

Moreover, as political sociologist Daniela Tepe-Belfrage has argued, gender is a key marker in determining :

the largest drop in disposable income since the crisis has been experienced by women. Women are also more likely to be employed in the public sector or be subcontracted to the state via private-sector organisations (for example, in the form of cleaners or carers). As the UK's austerity policy regime has especially targeted public services, women have been particularly affected, facing wage drops and job losses. Austerity also has a 'double-impact' on women as, by virtue of being disproportionally in caring roles, they tend to be more likely to depend on the public provision of social services such as childcare services or care provision.[45]

Research published by the Northern Rock Foundation and Trust for London found that austerity has had a sudden and dramatic impact on services supporting women victims of domestic violence. Between 2009/10 and 2010/11 there was a 31 per cent cut in the Local Authority funding for domestic and sexual violence support. The report stated clearly that: 'These cuts in service provision are expected to lead to increases in this violence'.[46] The report noted that 230 women were being turned away by the organisation Women's Aid because of a lack of provision in 2011.

The multiple and intersectional nature of class, gender, disability and race means that, for example, black women will be exposed to austerity policies differently to white women. Social support for black women, already paltry, has been cut to the bone in the austerity period (see Chapter 11 by Akwugo Emejulu and Leah Bassel), just as support for refugees and people seeking asylum has been subject to the confluence of a range of policy prejudices (see Chapter 5 by Victoria Canning).

At the same time, what we are witnessing is a much more naked form of class politics. Rapidly growing levels of inequality have produced some ugly political phenomena, not least the racism that has been linked to the Brexit vote. But in many ways, Brexit merely brought to the surface the tensions being felt amongst the most marginalised. And, of course, some of the groups who have suffered racist and anti-poverty attacks in the wake of the Brexit vote were precisely the same people that suffered the most under the axe of austerity (see Chapter 24 by Jon Burnett). Crown Prosecution Service (CPS) data, for example, shows that hate crimes against people with disabilities more than doubled between 2008 and 2014. This trend has been widely attributed to 'benefits propaganda'.[47] Although it is estimated that around 4000 disability hate crimes have been prosecuted by the CPS since 2007, the Disability Hate Crime Network believes that up to 60,000 disability hate crimes occur every year in the UK.[48]

The fiscal policies implemented in the period following the 2007/08 crash have served as a pincer movement: drawing back even more of the social wage entitlements of the working class while at the same time ring fencing the elite wealth that remains intact at the top of the social structure. Nothing could be clearer: we certainly are *not* all in this together; we have all experienced austerity very differently.

The real politics of austerity 1: fortress austerity

Ultimately, the purpose of the violence of austerity is not simply to stabilise the economic system in the aftermath of the financial crisis but to stabilise it in a particular form that enables the rich to sustain opportunities for wealth generation. As Mark Blyth puts it, 'Austerity is not just the price of saving the banks. It's the price that the banks want somebody else to pay.'[49] And this 'somebody' is pretty much certain to be poor or working class. The fiscal consolidation policies implemented in the period following the 2007/08 crash have ensured even greater levels of inequality, ideologically supported by a crude trickle-down rationale. The idea of the trickle-down effect is commonly associated with supply-side economics, a theory that sets out how economic benefits for all can be most effectively created by making it easier for businesses to produce (or supply) goods and services. In fact, there are very few economists who have ever actually been stupid enough to advocate 'trickle-down' economics, since there is virtually no evidence anywhere that can conclusively support trickle-down or supply-side economic theory, even when the research has been conducted by right-wing economists. Prominent neoliberal economist Thomas Sowell, has gone so far as denying that trickle-down theory has *ever* existed as a serious idea in economics.[50] As supply-side economics is palpably revealed as little more than a convenient untruth, even the most die-hard of die-hard neoliberals are now 'trickle-down' deniers.

Indeed, we find a similar contradiction in the public statements made by the key International Financial Institutions (IFIs), the IMF and the World Bank. On the one hand, speeches are made, and position papers are published that disavow austerity, arguing that it has had a negative impact on economic recovery.[51] On the other hand, those IFIs continue to force austerity measures through structural adjustment programmes and loan conditions (see Chapter 19 by Rob Knox). This apparent contradiction stems from the inability of politicians to defend austerity on economic grounds, rather than on political or moral grounds. In other words, national governments and IFIs design and push policies that their economists cannot now credibly defend in public.

As we have argued, austerity is basically a strategy for the advancement of neoliberal policies that maintain and indeed worsen social inequality. For neoliberal governments and the various international institutions, dealing with public debt is not necessarily an intractable problem, but rather an opportunity that has allowed austerity to enhance the dominance of corporate and political elites. The winners and losers are clear. This book is mainly about the losers. However, we cannot ignore the fact that austerity has had its winners. As social theorist Andrew Sayer has noted, austerity policies imply a switch from taxing the rich to borrowing from them.[52] A deepening cycle of indebtedness and the need to pay off the deficit exposes governments to private bond lenders (as well as to future repayment of government bonds). Of course, interest rates vary wildly so that, currently, we find the UK government paying interest rates of around a quarter those paid by the Greek government to service its loans. As the welfare state is squeezed and wages are forced down, this also places employers in a structurally strong position. The rich thus stand to gain either way: as employers or as lenders.

As an ideological set of 'truths', then, austerity enables governments and politicians to advance spurious claims that economic consolidation leads to recovery, to downplay the counter-evidence exposing these myths, to foreground the predatory demands of business, and to politically cut out marginalised groups who fail to adjust to the impossibly harsh conditions of austerity. If one fact stands above all others as an indication that austerity is not all it claims to be it is that the UK's national debt has risen by at least 50 per cent since the austerity programme began in 2010.[53] It is this fact that demonstrates most clearly that the politics of austerity is less concerned with reducing the deficit than it is with preserving the wealth of those at the top.

The real politics of austerity 2: extending wealth by growing inequality and enabling dispossession

Of course, none of this is new; none of this deviates from the general path of economic development that the UK and the rest of the 'developed' world has followed for over 40 years. More than a decade before the 2007/08 financial crisis, philosopher John McMurtry noted that cuts to public services were attacking the 'life-serving systems of social bodies' in order to ensure public resources are 're-channelled to the expansion of money-to-more-money circuits with no commitment to life function'. The pattern of redistributing resources from public to private hands is so aggressive, he argued, 'that the signifiers of its agents do not disguise the underlying violence of the appropriation – "axing social programmes", "slashing public services", "subjecting societies to shock treatments" and so on'.[54]

According to the geographer, David Harvey, state reform involving 'corporatization and privatization of hitherto public assets'[55] represent the 'cutting edge' of accumulation in advanced capitalist societies. In his reappraisal of Karl Marx's concept of primitive accumulation, Harvey introduced the widely cited concept of 'accumulation by dispossession'.[56] It is a concept that is used to explain the connection between processes of 'accumulation' and 'dispossession' in the production of capital. Harvey claims that the transfer of state assets to private ownership always implies a process of dispossession and general loss of rights. Thus, aspects of neoliberal reform that we are all now familiar with – privatisation, commodification, financialisation and the recalibration of people's entitlement to state services and funds – result in the redistribution and accumulation of wealth for some, while ensuring the loss of rights for others. Harvey claims that accumulation by dispossession is the driving force of contemporary capitalism, and that this process of capital accumulation has become more predatory and violent under austerity programmes.

As journalist Aditya Chakrabortty has noted, even if it is rarely mentioned, privatisation in this period of austerity has enabled the government to 'bring much-needed cash into the Treasury and make [the Chancellor's] sums add up'.[57] Perhaps the most significant privatisations since 2010 have been the selling off of Royal Mail, and the re-sale of the public shares of banks that the taxpayer bailed out. Other privatisations central to the austerity drive have been the privatisation of probation and other criminal justice services (see Chapter 20 by Maureen Mansfield and Vickie Cooper) and the 2015 sell-off of the government-owned Remploy. Remploy was originally established under the terms of the Disabled Persons (Employment) Act 1944 to employ disabled persons in specialised factories. It has now been grotesquely transformed to play a central role in driving the government's welfare-to-work strategy targeted at disabled people. Remploy was sold to the US firm Maximus.

There is a more silent privatisation underway involving the drip-drip transfer of responsibility for delivery to the private sector as the space vacated by public sector providers opens up new markets. Those new markets that have been created as a result of welfare reforms include the creation of a significant new section of the labour market through the introduction of workfare placements (see Chapter 4 by Jon Burnett and David Whyte) and the recruitment of private sector providers to assess people as fit to work. The company ATOS that so spectacularly failed to implement government policy in this latter function walked away relatively unscathed, despite widespread public and political anger over the way it assessed people. The company that followed in ATOS' profitable footsteps, Maximus (yes, the same company that now owns Remploy), has a contract reportedly worth half a billion pounds.

Following the 2010 'emergency budget', The government warned that the welfare state must make do with cuts totalling £11 billion over the following five years, while the business community were offered a suite of reforms – including 'lower [tax] rates, simpler rules and greater certainty'[58] – to ensures their prosperity and longevity in the market.

Corporation tax has been cut from 30 per cent to 20 per cent since 2008, a direct policy translation of trickle-down economics that can not merely be attributed to austerity policies, but is part of the wider package of measures that are supposed to encourage economic recovery.

Indeed, some sectors have been seen as a vehicle for economic recovery and therefore singled out for special treatment. This partly explains the lack of any meaningful regulatory change in the financial sector but also why some high revenue sectors, such as unconventional oil and gas – or 'fracking', are being singled out for special treatment (see Chapter 16 by Will Jackson, Helen Monk and Joanna Gilmore). In July 2013 the government announced that the fracking industry would receive a major reduction in its tax burden. Shale gas producers were told that they would be asked to pay just 30 per cent tax on profits compared to 62 per cent normally paid by the oil and gas industry. In response, Andrew Pendleton of UK Friends of the Earth observed:

> Promising tax hand-outs to polluting energy firms that threaten our communities and environment, when everyone else is being told to tighten their belts, is a disgrace.[59]

The security sector has also reaped the rewards, with private companies recruited to police evictions, repossessions and anti-austerity protests (see Chapter 17 by Kirsteen Paton and Vickie Cooper and Chapter 22 by Steven Speed). Private rental companies and landlords have significantly increased their share of earnings. The relatively unprotected housing market, which renders tenants vulnerable, has remained lucrative. While wages have stagnated and average incomes have fallen in real terms, private rents have risen at a steady pace, uninterrupted, since April 2010.[60] As the author of *Austerity Bites*, and contributor to this book, Mary O'Hara noted, so-called payday lenders – the companies that provide high interest, high risk loans to people with low credit ratings – have been recording windfall profits. In 2013 Wonga, for example, issued £1.2 billion worth of loans to 1 million lenders, and had a total value worth more than three times the entire credit union sector[61] (see also Chapter 10 by David Ellis).

Meanwhile, as a number of commentators have noted, the major corporations that are not finding the opportunities to profit are simply sitting it out, and hording large amounts of cash, as the public sector crumbles.[62] Ultimately, the most powerful players in corporate capitalism have emerged from this crisis largely unscathed and intact. Since July 2011, the share value of FTSE 250 – the largest 250 companies trading on the London stock exchange – has risen by 60 per cent.[63] The system of financialisation that has brought us to this point has been the standout beneficiary of austerity. Financial markets and financial institutions were prioritised for emergency spending protection, demonstrating that the reflex of the political system is to preserve and defend the key actors in the financial system even when those being preserved are the greatest threats to our social and economic sustainability. In other words, austerity has consolidated and maintained the pace of capital accumulation in dominant sectors of the economy.

The real politics of austerity 3: permanently dissembling the 'protection state'

Underlying austerity is exactly the same model of fiscal purging that modern liberal states have been rolling out since the early 1980s. Austerity's fiscal consolidation policy stems from the same economic model that promotes growth through private investment and freeing-up the movement of capital. Austerity policies enable governments to accelerate neoliberal programmes and advance modern capitalism like never before. Now, in austerity Britain, the scale of cutbacks has resulted in a permanent 'disassembling of the state'[64] whereby the former Coalition and Conservative governments have introduced a suite of irrevocable reforms to welfare benefits, housing, pensions, higher education, privatisation and so forth. As economist Paul Krugman succinctly put it:

> the austerity drive in Britain isn't really about debt and deficits at all; it's about using deficit panic as an excuse to dismantle social programs … the drive for austerity was about using the crisis, not solving it.[65]

Around 631,000 jobs in the public sector have been lost since 2010. It is anticipated that an additional million public sector jobs will be lost in the UK before 2020.[66] Such a sudden and brutal axing of public sector funding and jobs is unprecedented in the UK and probably in Northern Europe.

However, as austerity analyst Mark Blyth has noted, the cuts have not hit all parts of the public sector equally.[67] Indeed, central government and centralised public services have remained relatively unscathed. Around 50 per cent of the cuts have been targeted at the welfare system and local government. In other words, the services most required by the vulnerable have been those singled out for disassembling. At the time of writing, the fallout of a decimated care sector has left many older people and the most vulnerable without even skeleton support provision. Indeed, one of the best estimates shows that 24 per cent fewer elderly people now receive support than in 2011, and those estimates project that an ever increasing proportion of people will be effectively removed from the care system for years to come.[68] And of course there is a process of double victimisation in which the most vulnerable people living in Local Authority areas where needs are greatest will suffer disproportionately more than elsewhere. As commentator Tom Crewe has observed, in Liverpool the cuts have resulted in a reduction of council spending per head of £390 compared with £2.29 in Wokingham in the South East of England.[69] The patterns of wealth and poverty that the austerity agenda embeds are so predictable that it no longer makes sense to talk of a 'postcode lottery'; those patterns look more like a 'postcode certainty' in which your chances of winning or losing are greatly magnified by the determining factor of the Local Authority area in which you live and work.

Some key decisions have been made to determine which public services are targeted the most. Compare, for example, cuts to the police budget with cuts to regulatory authorities – the bodies that we expect to police the business sector. Cuts to police spending since 2011 have amounted to 14–20 per cent of the total budget.[70] Contrast this with the Health and Safety Executive, facing a 46 per cent cut to its budget[71] (see Chapter 14 by Hilda Palmer and David Whyte). Moreover, some Local Authorities have been so decimated they are now left without any environmental health inspectors (see Chapter 13 by Steve Tombs). The Department for Environment, Food and Rural Affairs is said to be the most severely targeted government department, with a real term cut of 57 per cent.[72] The Environment Agency which sits within this department is facing paralysing cuts (see Chapter 15 by Charlotte Burns and Paul Tobin). Austerity, by targeting the areas of public spending that protect us the most from threats to our well-being and our lives, has wholly unravelled our system of social protection. In many ways, this is the ideological dream of neoliberal technicians: to unravel the 'flabby' sectors of the state that get in the way of enterprise.

It is clear that the axe has not fallen with equal force across public services. Cuts to the police in the UK since austerity measures were introduced do not come close to the level of cuts dealt out to Local Authority services and welfare support, and have by no means interrupted the expansive control functions of policing or the prisons significantly (see Chapter 23 by Rizwaan Sabir, Chapter 21 by Joe Sim, Chapter 20 by Maureen Mansfield and Vickie Cooper and Chapter 6 by Emma Bond and Simon Hallsworth).

The real prize that austerity offers neoliberal governments is the opportunity to complete the core project of the neoliberal governments of the 1980s: to simultaneously eradicate the areas of state provision and expenditure that are seen as a threat to neoliberal structural adjustment.[73] The priority, then as now, is not the complete 'rollback' or eradication of the state but to diminish the parts of the state that stand in the way of structural adjustment. The effect of ensuring that the burden of cuts falls on Local Authorities and on essential social services that are locally administered is to concentrate the power and authority of whatever is left of the public sector in Whitehall and the Cabinet.

Austerity, then, is a political strategy based on myth, deception and misinformation. In this sense, it is a moralising discourse that supports a viciously immoral politics. Florian Schui's long history of 'austerity' argues:

> Arguments for and against austerity have undergone many permutations but the basic pattern has remained unchanged: proponents of austerity argue on the basis of morality and politics, while their critics use the language of economic efficiency to challenge their viewpoint.[74]

The sophistication of the austerity narrative, then, is that it enables a kind of smash and grab politics to be supported by a deeply moral and ideological set of principles. Austerity is about class domination, but it is also about providing a narrative that is apparently more plausible and more complex than class domination; a narrative that brings us all together around a common sense:[75] *we* maxed out our credit card; *we* are all in this together; and *we* all stand to gain after the dust has cleared.

As we have seen, twenty-first-century austerity policies in the UK cannot be defended on grounds of economic efficiency or necessity. However, in being able to see the real aims and desires of the political elite, and how those aims and desires are connected intimately to the interests of the financial and business elites, we begin to understand austerity as little more than a cruel and violent strategy of class domination.[76]

INSTITUTIONAL VIOLENCE

One of the consequences of understanding austerity as a profoundly violent set of policies is that we need to rethink how we talk about and respond to this violence. Violence committed at the institutional level is not always considered in the same way as 'interpersonal' violence. The violence of austerity is not delivered by 'street gangs' or by the individuals that are typically the focus of public anxieties and tabloid moral panics. The violence of austerity is delivered by smartly dressed people sitting behind desks. And if we are looking for people to blame for the violence of austerity, we may not get very far. In front of the very obvious rogues gallery of politicians who designed this agenda – and refused to change course when its human consequences were in clear view – from David Cameron and George Osborne to Theresa May and Phillip Hammond, stand the armies of civil servants, government departments and Local Authorities. And in front of them stand the armies of private officials in companies like G4S and ATOS and public officials in benefits offices and housing trusts.

If nothing else, austerity reveals the 'ordinary' and 'mundane' bureaucratised face of violence. This is the common thread that runs through every chapter in this book. Each contribution has in some way uncovered the intricate relationship between political violence and institutions that are tasked with implementing and administering key political objectives. It is *institutional* violence.[77] This is a form of violence that can be understood as a means of force which is not simply acted upon, but organised and administered through *legitimate* means.

'Institutional violence' therefore describes the ordinary and mundane violence that make up the lived experience of austerity; the lived experience of feeling humiliated, anxious and vilified. To talk about institutional violence means that we need to see violence not as 'exceptional' or 'unusual' events but 'ordinary' and 'mundane' processes that routinely and over time deteriorate our mental and physical health. Governments rely on the institutional machinery to translate economic reforms into policy and administer them in ways that achieve their main goals.

The very long line of twentieth-century thinkers that have exposed in detail the intrinsically violent foundations of the state's political power include Walter Benjamin,[78] Emma Goldman,[79] Vandana Shiva,[80] Max Weber[81] and C. Wright Mills.[82] Hannah Arendt, whose essay *On Violence* sought to dissect the relation between political power and the organisation of violence, argued that the use of force to achieve political ends had become so normalised that the 'enormous role that violence plays in human affairs' had become 'taken for granted and therefore neglected'.[83]

Perhaps we have become so accustomed to the ease with which people are evicted and made homeless, or to the food banks, the street-begging and the epidemics in suicides, that we do not make the most obvious of observations: that the age that we live in is one in which the political violence of the state is becoming normalised. One consequence of this process of normalisation is that the violent effects of austerity are not always immediately visible. Institutional violence does not always inflict sudden pain in the way that interpersonal violence might (although in some instances it does); the pain inflicted by austerity generally unfolds over time, at a deteriorative pace. In this sense, the violence of austerity is best understood as 'slow violence'.[84] Indeed, social policy scholars are now predicting that the most damaging effects of austerity will take years to be fully realised because of the time lag between the implementation of austerity policies and the way in which they impact.

It is the slow, deteriorative process of institutional violence imposed by austerity that gives it its force. It is precisely because this violence pervades people's lives over long periods of time that the violence of austerity carries an ever present *threat* of physical and/or psychological harm. The various forms of violence detailed in this book (destitution, eviction, the seizure of possessions, homelessness, deportation, going without a meal or having electricity or gas cut off) have now become a very real possibility for a fast-growing section of the population, and, as a number of chapters in this book document, it is the threat of violence that has become absolutely central to the power that *institutional* violence wields over its targets.

CONCLUSION: CHALLENGING THE VIOLENCE OF AUSTERITY

The violence of austerity does not have to be viewed as a natural or normal response of governments. Indeed, the task of opponents of austerity is to ensure that its violence is not normalised or taken for granted as a legitimate political strategy. It is not normal to subject the most vulnerable sections of the population to such pain, humiliation and degradation. Elsewhere, political strategies have been successful in holding the political class accountable, rather than scapegoating and vilifying the poor. After the 2008 crash and following 16 weeks of public protests in Iceland, the then Prime Minister Haarde became the first political casualty of the financial crisis. In January 2009, Geir Haarde announced his resignation after discovering a malignant tumour in his throat. Thus, a 'great cannibalistic frenzy'[85] began within his party as other politicians and key players in the crisis also resigned, until finally the government was dissolved in February 2009.

To protect public expenditure, safeguard health, education and welfare systems and maintain dignity in the workplace and the home, we need to reverse the effects of the GFC and hold the main winners of financialisation responsible. It is imperative that we reverse the effects of the crisis. Indeed, abandoning the literally suicidal course that we are currently on and finding real ways of addressing inequalities and the concentration of wealth is our only hope of protecting against the coruscating violence that another economic crisis will certainly bring. And we hope that one contribution made by this book is to show that there is no shortage of opportunity for building solidarity around resistance to the violence of austerity.

An impressively diverse body of activist groups and campaigns that have directly confronted the government in the courts and on the streets include groups defending the NHS (Keep Our NHS public[86]), housing, homeless and welfare rights organisations (Anti Bedroom Tax Federation for Greater Manchester,[87] Radical Housing Network,[88] Axe the Housing Act,[89] Black Triangle[90] and Generation Rent[91]), women's campaign groups (including Sisters Uncut,[92] the Fawcett Society,[93] Women's Aid[94] and Rape Crisis[95]), black community organisations (including Black Activists Rising Against the Cuts,[96] Imkaan[97] and Southall Black Sisters[98]), economic justice activists (including UK Uncut,[99] the Tax Justice Network[100] and Debt Resistance UK[101]) and trade unionists (including the People's Assembly Against Austerity[102] and the Anti-Cuts campaign[103]).

Some campaign groups that have taken their anti-austerity demands to the government are represented in this book (including Boycott Workfare,[104] Fuel Poverty Action,[105] Disabled People Against the Cuts,[106] the Hazards Campaign[107]) alongside campaign groups who work closely with some of the book's contributors (including Psychologists Against Austerity,[108] Focus E15 Mothers[109] and The Ark Manchester[110]).

There is, then, no shortage of organised opposition to the austerity agenda. Some of the chapters in this book help to shine a light on those anti-austerity strategies of resistance. It is in this spirit of resistance that the book asks how the violence of austerity can be turned back on its architects.

NOTES

Websites were last accessed 31 December 2016.

1. Mary O'Hara, *Austerity Bites: A Journey to the Sharp End of Cuts in UK*, Bristol: Policy Press, 2015; Jeremy Seebrook, *Cut Out: Living Without Welfare*, London: Pluto Press, 2016; Kerry-Anne Mendoza, *Austerity: The Demolition of the Welfare State and the Rise of the Zombie Economy*, Oxford: New Internationalist, 2015.

2. We are influenced by a number of authors who develop a similar argument, including Kelly Anne Mendoza, Barry Kushner, Mark Blyth, Richard Seymore and Chunky Mark whose film *Austerity is a Scam* should be seen by everyone who wants to understand the violence of austerity.

3. Pasquale Foresti and Ugo Marani, 'Expansionary fiscal consolidations: theoretical underpinnings and their implications for the Eurozone', *Contributions to Political Economy*, 33 (1), 2014, 19–33.

4. A. Alesina and R. Perotti, 'Fiscal expansions and adjustments in OECD countries', Working paper No. 5214, National Bureau of Economic Research, Cambridge, MA, 1995, p. 23.

5. Ibid.

6. This speech, made at the offices of Bloomberg, the financial news and media firm, on 17 October 2008 can be found in full at: www.theguardian.com/politics/2008/oct/17/davidcameron-economy

7. B. Kushner and S. Kushner, *Who Needs the Cuts? Myths of the Economic Crisis*, London: Hesperus, 2013.

8. D. Blanchflower, 'An economics lesson for David Cameron', *New Statesman*, 11 June 2011, available at: www.newstatesman.com/blogs/david-blanchflower/2011/06/credit-card-cameron-basi

9. A useful summary of this process, conceptualised as the 'ubiquity of blame' is set out in Steve Tombs, '"After" the crisis: morality plays and the renewal of business as usual', in David Whyte and Jorg Weigratz (eds), *Neoliberalism and the Moral Economy of Fraud*, London: Routledge, 2016, pp. 31–44; on how an 'ambiguous indebtedness' has helped narrate a crisis of the 'public', see Liam Stanley, '"We're reaping what we sowed": everyday crisis narratives and acquiescence to the age of austerity', *New Political Economy*, 19 (6), 2014, 895–917.

10. John Clarke and Janet Newman, 'The alchemy of austerity', *Critical Social Policy*, 32 (3), 2012, 299.

11. G. Brown, *Beyond the Crash*, London: Simon and Schuster, 2010.

12. National Audit Office, *HM Treasury: The Comptroller and Auditor General's Report on Accounts to the House of Commons*, London, 2011.

13. See, for example, J. Traynor, 'UK government starts Royal Bank of Scotland sell-off', *Guardian*, 3 August 2015, available at: www.theguardian.com/business/2015/aug/03/uk-government-starts-royal-bank-of-scotland-sell-off-rbs

14. D. McNally, *Global Slump: The Economics and Politics of Crisis and Resistance*, Oakland, CA: PM Press, 2010.

15. The full text of George Osborne's speech is available at: www.telegraph.co.uk/finance/budget/7846849/Budget-2010-Full-text-of-George-Osbornes-statement.html

16. For example, see David Cameron's speech, 17 May 2012, available at: www.gov.uk/government/speeches/prime-minister-a-speech-on-the-economy

17. Quote taken from the 2010 George Osborne speech.

18. See also Mark Blyth, *Austerity: The History of a Dangerous Idea*, Oxford: Oxford University Press, 2013.

19. 2010 George Osborne speech.

20. For indicative statements, see former US Treasury Secretary Larry Summers at: www.ft.com/content/dbb65da8-9062-11e1-8adc-00144feab49a; Nobel Prize-winning economist Paul Krugman at: http://krugman.blogs.nytimes.com/2012/04/15/insane-in-spain/?_r=0; and even the conservative *The Economist* at: www.economist.com/blogs/freeexchange/2012/05/growth

21. UN Human Rights Council, *Report of the Special Rapporteur on Adequate Housing as a Component of the Right to an Adequate Standard of Living, and on the Right to Non-discrimination*, Geneva, 2013, p. 20.

22. P. Butler, 'Bedroom tax: Raquel Rolnik's uncomfortable truths', *Guardian*, 3 February 2014, available at: www.theguardian.com/society/patrick-butler-cuts-blog/2014/feb/03/bedroom-tax-raquel-rolnik-uncomfortable-housing-truths

23. Ibid.; Stewart Jackson, by the way, is the MP who, when asked whether MPs should be entitled to a second home, said that cutting funds for second home entitlement for MPs would be 'draconian and unfair'. See, for example, P. Sawer, 'MPs' expenses: MPs who milked the expenses system now complain

about attempts to reform it', *Telegraph*, 29 August 2009, available at: www.telegraph.co.uk/news/newstopics/mps-expenses/6112443/MPs-expenses-MPs-who-milked-the-expenses-system-now-complain-about-attempts-to-reform-it.html

24. V. Ingimundarson, P. Urfalino and I. Erlingsdóttir (eds), *Iceland's Financial Crisis: The Politics of Blame, Protest, and Reconstruction*, Basingstoke: Routledge, 2016.

25. Ibid.

26. Ibid.

27. Kushner and Kushner, *Who Needs the Cuts?*

28. Michael Meacher, 'Why is the alternative to austerity kept such a secret?', *New Statesman*, 3 June 2015, available at: www.newstatesman.com/politics/2014/06/why-alternative-austerity-kept-such-secret

29. Tom MacInnes, Hannah Aldridge, Sabrina Bushe, Adam Tinson and Theo Barry Born, *Monitoring Poverty and Social Exclusion 2014*, York: Joseph Rowntree Foundation, 2014, available at: www.jrf.org.uk/sites/default/files/jrf/migrated/files/MPSE-2014-FULL.pdf

30. Ibid.

31. Ibid.

32. BBC News, 'Budget 2012: George Osborne cuts 50p top tax rate', 21 March 2013.

33. Mark Blyth, 'Foreword', in O'Hara, *Austerity Bites*, pp. xiv–xviii.

34. Jamie Peck, 'Austerity urbanism', *City*, 16 (6), 2012, 626–55, emphasis in the original.

35. S. Hodkinson and G. Robbins, 'The return of class war conservatism? Housing under the UK Coalition government', *Critical Social Policy*, 33 (1), 2013, 57–77.

36. Kirsteen Paton, *Gentrification: A Working-class Perspective*, Farnham: Ashgate, 2014.

37. Trade Union Congress, 'UK workers experienced sharpest wage fall of any leading economy, TUC analysis finds', Press release, 27 July 2016, available at: www.tuc.org.uk/economic-issues/labour-market/uk-workers-experienced-sharpest-wage-fall-any-leading-e

38. Kirsteen Paton and Vickie Cooper, 'It's the state, stupid: 21st gentrification and state-led evictions', *Sociological Research Online*, 21 (3), 2016.

39. BBC News, 'Housing benefits: changes "see 6% of tenants move"', 28 March 2014, available at: www.bbc.co.uk/news/uk-26770727

40. Joe Halewood, 'Overall benefit cap – the HB (£) cut is 3 times the bedroom tax', 23 February 2016, available at: https://joehalewoodblog.wordpress.com/2016/02/23/overall-benefit-cap-the-hb-cut-is-3-times-the-bedroom-tax/

41. Patrick Butler, 'Benefit cap will pitch thousands more British children into poverty', *Guardian*, 7 July 2015, available at: www.theguardian.com/

society/2015/jul/07/benefit-cap-pitch-children-poverty-12bn-cuts-tory-budget

42. Department for Work and Pensions, *Households Below Average Income: An Aanalysis of the Income Distribution: 1994/95–2015/16*, London, DWP, 2016.

43. Oxfam, *The True Cost of Austerity and Inequality: Oxfam Case Study*, Oxford: Oxfam, 2013, available at: www.oxfam.org/sites/www.oxfam.org/files/cs-true-cost-austerity-inequality-uk-120913-en.pdf

44. And here she is referring to figures generated by the government's own impact assessment; see Mendoza, *Austerity*, p. 63.

45. Daniela Tepe-Belfrage, 'The intersectional consequences of austerity', Political Economy Research Centre blog, 27 April 2015, available at: www.perc.org.uk/project_posts/the-intersectional-consequences-of-austerity/

46. J. Towers and S. Walby, *Measuring the Impact of Cuts in Public Expenditure on the Provision of Services to Prevent Violence Against Women and Girls*, Lancaster: Lancaster University, Northern Rock Foundation and Trust for London, 2012.

47. Welfare Weekly, '213% rise in disability hate crime "fuelled" by benefits propaganda, say campaigners', 12 January 2015, available at: www.welfareweekly.com/disability-hate-crime-fuelled-by-propaganda/

48. Hansard, Debate on 'CPS and disability hate crime', 8 November 2016, column 493WH, Vol. 616.

49. Blyth, *Austerity: A History of a Dangerous Idea*, p. 7.

50. Thomas Sowell, *'Trickle Down' Theory and 'Tax Cuts for the Rich'*, Stanford, CA: Hoover Institution, 2012.

51. Such statements have been fairly frequent, beginning in 2012; see Associated Press report, 12 October 2012 in which 'IMF, World Bank warn against growth-stifling austerity', available at: www.macleans.ca/general/imf-world-bank-warns-against-growth-stifling-austerity/; for a concise summary of this contradictory position, see Larry Elliot, 'The World Bank and the IMF won't admit their policies are the problem', *Guardian*, 9 October 2016, available at: www.theguardian.com/business/2016/oct/09/the-world-bank-and-the-imf-wont-admit-their-policies-are-the-problem

52. Andrew Sayer, *Why We Can't Afford the Rich*, Bristol: Policy Press, 2015.

53. A useful analysis of UK Treasury data can be found at: www.ukpublicspending.co.uk/spending_chart_2005_2016UKr_XXc1li111mcn_Got_Total_National_Debt

54. John McMurtry, *The Cancer Stage of Capitalism*, London: Pluto Press, 1999, p. 115.

55. David Harvey, *The New Imperialism*, New York: Oxford University Press, 2003, p. 148.

56. Ibid., pp. 137–82.

57. Aditya Chakrabortty, 'Austerity is far more than just cuts. It's about privatising everything we own', *Guardian*, 24 May 2016, available at: www.

theguardian.com/commentisfree/2016/may/24/austerity-cuts-privatising-george-osborne-britain-assets

58. From George Osborne's 2010 speech.
59. BBC News, '"Generous" tax breaks for shale gas industry outlined', 19 July 2013.
60. Office for National Statistics, *Index of Private Housing Rental Prices (IPHRP) in Great Britain: October 2016*, London, 2016.
61. O'Hara, *Austerity Bites*.
62. For example, Richard Seymour, *Against Austerity: How We can Fix the Crisis They Made*, London: Pluto Press, 2014.
63. This calculation is made using the data analysis tool available at ft.com: https://markets.ft.com/data/indices/tearsheet/summary?s=FTSM:FSI
64. O'Hara, *Austerity Bites*, p. 8.
65. Paul Krugman, 'The austerity agenda', *New York Times*, 31 May 2012, available at: www.nytimes.com/2012/06/01/opinion/krugman-the-austerity-agenda.html
66. S. Lavery, 'Public and private sector employment across the UK since the financial crisis', SPERI British Political Economy Brief No. 10, University of Sheffield, Sheffield, 2015.
67. Blyth, 'Foreword', in O'Hara, *Austerity Bites*.
68. R. Humphries, R. Thorlby, H. Holder, P, Hall and A. Charles, *Home Truths: Social Care for Older People*, London: King's Fund and Nuffield Trust, 2016.
69. Tom Crewe, 'The strange death of municipal England', *London Review of Books*, 38 (4), 15 December 2016, 6–10.
70. Her Majesty's Inspectorate of Constabulary, *Policing in Austerity: Meeting the Challenge*, London, 2015, available at: www.justiceinspectorates.gov.uk/hmic/wp-content/uploads/policing-in-austerity-meeting-the-challenge.pdf
71. C. Warburton, 'HSE business plan reveals further budget cuts', *Health and Safety at Work*, 1 April 2016, available at: www.healthandsafetyatwork.com/hse/business-plan-reveals-further-budget-cuts
72. E. Howard, 'Defra hit by largest budget cuts of any UK government department, analysis shows', *Guardian*, 11 November 2015, available at www.theguardian.com/environment/2015/nov/11 that/defra-hit-by-largest-budget-cuts-of-any-uk-government-department-analysis-shows
73. See Crewe, 'The strange death of municipal England', 63.
74. Florian Schui, *Austerity: The Great Failure*, New Haven, CT and London: Yale University Press, 2014, p. 6.
75. On this process, see Richard Seymour's brilliant analysis of the politics of austerity as a hegemonic process in chapter 3 his book *Against Austerity*.
76. See also Seebrook, *Cut Out*, p. 174.
77. Jamil Salmi, *Violence and Democratic Society*, London: Zed, 1993.

78. Walter Benjamin, 'Critique of violence', in Peter Demetz (ed.), *Reflections: Essays, Aphorisms and Autobiographical Writings*, New York: Schocken, 1978, pp. 277–300.
79. Emma Goldman, *My Disillusionment in Russia*, Mineola, NY: Dover, 2003.
80. Vandana Shiva, *Staying Alive: Women, Ecology, and Survival in India*, New Delhi: Kali for Women, 1988.
81. Max Weber, *The Vocation Lectures*. Indianapolis: Hackett, 2004.
82. C. Wright Mills, *The Power Elite*, Oxford: Oxford University Press, 2000.
83. Hannah Arendt, *On Violence*, New York: Harcourt, 1970, p. 8.
84. Rob Nixon, *Slow Violence and the Environmentalism of the Poor*, Cambridge, MA: Harvard University Press, 2011.
85. R. Boyes, *Meltdown Iceland: How the Global Financial Crisis Bankrupted an Entire Country*, London: Bloomsbury Publishing, 2010.
86. http://keepournhspublic.com/
87. www.facebook.com/NBTGM/
88. https://radicalhousingnetwork.org/
89. www.axethehousingact.org.uk/
90. http://blacktrianglecampaign.org/
91. www.generationrent.org/
92. www.sistersuncut.org/
93. www.fawcettsociety.org.uk/
94. www.scottishwomensaid.org.uk/
95. http://rapecrisis.org.uk/; www.rapecrisisscotland.org.uk/
96. http://blackactivistsrisingagainstcuts.blogspot.co.uk
97. http://imkaan.org.uk/
98. www.southallblacksisters.org.uk/
99. www.ukuncut.org.uk/
100. www.taxjustice.net/
101. http://lada.debtresistance.uk/
102. www.thepeoplesassembly.org.uk/
103. Ibid.
104. www.boycottworkfare.org/
105. https://fuelpovertyaction.org.uk/
106. dpac.uk.net/
107. www.hazardscampaign.org.uk/
108. https://psychagainstausterity.wordpress.com/
109. https://focuse15.org/
110. www.facebook.com/thearkmcr/

PART I

Deadly Welfare

1

Mental Health and Suicide

Mary O'Hara

In the aftermath of the meltdown that was the 2007/08 financial crisis, millions of people – millions of ordinary people on low to moderate incomes – paid an enormous price. They paid that price, however, not just in terms of job losses or employment security and wages, or indeed the loss of their homes and vital services. As savage austerity measures were rolled out in the UK after the crash, huge numbers of people paid the price way beyond their pockets. They paid it with something much more valuable – their mental health.

No matter where in the world you are, look at the research and the evidence is clear: economic strain contributes to mental health difficulties – especially during recessions when unemployment and poverty tend to jump. What's more, people already living with mental health difficulties are likely to suffer disproportionately in times of recession – not just because funding for services might be cut but also because they are at higher risk of losing their jobs and homes.[1]

The so-called age of austerity has shown just how serious and widespread the impact of economic turmoil on mental health could be. One US study found a 'significant and sustained' increase in major depression among adults between 2005–06 and 2011–12, during which time millions of Americans lost their jobs and their homes.[2] Another study exploring the effects of the 2008 financial crash[3] reached some stark conclusions. Analysing data from 24 European Union (EU) countries, the USA and Canada, the researchers reported that by 2011, the economic crisis had already led to over 10,000 more suicides than would have been expected – a figure they called a 'conservative estimate'. The downward trend in suicide rates seen in the EU before 2007 went into reverse when the financial crisis hit, rising 6.5 per cent by 2009. In the USA the rate increased by 4.8 per cent over the same period. Yet the study also showed that the trends were not uniform: many countries did not see any increase in suicide rates. The researchers suggested that a range of interventions – from back-to-work programmes to prescriptions for antidepressants – may reduce the risk of suicide during economic downturns. In the USA, figures published in April 2016 showed a suicide rate at its highest for 30 years with researchers linking[4] the surge in part to financial woes, poverty and job insecurity.

One study in the UK published in November 2015[5] concluded that austerity, financial strain and unemployment following the financial crash of 2008 were significant factors in suicide rates. The work, by academics at the Universities of Bristol, Manchester and Oxford, estimated that around 1000 additional deaths by suicide occurred between 2008 and 2010 while something like 30 to 40,000 extra suicide attempts may have taken place.

In their important book, *The Body Economic*, Sanjay Basu and David Stuckler examined health and economic data over decades, concluding that austerity was bad for both physical and mental health.[6] 'If austerity were tested like a medication in a clinical trial, it would have been stopped long ago, given its deadly side effects … One need not be an economic ideologue – we certainly aren't – to recognise that the price of austerity can be calculated in human lives', was their damning conclusion in the *New York Times*. They went on to argue that countries that have chosen stimulus over austerity, such as Germany, Sweden and Iceland, have had better health outcomes than countries such as Greece, Italy and Spain, where austerity measures have been used. 'If suicides were an unavoidable consequence of economic downturns this would just be another story about the human toll of the Great Recession', they concluded. 'But it isn't so.'

Greece – a country with traditionally lower suicide rates than other European nations – has felt the impact of austerity more than most. A landmark study led by Professor Charles Branas of the University of Pennsylvania incorporated a 30-year month-by-month analysis[7] of suicides in Greece, ending in 2012. The researchers looked at possible links between suicide data and particular prosperity- and austerity-related events over the three decades, including the acceptance of Greece into the EU, the 2004 Athens Olympic Games and the passing of austerity measures by the government.

While cautious not to link the cause directly to austerity, the researchers found 'a significant, abrupt and sustained increase' in suicides following austerity-related events like announcements of spending cuts and violent protests against them. Across the decades studied, 2012 was the peak year for suicides in Greece.

In the UK, from as early as 2011, the charities Sane and the Depression Alliance were reporting concerns about links between financial woes, austerity policies and rising stress and depression.[8] Many organisations and activists began flagging up how a plethora of local government cuts and welfare reforms such as the Work Capability Assessment were creating unnecessary and sometimes intolerable stress for both physically disabled and mentally ill people.[9] The Work Capability Assessment in particular was generating widespread tension, according to many frontline welfare workers and campaigners (see Chapter 3 by John Pring and Chapter 4 by Jon Burnett and David Whyte).

Nick Dilworth[10] is a frontline welfare advice worker and long-standing critic of the government's back-to-work strategy who also monitors and analyses welfare statistics. He summed up the reality of dealing with the consequences: 'People are coming in with multiple problems. You get grown men crying. What you see are broken lives.'

In addition, sanctions, which were causing significant stress, soared after 2010, while JobCentre workers began speaking out about what they say was an increasingly punitive regime that was adding to the mental stress of both claimants and workers.[11] As Angela Neville, a JobCentre worker who went on to write a play about it, explained to me[12] in February 2015: 'From my own experience, staff are subjected to constant and aggressive pressure to meet and exceed targets. Colleagues would leave team meetings crying.' On the fallout after sanctions were applied, she said: 'It was very distressing to have customers literally without food, without heat, without resources – and these are unwell [and] disabled customers.'

Mental health services in the UK are notoriously underfunded and often referred to as a 'Cinderella service'. According to the Centre for Economic Performance, mental health services receive just 13 per cent of the total NHS budget, while mental illness is responsible for 23 per cent of the loss of years of healthy life caused by all illness nationwide.[13] Despite this, and despite numerous reassurances from government, services fell foul of austerity policies. Mental health provision was hit hard and early by austerity measures and this pattern has continued into 2016. Figures released in April 2016[14] by the charity Mind revealed that almost half of people (46 per cent) with mental health problems had considered or attempted to take their own life due to social factors such as debt and welfare difficulties.

Despite rising demand for help, including from people in crisis or feeling suicidal who were turning up at A&E departments ill-equipped to provide help, mental health services and the people relying on them were feeling the impact.[15] Organisations from Oxfam to activist groups such as Disabled People Against Cuts and War on Welfare warned of an unprecedented 'perfect storm' of falling incomes, rising costs and the removal of vital safety nets, including for mental health and disability, just when the pressure on individuals and families was skyrocketing.[16]

The figures back this up. In 2011, three years after the financial crisis, the number of prescriptions for antidepressants rose sharply, up 43 per cent on the previous year.[17] One investigation found that more than 2000 acute mental health beds were lost in England between 2011 and 2013. This meant that many people in crisis who didn't have a safe place had to be transported hundreds of miles to wherever a bed became available.[18]

By 2015, funding for mental health services was estimated to have fallen in real terms by 8.25 per cent over four years.[19] Three quarters of children and young people with a mental health issue could not access treatment when they needed it. Charities warned that this was also storing up problems for the future because it prevented early intervention, something proven to be crucial for young people's recovery prospects.[20] Meanwhile, it was reported that calls to mental health helplines from people citing financial problems shot up in line with personal indebtedness.[21] GPs reported a surge in patients with stress and anxiety due to worsening economic predicaments and joblessness.[22]

When discussing the impacts of austerity in the UK, deaths feature prominently.[23] Like 44-year-old Mark Wood – who was found dead after learning that his benefits were being cut and whose story of struggle drew outrage from campaigners – some of the people who have died had a history of mental health problems. Others didn't. And there are many, many stories.[24] The violence of some of the deaths and distress can be truly shocking. In one case, a man doused himself in petrol outside a JobCentre after being declared fit for work and experiencing benefits delays. Police arrived in time to save him. One woman died two days after trying to take her own life. Her doctor told the inquest that a letter stating that her incapacity benefits were to be withdrawn had precipitated the suicide attempt. A pensioner in his seventies was believed to have killed himself due to fears about the 'bedroom tax' (see also Chapter 17 by Kirsteen Paton and Vickie Cooper). Witnesses testified to the inquest that he was frightened by news reports that said people might lose their homes if they couldn't pay it.

On the frontline of mental health, the strain of five years of austerity became such that hundreds of health professionals took to writing to newspapers about it. In one highly critical letter to the *Guardian*[25] on the government's public health record, senior physicians linked austerity policies to rising suicides, concluding that 'over the last five years, there have been avoidable deaths and much unnecessary damage to health'.

In another letter,[26] published just before the 2015 election, 442 professionals ranging from psychologists to epidemiologists wrote:

The past five years have seen a radical shift in the kinds of issues generating distress in our clients: increasing inequality and outright poverty, families forced to move against their wishes, and, perhaps most important, benefits claimants (including disabled and ill people) and those seeking work being subjected to a quite new, intimidatory kind of disciplinary regime.

Psychologists Against Austerity,[27] an alliance of mental health professionals, formed with the aim of directly challenging the cuts and welfare changes that they said were adding to mental distress. The group produced a briefing paper[28] that includes five 'austerity ailments' it believes contribute to worsening mental despair. These are: humiliation and shame; instability and insecurity; isolation and loneliness; being trapped or feeling powerless; and fear and distrust. The authors conclude: 'Mental health problems are being created in the present, and further problems are being stored for the future.'

One group of researchers believes that a serious political-cultural shift is taking place within the welfare system, and that it is having serious ramifications for mental health. In a paper published in 2015,[29] Dr Lynne Friedli and colleagues documented their findings on the impact of back-to-work policies, notably psychological assessments of unemployed individuals' fitness for work. 'Psychological explanations for unemployment ... isolate, blame, and stigmatise unemployed people. They reinforce myths about "cultures of worklessness"', Frieldli wrote. 'They obscure the realities of the UK labour market and the political choices that underpin it.'

There have been ongoing calls from families and campaigners for a full public investigation into deaths that followed cuts to benefits or the implementation of sanctions in order to find out what connections there may be.[30] And when, in September 2015, a coroner in north London concluded that the suicide in 2013 of 60-year-old disabled man Michael O'Sullivan was a direct result of having been wrongly found fit for work, there were yet more calls for the Department for Work and Pensions to overhaul fitness-for-work assessments. The coroner said: '[His] anxiety and depression were long-term problems but the intense anxiety that triggered his suicide was caused by his recent assessment ... as being fit for work, and his view of the likely consequences of that.'

More research and better data are needed to ascertain fully the connections between recessions and austerity and suicide, but mental health strains are clearly exacerbated by economic factors, according to Joe Ferns, Director of Policy and Research at the Samaritans. Part of the problem, he says, is that stresses such as financial pressures or losing a job make people feel 'disempowered' and 'less able to cope'. But people can be affected by the community around them too. Says Ferns: 'The social impacts spread far wider and last far longer than the economic ripples.'

Sanjay Basu has pointed out that there is already considerable evidence of serious and deleterious effects of austerity which as a matter of urgency require robust policy responses. Basu told me in an interview that his work has persuaded him that the stakes of austerity for mental health are very high indeed:

I think the real decision for us is whether we want to pay now or pay later. I think we can either pay now in terms of creating the social safety nets in order to avoid a real dismantling of some of the key parts of our communities or we'll face the consequence for many years.

Charities, healthcare professionals, academics and those on the frontline agree: act now or suffer more later. The Department of Health told me that it was tackling 'historic underfunding' in mental health, yet time and again it is pointed out that many services are on their knees.

As anyone who has suffered directly as a result of austerity or who has lost a loved one because of policies implemented under its banner will tell you, harm to mental health and loss of life constitute a serious violation. Almost a decade after the financial crisis, people continue to suffer under aggressive austerity policies even in the face of evidence of the human cost.

NOTES

Websites were last accessed 30 November 2016.

1. S. Evans-Lacko, M. Knapp, P. McCrone, G. Thornicroft and R. Mojtabai, 'The mental health consequences of the recession: economic hardship and employment of people with mental health problems in 27 European countries', *PLoS One*, 8 (7), 2013, available at: http://journals.plos.org/plosone/article?id=10.1371/journal.pone.006979222

2. Loyola University Health System, 'Significant increase in major depression reported during recent recession', *PsyPost*, 24 April 2015, available at: www.psypost.org/2015/04/significant-increase-in-major-depression-reported-during-recent-recession-33753

3. University of Oxford News, 'Recession "linked with" over 10,000 suicides across Europe and North America', 12 June 2014, available at: www.ox.ac.uk/news/2014-06-12-recession-'linked-with'-over-10000-suicides-across-europe-and-north-america#

4. S. Tavernise, 'U.S. suicide rate surges to a 30-year high', *New York Times*, 22 April 2016, available at: www.nytimes.com/2016/04/22/health/us-suicide-rate-surges-to-a-30-year-high.html

5. K. McVeigh, 'Austerity a factor in rising suicide rate among UK men – study', *Guardian*, 12 November 2015, available at: www.theguardian.com/society/2015/nov/12/austerity-a-factor-in-rising-suicide-rate-among-uk-men-study

6. K. Allen, 'Austerity kills, economists warn', *Guardian*, 29 April 2013, available at: www.theguardian.com/business/economics-blog/2013/apr/29/austerity-kills-health-europe-us

7. C.C. Branas, A.E. Kastanaki, M. Michalodimitrakis, J. Tzougas, E.F.Kraniot., P.N.Theodorakis, B.G. Carr and D.J. Wiebe, 'The impact of economic austerity and prosperity events on suicide in Greece: a 30-year interrupted time-series analysis', *British Medical Journal*, 5:e005619, 2015.

8. N. Triggle, 'Money woes linked to rise in depression', BBC News, 7 April 2011, available at: www.bbc.co.uk/news/health-12986314

9. A. Gentleman, 'Fitness-for-work tests unfair on people with mental health problems, court says', *Guardian*, 22 May 2013, available at: www.theguardian. com/society/2013/may/22/fitness-work-tests-mental-health-unfair

10. M. O'Hara, 'The welfare rights adviser on a mission to shame Iain Duncan Smith', *Guardian*, 30 September 2014, available at: www.theguardian. com/society/2014/sep/30/welfare-rights-shame-iain-duncan-smith-nick-dilworth-reform

11. P. Scott and J. Rampen, '"Harmful" ESA benefit sanctions double in one year – who's at risk and why', *Mirror*, 9 June 2015, available at: www.mirror.co.uk/money/harmful-esa-benefit-sanctions-double-5849195

12. M. O'Hara, 'As a jobcentre adviser, I got "brownie points" for cruelty', *Guardian*, 4 February 2015, available at: www.theguardian.com/society/2015/feb/04/jobcentre-adviser-play-benefit-sanctions-angela-neville

13. M. O'Hara, 'Mental health cuts are "driving people to the edge"', *Guardian*, 13 May 2015, available at: www.theguardian.com/society/2015/may/13/mental-health-cuts-driving-people-edge-mark-winstanley

14. Mind, 'One in two people with mental health problems have felt suicidal because of money, housing or benefits issues', 7 April 2016, available at: www. mind.org.uk/news-campaigns/news/one-in-two-people-with-mental-health-problems-have-felt-suicidal-because-of-money-housing-or-benefits-issues/#. WGOsNIXls9m

15. H. Siddique, 'Mental health treatment failings adding to strain on A&E, says minister', *Guardian*, 25 December 2014, available at: www.theguardian. com/society/2014/dec/25/mental-health-treatment-failings-adding-to-casualty-strain

16. Oxfam, 'Work no longer pays for Britons caught in "perfect storm" of falling incomes and rising costs', 14 June 2012, available at: www.oxfam.org.uk/media-centre/press-releases/2012/06/work-no-longer-pays-for-britons-caught-in-perfect-storm-of-falling-incomes-and-rising-costs

17. M. Evans, 'Recession linked to huge rise in use of antidepressants', *Telegraph*, 7 April 2011, available at: www.telegraph.co.uk/news/health/8434106/Recession-linked-to-huge-rise-in-use-of-antidepressants.html

18. The Mental Health Taskforce, *The Five Year Forward View for Mental Health*, London: NHS England, 2016, available at: www.england.nhs.uk/wp-content/uploads/2016/02/Mental-Health-Taskforce-FYFV-final.pdf. See also Department for Work and Pensions, *Mortality Statistics: Employment and Support Allowance, Incapacity Benefit or Severe Disablement Allowance*, London, 2015, available at: www.gov.uk/government/uploads/system/uploads/attachment_data/file/456359/mortality-statistics-esa-ib-sda. pdfwww.gov.uk/government/uploads/system/uploads/attachment_data/file/456359/mortality-statistics-esa-ib-sda.pdf

19. M. Buchanan, 'Mental health service budgets "cut by 8%"', BBC News, 20 March 2015, available at: www.bbc.co.uk/news/health-31970871

20. YoungMinds, 'Stop cutting CAMHS services', n.d., available at: www. youngminds.org.uk/about/our_campaigns/cuts_to_camhs_services. See also M. O'Hara, 'Teachers left to pick up pieces from cuts to youth mental health services', *Guardian*, 15 April 2014, available at: www.theguardian. com/education/2014/apr/15/pupils-mental-health-cuts-services-stress-teachers

21. R. Reilly, 'Number of people calling mental health helplines soars by 50% in one year – and "financial pressures" are to blame', *Daily Mail*, 18 July 2013, available at: www.dailymail.co.uk/health/article-2368512/Number-people-calling-mental-health-helplines-soars-50-year--financial-pressures-blame. html

22. M. O'Hara, 'Cut off: how austerity relates to our mental health', *New Statesman*, 6 October 2015, available at: www.newstatesman.com/politics/ welfare/2015/10/cut-how-austerity-relates-our-mental-health

23. R. Jones, 'Remember those killed by Tory austerity when you cast your vote on Thursday', *Mirror*, 5 May 2015, available at: www.mirror.co.uk/ news/uk-news/remember-those-killed-tory-austerity-5642530. See also A. Cowburn, 'Suicides highlight the grim toll of benefits sanctions in austerity Britain', *Guardian*, 3 January 2015, available at: www.theguardian.com/ society/2015/jan/03/benefits-sanctions-leading-suicides-dwp-depression

24. M. O'Hara, *Austerity Bites: A Journey to the Sharp End of the Cuts in the UK*, Bristol: Policy Press, 2015.

25. D. Campbell, 'Austerity policies and failures on public health have cost lives, say senior doctors', *Guardian*, 5 May 2015, available at: www.theguardian. com/politics/2015/may/03/austerity-policies-failures-public-health-cost-lives-senior-doctors-coalition-obesity-alcohol-welfare-letter

26. 'Austerity and a malign benefits regime are profoundly damaging mental health', *Guardian*, 17 April 2015, available at: www.theguardian.com/ society/2015/apr/17/austerity-and-a-malign-benefits-regime-are-profoundly-damaging-mental-health

27. See campaign website: https://psychagainstausterity.wordpress.com

28. 'The psychological impact of austerity: a briefing paper', Psychologists Against Austerity, London, 2015, available at: https://psychagainstausterity. files.wordpress.com/2015/03/psychological-costs-of-austerity-briefing-paper-compressed.pdf

29. L. Friedli and R. Stearn, 'Positive affect as coercive strategy: conditionality, activation and the role of psychology in UK government workfare programmes', *Critical Medical Humanities*, 41, 2015, available at: http:// mh.bmj.com/content/41/1/40.fulll

30. J. Pring, 'One in five benefit-related deaths involved sanctions, admits DWP', Disability News Service, 15 May 2015, available at: www. disabilitynewsservice.com/one-in-five-benefit-related-deaths-involved-sanctions-admits-dwp/

2

Austerity and Mortality

Danny Dorling*

In 2015, the UK suffered one of the largest rises in overall mortality measured since reliable annual records were first collected of the population in the late 1830s. What has taken place in Britain recently has few precedents since the 1930s and the Second World War.[1] To discover the reasons why there might be a fall in life expectancy among the elderly in England now, we need to look for where a similar fall has occurred in the past.

One such spike in mortality rates occurred in the early 1950s. It took just four months, in the midst of Britain's post-war austerity period from December 1952 to March 1953, for some 12,000 residents to perish in what was then modern London's most deadly civilian disaster. The initial public reaction was to attribute the deaths to air pollution. At the time, most Londoners kept warm by burning dirty coal. Cool air had settled over the Thames Valley in early December 1952 and did not move for weeks. The air turned thick with smog. In one week alone 4703 people died, many more than the 1852 people who had died during the same week the previous year.

In early 1953, a Member of Parliament put this episode into context when he asked the Minister of Housing, Harold Macmillan:

> Does the minister not appreciate that last month, in Greater London alone, there were literally more people choked to death by air pollution than were killed on the roads in the whole country in 1952?

*   This chapter is a revised and updated version of D. Dorling, 'Why are the old dying before their time? How austerity has affected mortality rates', *New Statesman*, 7 February 2014. A fully referenced version with all the evidence known to this author and available from early 2014 is available at: www.dannydorling.org/?page_id=3970

Macmillan may well have appreciated the likelihood that it was the smog, but he was also averse to spending more on making smokeless fuel available for the poor at a time of austerity. He ordered that an official government report be conducted; it conveniently proposed the hypothesis that influenza had caused all the excess winter deaths. Many MPs and the public remained suspicious. They did not think it had been just another outbreak of flu. They agitated and, within three years, laws had been passed requiring the burning of cleaner, more expensive coal in cities such as London.

There are clear parallels with the current spike in mortality rates and the 1953 smog. Public Health England's explanation for the current rise in the death toll has been to assert that 'influenza has contributed significantly'. However, the rise in 2015 does not have the characteristics of previous cold weather snaps and influenza epidemics. It is austerity that is linked most closely with the rising old-age mortality and its timing coincides with the population reporting worse health and rises in mortality over several years. Influenza is an easy scapegoat.[2]

Between 2008 and 2013, public sector cuts led to some 483,000 old and disabled people in the UK either losing their care support or becoming no longer eligible to claim it. According to the Personal Social Services Research Unit, the 'reductions ... are particularly acute for older people'. By 2014, there were millions fewer social care visits a year to the elderly than took place five years before. These were visits to elderly people who would have been assessed as vulnerable, visits that could result in the carer setting in motion a course of action leading to the prevention of an unnecessary death. The big cuts to visits came after the general election of May 2010, and became deeper each year after that.

In July 2013, an internal Public Health England report was leaked by the *Health Service Journal*. In a repeat of events six decades earlier, the report revealed that, 'since December 2012, both male and female mortality are estimated to have increased'. This was no normal increase; and for the group most severely affected – the very elderly – death rates, already unusually high during most of 2012, were reported to be rising. It is important to point out that the deathly consequences of the cuts were becoming apparent so early on. What the Public Health England report found was shocking. Here, in its own words, is what it said:

When we focus on mortality over 75, we observe rapidly increasing mortality for both males and females, presenting throughout 2012, and continuing into 2013. Female 12-month mortality[3] over 75 is currently higher than in any year since 2009; and April 2013 saw a particularly sharp increase. Worryingly, female 75-plus mortality trends appear to have been worse in the Spearhead areas.[4]

In plain English what this means is that elderly people in the UK in 2012 and 2013 were dying a few weeks and in some cases a few months earlier than they had been before. The next year, 2014 was also bad compared to the improving trend which had existed from 1990 through to 2010, but it was what occurred in late 2014 and through many months of 2015 that was most shocking.

Spearhead areas are some of the poorest parts of the country. They are those places that had the highest premature mortality rates in the very recent past, and were targeted by the last Labour government for special intervention to try to bring down health inequalities in England. However, by 2015 the rise in death rates among the elderly was occurring across the UK and in early 2016 some of the highest elevated rates were in the South of England. These rises may have been so widely ignored because the deaths were of people in old age who would be expected to 'die anyway' just a few years later. But if we look back to what was known in 2013 we can see that an opportunity to properly address the issue was missed.

According to the leaked Public Health England report, by mid 2013 there had been, 'if anything, a further deterioration in mortality compared with that observed [in the same period in 2012]'. The number of excess deaths in England in 2012–13 had been 23,400 (5 per cent) above Office for National Statistics (ONS) expectations. However, a seemingly unperturbed anonymous official reacting to the story told the *Health Service Journal* that 'if increased mortality continues through 2013 and into 2014, there will have to be more detailed consideration'.[5]

In early 2015 there was a 5 per cent rise in total mortality in absolute numbers in England and Wales compared to 2014. In Scotland the rise was nearer 9 per cent. This was unprecedented. No public officials spoke out at a national level as this became evident in January, February and March 2016. They muttered about waiting for the 2015 population mid-year estimates, to be published by July 2016, before pronouncing, as if they thought some unnoticed mass immigration of the very elderly might have occurred. But at least by then the picture should be clear, or so we thought. And at least by then a choice would be made regards emergency funding of the services required in winter 2015/16, of the nurses, of visits to pensioners, of pensioner benefits. To not do would be choosing to let the cull continue. More and more academic papers began to be published in 2015 and early 2016 demonstrating that the geography and social association with austerity was so high that this clearly was not due to some new especially virulent strain of flu.

How did Public Health England react to its internal report being leaked? It shot the messenger. On 15 August 2013 the Orwellian-styled 'chief knowledge officer' of Public Health England issued an open letter suggesting there had been methodological weaknesses in the leaked internal report and explaining that: 'The analyst was therefore asked to stop circulating the reports.' The reports stopped. But the deaths didn't. And the need to explain the increase remained. The chief knowledge officer's letter was accompanied by a new, eight-page Public Health England report – *Excess Winter Mortality 2012–13* – which did not explain why there were any methodological weaknesses in the original internal report, but said instead that 'the temporal coincidence with influenza A(H3N2) across the UK and Europe suggests that influenza has contributed significantly'. And that influenza was 'a major explanatory factor'.[6]

Contrast the official message (that it's probably just mostly flu) with what was proved in the leaked internal reports. Those reports showed that the long-term trend in England of many years of falls in mortality coupled with rises in life expectancy appeared to have been halted in 2012; and that the situation was deteriorating throughout 2013. It was hard to know what to believe. Then the ONS produced its own report in November 2013 which showed the scale of excess deaths to be even greater.[7] The ONS report said it was not necessarily because the winter of 2012/13 had been cold that death rates had risen among the elderly. The government statisticians explained that during the exceptionally cold winter of 2009/10, the number of excess winter deaths had been 'similar to years with mild winters'. Thus, it is not so much the cold as the extent to which people can afford to heat their homes, and probably much else, such as whether they are visited that matters. According to the ONS, in 2012/13 there had been a 29 per cent increase in deaths, compared to 15.5 per cent the previous winter, with roughly 31,100 more people dying than the average for non-winter months. It highlighted that the great majority of these untimely deaths occurred among people over the age of 75. The ONS also cast doubt on flu being the main cause of the spike, saying: 'Influenza activity in 2012/13 was relatively low.' In the final version of the report that was later posted on the web this sentence read: 'Influenza activity in 2012/13 was relatively low, but activity was prolonged and reached levels higher than those seen in 2011/12.'[8] The officials stuck to their flu explanation for as long as possible.

The one thing we can now be sure of is the chief reason for the spike in deaths in 2012/13 was not flu. Researchers David Stuckler and Martin McKee had already determined that the rise was not due to influenza and pneumonia. They estimated that influenza and pneumonia respectively contributed only 5.8 and 3.5 per cent of the rapid absolute increase in elderly mortality in the UK since early 2012. The European Centre for Disease Control also announced that the UK had one of the lowest reported intensities of influenza across Europe in winter 2012/13.[9]

People may in future decades look back at the huge increase in deaths among the elderly from 2012 to 2016 and be amazed that the authorities initially just blamed the cold weather. They might reflect on the fact that there is no large rise in mortality when flu hits countries like Norway and Sweden because of their much better funded health and social service systems.

Cold weather is no excuse for more deaths. We know that countries with frequently low winter temperatures, such as Finland and Germany, where most housing has adequate insulation and heating, have very low rates of excess winter mortality. We have to search for more clues. Maybe, as the price of fuel for cars rises, we pay fewer visits to elderly relatives? There are many factors that matter, but the timing suggests it is the cuts, austerity and not all being in it together that matter most this time.

In 2014, I wrote that it will be those who are poorer and living in poorer areas who will comprise the majority of the prematurely dead, and who will comprise the majority of the thousands more who will die between now and May 2015, should the situation not improve. These are the last of all those people who, in their millions, voted for Labour in the landslide election victory of 1945. This is the generation that experienced post-war austerity – now being killed by post-crash austerity. Ironically given their old age, many will have been or become middle class during the 1960s and 1970s and may well have voted Conservative in the fatal 1979 general election which ushered in three decades of rising inequality and public service cuts.

The most deadly violence is quiet violence, violence that kills you softly. The middle class mass-murderer Harold Shipman killed his elderly and mostly female victims with the quiet violence of a lethal injection. For an action to be described as violent it is often required that there be an intention to hurt, to damage or to kill. If you know that what you are doing or choosing not to do will result in harm that increases mortality, then you are acting in a violent way (see also Vickie Cooper and David Whyte's Introduction to this book). It may be 30 years or more before the official documents are released to reveal what officials actually knew in 2011, 2012 and 2013.

In 1953, 60 years ago, when it began to emerge that people were dying in numbers who would not normally die, Londoners knew it was the smog. Their MPs knew too, but the Conservative government of the day and its housing minister, Harold Macmillan, did not want the hassle of having to sort out the problem of urban air pollution. The similarities with the British Prime Minister David Cameron are shocking, but the death toll today is far higher. David Cameron left office in June 2016 with UK life expectancy falling. No other post-war prime minister has achieved such a terrible outcome. It is hard not to conclude that patricians had again viewed the rising deaths among the elderly as a price worth paying for the greater good of 'balancing the books' and making Britain 'great' again, ready to win that 'global race'. Along the way, thousands will have to shiver in the cold or receive increasingly inadequate care in their old age as budgets are slashed. Over recent years, as the 1 per cent has become ever richer, the poorest have had their income or benefits cut even further. Most of the poor who do get to 65 then do make it to age 80 or 85, however, and it is those age groups that have seen the greatest rises in deaths in recent years. You reap what you sow.[10]

NOTES

Websites were last accessed 19 August 2016.

1. See rapid response of 29 July 2016 to the *British Medical Journal* editorial on the deaths, available at: www.bmj.com/content/354/bmj.i3697/rapid-responses

2. D. Dorling, 'Austerity, rapidly worsening public health across the UK, and Brexit', Political Insight blog, Political Studies Association, 11 July, available at: www.psa.ac.uk/insight-plus/blog/austerity-rapidly-worsening-public-health-across-uk-and-brexit-0

3. The 12-month mortality rate measures the death rate of a specified age population in a given period of twelve months.

4. www.newstatesman.com/politics/2014/02/why-are-old-people-britain-dying-their-time

5. The quote appears in the version of my original *New Statesman* article which is available at: www.dannydorling.org/?page_id=3970. This article gives 32 references including: D. West, 'EXCLUSIVE: unexpected rise in deaths among older people', *Heath Service Journal*, 25 July 2013, available at: www.hsj.co.uk/news/exclusive-unexpected-rise-in-deaths-among-older-people/5061540.article#.UoyrZtK-06Y

6. Public Health England, *Excess Winter Mortality 2012–13*, London, 2013, available at: www.gov.uk/government/publications/excess-winter-mortality-2012-to-2013

7. Office of National Statistics, *Excess Winter Mortality in England and Wales, 2012/13 (Provisional) and 2011/12 (Final)*, London, 26 November 2013, p. 5, available at: www.ons.gov.uk/ons/rel/subnational-health2/excess-winter-mortality-in-england-and-wales/2012-13--provisional--and-2011-12--final-/stb-ewm-12-13.html

8. The final version is available at: www.ons.gov.uk/peoplepopulationand community/birthsdeathsandmarriages/deaths/bulletins/excesswinter mortalityinenglandandwales/2013-11-26

9. European Centre for Disease Control (ECDC), *Influenza in Europe, Season 2012–2013, Latest Surveillance Data Reports*, Solna, Sweden, 2013, available at: http://ecdc.europa.eu/en/publications/Publications/influenza-season-risk-assessment-europe-2013.pdf

10. See: Hiam, L., Harrison, D., Dorling, D., McKee, M. (2017) Why has mortality in England and Wales been increasing? An iterative demographic analysis, *Journal of the Royal Society of Medicine*, http://dx.doi.org/10.1177%2 F0141076817693599 and Hiam, L., Harrison, D., Dorling, D., and McKee, M. (2017) What caused the spike in mortality in England and Wales in January 2015?, *Journal of the Royal Society of Medicine*, February 17th, http://dx.doi.org/10.1177%2F0141076817693600

3

Welfare Reforms and the Attack on Disabled People

John Pring

Part of the disdain that the current and previous governments show for disabled people is exemplified by their refusal to conduct basic research on the impact of their welfare policies. We therefore have no understanding of the devastating human impacts of policies such as the introduction of Personal Independence Payment (PIP); the intensified use of the work capability assessment (WCA) (possibly the most violent and discriminatory tool ever handed to a government department); the increased use of benefit sanctions to punish people in vulnerable situations; or any number of other reckless and ill-evidenced policies (see also Chapter 4 by Jon Burnett and David Whyte).

Where we do have independent research, the evidence is shocking. For every policy, there is testimony from friends or family of the harm caused to individual disabled people who have been powerless to protect themselves, have had their freedom catastrophically affected, and have seen their dignity, health, choices and ability to control their own lives restricted in a way that can only be described as damaging and violent, and where some have lost their lives.[1]

George Osborne's 'emergency budget' on 22 June 2010[2] signalled the first in a series of brutal cuts to disabled people's support that would, six years later, lead to calls for a criminal investigation into the actions of two ministers at the centre of the austerity programme Osborne's government was setting in motion. In all, the Tory-led Coalition government brought in £21 billion in cuts to working-age social security, while the Conservative government that followed announced another £12 billion cuts by 2017–18. These cuts had a brutal impact on disabled people's income, and their rights. The think-tank Demos estimated[3] that disabled people risked losing £28 billion in income support by 2018.

Budget documents[4] show that the Coalition planned to cut 20 per cent of spending on working-age Disability Living Allowance (DLA) by introducing PIP as a replacement benefit, which would be designed to make it harder to claim. The psychological impact was felt almost immediately. A survey in 2011 found that nearly one in ten respondents believed death or suicide were possible outcomes of people losing their DLA.[5] PIP was introduced in 2013, and by July 2016 up to 700 disabled people a week who had previously claimed DLA were being forced to hand back their Motability vehicles.[6]

The DLA cuts were just one element of what began to feel like an unceasing attack on the support disabled people relied on to remain independent, healthy and alive. But some of the most damaging cuts were those made to the out-of-work disability benefit, Employment and Support Allowance (ESA). ESA eligibility was decided through the WCA. Disability News Service (DNS) had begun to report on emerging flaws within the WCA process in September 2009, a year after its introduction by the Labour government as a replacement for incapacity benefit (IB). Labour ministers had pushed the idea that 'people who scrounge from the system' through IB were taking money from 'legitimate' claimants,[7] and vowed to 'rip up sicknote Britain'.[8] This pressure to find claimants 'fit for work' fed through into the WCA system. Citizens Advice Scotland marked the assessment's first anniversary by warning that it had been 'flooded' with complaints about the WCA.[9] By the spring of 2012, GPs were calling for it to be scrapped and replaced with a 'rigorous and safe system that does not cause avoidable harm'.[10]

Since 2010, countless disabled people have come forward to testify to the WCA's impact on their health, but it was not until September 2015 that the first case emerged of a coroner drawing a direct link between the WCA and the death of a benefit claimant. DNS found the case of Andrew Davidson[11] after searching a database of reports written by coroners.[12] A coroner had stated that Davidson's decision to take his own life had been triggered by being found 'fit for work', questioned the failure of the assessor and the Department for Work and Pensions (DWP) to seek medical evidence from his GP, psychiatrist or clinical psychologist, and called for the necessary improvements to prevent such deaths in the future.

Campaigners pushed the DWP to release statistics showing how many disabled people had died following a WCA, believing this would prove that the assessment system had caused thousands of deaths. When the figures were finally released,[13] they were striking. Between December 2011 and February 2014, 2650 ESA and IB claimants had died soon after being found 'fit for work', and another 7200 died after being placed in the ESA Work-Related Activity Group (WRAG). But the DWP insisted that these figures showed no 'causal effect' and that many of these people would have died whether or not they had been assessed. A month later, it became much harder to maintain this position. A study showed that for every 10,000 IB claimants reassessed between 2010 and 2013, there were an additional six suicides and more than 7000 extra cases of antidepressants being prescribed.[14] The same study showed that across England the reassessment process was 'associated with' an extra 590 suicides (see also Chapter 1 by Mary O'Hara).

One of the weapons used by successive governments to force benefit claimants to comply with their reforms has been the use of sanctions. The use of sanctions against ESA claimants increased rapidly after its introduction in October 2008 and while the number of sanctions issued dropped in the period 2010–12, they increased after the welfare reforms came into full effect. Ministers continued to insist that sanctions were used 'as a last resort in a small percentage of cases',[15] but evidence shows that they have been used punitively, with violent, and even fatal, impacts. A survey by the Benefits and Work website produced hundreds of comments about their impact.[16] One welfare rights adviser said:

> Frequently clients do not know they've been sanctioned until they don't receive their benefit. They've received no letter and given no information on the right of appeal. No advice has been provided on hardship payments and we are regularly issuing food vouchers. I've had an increase in referrals from courts due to shoplifting offences. Clients have told me they are shoplifting to eat.[17]

Despite the overwhelming evidence highlighting the violent outcomes of welfare reforms, the last two governments refused to accept that their cuts and reforms have any harmful effect on disabled welfare claimants. Not only do ministers refuse to accept the anecdotal evidence and research reports that demonstrate harm, they refuse to carry out 'cumulative impact assessments' that would prove the overall effects of austerity cuts, claiming that this would be impossible, and repeatedly argue that this view is shared by the Institute for Fiscal Studies. But it is not.[18] And nor is it shared by the Equality and Human Rights Commission,[19] the UK Parliament's joint committee on human rights, DWP's own social security advisory committee,[20] the National Institute of Economic and Social Research or the UN Committee on Economic, Social and Cultural Rights.[21] They all concur that such a cumulative impact assessment can and should be carried out.

In mid 2014, DNS became interested in how the DWP responded to deaths linked to the social security system. Following a freedom of information request submitted by DNS, the DWP insisted that it kept no record of deaths found to be 'connected to, or linked to, or partially caused by, the withdrawal or non-payment of disability benefits'. The DWP eventually admitted that it carried out internal, confidential reviews into the deaths of some claimants. Fresh freedom of information requests revealed that between February 2012 and October 2014, the DWP had carried out 49 internal 'peer reviews' into such deaths. It later admitted that in ten cases the claimant had had their benefits sanctioned, while 33 reviews contained recommendations for improvements to DWP policies or procedures.

But the DWP still refused to release the reviews, until the information rights tribunal forced it to publish them; even then they were heavily redacted.[22] All that was released were the recommendations for improvements, many following the deaths of IB claimants who had been reassessed through a WCA. What the reviews did show was that ministers had been warned repeatedly that their policies were risking the lives of 'vulnerable' claimants.

DWP admissions of responsibility for harm caused to claimants have been grudging. The DWP repeatedly insisted that linking a death to someone's benefit claim was 'misleading' and 'wrong'. But after the reviews were released, the DWP began telling journalists: 'Any suicide is a tragedy and the reasons for them are complex, however it would be inaccurate and misleading to link it solely to a person's benefit claim.'[23] A small victory, but a sign that ministers had finally accepted that their actions could, partly, be responsible for claimants losing their lives.

The birth of the disabled people's anti-cuts movement can be traced back to the austerity protests held outside the Conservative Party conference in Birmingham in October 2010.[24] Disabled activists wore t-shirts warning that 'Cuts Kill'. The organisers of The Disabled People's Protest subsequently formed Disabled People Against Cuts (DPAC), set up to fight the austerity-driven erosion of disabled people's living conditions and human rights. DPAC's most significant achievement has been to persuade the UN Committee on the Rights of Persons with Disabilities to carry out – as a result of the austerity cuts to disabled people's support – an unprecedented, ongoing inquiry into 'grave or systemic violations' of the UN disability convention by the UK government.[25]

Other disabled people's groups have worked mainly online, including petitions on the UK Parliament website from the Pat's Petition and WOW (War On Welfare) Petition campaigns, both calling for a cumulative impact assessment. Disabled people also carried out their own high-quality research, including several reports by the Spartacus online network. Spartacus put together reviews of the WCA in 2012 and 2013.[26] The second review included pages of accounts from disabled people who had experienced anxiety, despair and hardship. Another user-led report revealed that 95 per cent of respondents said the WCA had damaged their health, with nearly a third reporting 'severe damage'.[27]

Disabled people are also fighting back through the criminal justice system, focusing on former Work and Pensions Secretary Iain Duncan Smith and former Employment Minister Chris Grayling. After their appointments as ministers in May 2010, Duncan Smith and Grayling assumed responsibility for responding to a letter written by coroner Tom Osborne. The letter followed the death of Stephen Carré, who took his own life in January 2010 after being wrongly found fit for work. Osborne asked the DWP to review its policy not to seek medical evidence for ESA claimants with mental health conditions, just as another coroner would in January 2014 following the death of Andrew Davidson.[28] Duncan Smith and Grayling failed to reply, and failed to share the letter with the expert they commissioned to review the WCA, Professor Malcolm Harrington.[29] They then rolled out the WCA to hundreds of thousands of IB claimants the following year, against Harrington's advice.

Black Triangle's[30] co-founder John McArdle also put together a dossier on three Scottish benefit claimants who he believed died as a direct result of those uncorrected flaws in the WCA, and took them to Police Scotland, suggesting that Duncan Smith and Grayling were guilty of the criminal offence of willful neglect of duty by a public official. The

Scottish criminal justice agencies decided in December 2016 to take no further action.

Deprived of government recognition of the damaged health, the restricted freedom, the despair and the lost lives, disabled people have looked instead to the criminal justice system and the United Nations. This chapter is too short to describe the many individual cases that should scar the consciences of ministers who recklessly sought cuts at the expense of rights, and of the media and private sector contractors who cheered them on. But many campaigners are determined that their names, and stories, will not go untold, and that the violence inflicted on them over the last seven years will be remembered.

NOTES

Websites were last accessed 28 October 2016.

1. See, for example, Disability News Service, 'Testimony for UN hears of food banks and suicides', 26 November 2013, available at: www.disabilitynews service.com/testimony-for-un-hears-of-food-banks-and-suicides/
2. George Osborne, MP, Financial Statement, Hansard, 22 June 2010, available at: www.parliament.uk/business/news/2010/06/emergency-budget-2010-statement/
3. C. Wood, *Destination Unknown: Summer 2012*, London: Demos, 2013.
4. HM Treasury and HM Revenue and Customs, *Budget 2010 Policy Costings*, London: HM Treasury, 2010.
5. Disability Alliance Survey, February 2011.
6. J. Pring, 'PIP reassessments mean 35,000 will lose motability vehicles in 2016', Disability News Service, 14 July 2016, available at: www. disabilitynewsservice.com/pip-reassessments-mean-35000-will-lose-motability-vehicles-in-2016/
7. 'Get-tough tests face the sick on benefit', *Liverpool Echo*, 9 April 2008.
8. 'Incapacity benefit set for axe', *Daily Mirror*, 5 November 2007.
9. Citizens Advice Scotland, 'A very un-happy birthday for Scotland's sick and disabled', 23 October 2009, available at: www.cas.org.uk/news/very-un-happy-birthday-scotlands-sick-and-disabled
10. A. Gentleman, 'GPs call for work capability assessment to be scrapped', *Guardian*, 23 May 2012.
11. Not his real name.
12. Courts and Tribunals Judiciary, *Prevention of Future Deaths*, Reference: 2014-0012, 13 January 2014.
13. Department for Work and Pensions, *Mortality Statistics: ESA, IB and SDA Claimants*, London, 2015, available at: www.gov.uk/government/uploads/system/uploads/attachment_data/file/459106/mortality-statistics-esa-ib-sda.pdf

14. B. Barr, D. Taylor-Robinson, D. Stuckler, R. Loopstra, A. Reeves and M. Whitehead, '"First, do no harm": are disability assessments associated with adverse trends in mental health? A longitudinal ecological study', *Journal of Epidemiology and Community Health*, 70 (4), 2015.

15. Department for Work and Pensions, 'Benefit sanctions down as more people helped into work', Press release, 13 May 2015, available at: www.gov. uk/government/news/benefit-sanctions-down-as-more-people-helped-into-work

16. Benefits and Work, 'Massive survey majority believes "inhuman" DWP causes and then covers-up claimant deaths', 23 March 2015, available at: www.benefitsandwork.co.uk/news/3049-massive-survey-majority-believe-dwp-causes-and-covers-up-claimant-deaths

17. Ibid.

18. See, for example, J. Pring, 'Ministers humiliated over cumulative impact assessment', Disability News Service, 11 July 2014, available at: www. disabilitynewsservice.com/ministers-humiliated-over-cumulative-impact-assessment/

19. H. Reed and J. Portes, *Cumulative Impact Assessment: A Research Report by Landman Economics and the National Institute of Economic and Social Research (NIESR) for the Equality and Human Rights Commission: Research Report 94*, Manchester: Equality and Human Rights Commission, 2014, available at: www.equalityhumanrights.com/sites/default/files/cumulative_impact_assessment_executive_summary_30-07-14_2.pdf

20. Social Security Advisory Committee, *SSAC Occasional Paper 12: The Cumulative Impact of Welfare Reform: A Commentary*, London, 2014, available at: www.gov.uk/government/uploads/system/uploads/attachment_data/file/324059/ssac_occasional_paper_12_report.pdf

21. See the Office of the High Commissioner for Human Rights, *UN Committee on Economic, Social and Cultural Rights, Findings on France, Sweden, Honduras, Burkina Faso, the Former Yugoslav Republic of Macedonia, Angola and the UK*, 28 June 2016, available at: www.ohchr.org/EN/NewsEvents/Pages/DisplayNews.aspx?NewsID=20191&LangID=E

22. Department for Work and Pensions, 'DWP FOI releases for May 2016', 12 May 2016, available at: www.gov.uk/government/publications/dwp-foi-releases-for-may-2016

23. S. Fenton, 'DWP repeatedly warned of failures to protect vulnerable benefit claimants, internal documents reveal', *Independent*, 14 May 2016, available at: www.independent.co.uk/news/uk/politics/dwp-repeatedly-warned-of-failures-to-protect-vulnerable-benefit-claimants-internal-documents-reveal-a7029691.html

24. J. Pring, 'Spending cuts protest sparks birth of new campaign', Disability News Service, 31 October 2010, available at: www.disabilitynewsservice.com/spending-cuts-protest-sparks-birth-of-new-campaign/

25. J. Pring, 'UN investigators begin taking evidence in UK on "rights violations"', Disability News Service, 16 October 2015, available at: www.

disabilitynewsservice.com/un-investigators-begin-taking-evidence-in-uk-on-rights-violations/

26. See, for example, 'Spartacus', *The People's Review of the Work Capability Assessment*, November 2012, available at: www.centreforwelfarereform.org/library/by-az/the-peoples-review-of-the-wca.html; 'Spartacus', *The People's Review of the WCA: Further Evidence*, December 2013, available at: www.centreforwelfarereform.org/library/by-az/peoples-review-of-wca-further-evidence.html

27. R. Burgess, S. Duffy, N. Dilworth, J. Bence, W. Blackburn and M. Thomas, *Assessing the Assessors*, Sheffield: The Centre for Welfare Reform, 2014, available at: www.centreforwelfarereform.org/uploads/attachment/433/assessing-the-assessors.pdf

28. Not his real name.

29. J. Pring, 'WCA death scandal: ministers "failed to pass 2010 suicide report to Harrington"', Disability News Service, 9 November 2015, available at: www.disabilitynewsservice.com/wca-death-scandal-ministers-failed-to-pass-2010-suicide-report-to-harrington/

30. Black Triangle is a Disability News Service subscriber.

4

The Violence of Workfare

Jon Burnett and David Whyte

This chapter documents first-hand accounts of people who have been forced to participate in UK 'workfare' schemes. These accounts were gathered by Boycott Workfare, a grassroots organisation that campaigns to end forced unpaid work for people who receive welfare. The chapter uses first-hand accounts to build a detailed exposure of government-organised workfare schemes and their encouragement of violent – and very often illegal – working practices.

A range of attacks on benefit entitlements have been central to austerity-led public sector cuts in which individuals have been punished and sanctioned for not 'actively seeking work'. Workfare is therefore a form of welfare conditionality, in which individuals are made to work without pay, or risk losing entitlement to benefit income for being defined as not maximizing their employment prospects. Workfare schemes are part of a much wider set of measures that place benefit claimants at the frontline of the government's so-called 'belt-tightening' public sector squeeze and intensification of 'welfare conditionality' in the current period of 'austerity'. There is much discussion around benefit sanctions, and the hardship that follows them, but there is less discussion about the increasingly common use of 'workfare schemes'.

Workfare has a history going back several decades in the UK.[1] First introduced as part of the 'community action' scheme, under John Major's Conservative government in 1993, workfare schemes became a central part of welfare policy reforms under the New Labour government's 'new deal' policy for the unemployed, launched in 1998. The last two governments have expanded these schemes. The Conservative's Mandatory Work Activity scheme, for example, compelling people to work without pay for between 4 and 26 weeks, was introduced in 2011 and by 2013 was reported to have been expanded to 70,000 placements per year.[2]

Current workfare schemes organised by the UK government come in various guises. The most well known include the phased out 'Community Work Placements' and 'Mandatory Work Activity' schemes and the current 'Help to Work' scheme. Those schemes share one thing in common: they are all compulsory work placements for people claiming social security benefits. In this chapter we will show, drawing on data provided by Boycott Workfare, how workfare schemes ruthlessly exploit welfare claimants and put them at risk of physical harm and violence.

Boycott Workfare is routinely contacted by claimants about workfare schemes and placements. In order to log information about claimants' experiences, the organisation uses a section of its website to gather information such as the name of the workplace, its location, the provider and other basic details. The website also provides a space for people to leave written descriptions of their experience. The spaces used for these descriptions do not specify what kind of information should be supplied. However, a review of written descriptions by Boycott Workfare volunteers in late 2015, revealed that those descriptions contained regular testimonies about the health and safety risks faced by people on workfare placements.

In order to document these experiences, Boycott Workfare asked us to analyse the testimonies provided by a total of 531 people logged between May 2011 and November 2015. Of this total, 97 people (18 per cent) specifically raised problems relating to workplace health and safety issues. These testimonies related to issues of varying severity. Some of the details consisted of very serious allegations indeed, and, as we show later in the chapter, many of the practices described in those accounts would be unambiguously regarded as illegal. These testimonies shed light on working practices in a section of the labour market which is hidden from public view. Common locations for workfare placements are recycling plants, warehouses, various types of Local Authority departments, charities and social enterprises, conservation centres and high street discount stores (Table 4.1).

In a great many cases, the testimonies revealed that claimants were expected to complete physical labour at an intense pace. This ruthless extraction of labour power is a consequence of being forced into the labour market under very particular conditions. A section of the labour

Table 4.1   Locations of workfare placements where complaints about health and safety were logged

Type of work	Number
Working in a discount store	5
Working for a charity or social enterprise, either in-store or in their warehouse	36
College/educational establishment, community centre, hotel, hospital	5
Conservation company/project (i.e. groundworks, agricultural work)	15
Warehouse, maintenance company, labouring project, plastics supplier	6
Local Authority	2
Recycling/waste disposal, transport or management company	20
Other	8

force that works under the threat of having its benefits sanctioned, and involves virtually no wage costs to the employer, can be readily exploited to meet the rise in demand as and when required. As part of this labour process, employers can make welfare claimants work 'faster' and 'harder', which can often mean them being refused respite or rest. In some cases, those that did not work hard enough or fast enough were sent back to the JobCentre. One claimant in our sample noted that:

> [There were] 10 workers all from JobCentre, none paid workers except management. Forced to recycle rubbish and cardboard and paper … at least 3 of the boys asked to leave and [were] sent back to JobCentre for not working at a fast enough pace.

Another described how his work involved:

> Hard labour on feet all day heavy lifting despite my medical conditions. Out of eight that started, only three remain after working all day in the heavy rain and getting soaked and chilled to the bone.

A number of claimants also reported that they were discouraged from taking lunch or rest breaks, and one reported only being allowed one

20-minute break per eight-hour shift. Another said he was charged several pounds per week to have access to the toilet facilities.

It was reported that employers would go out of their way to find work for claimants even when it was clear that there were no jobs that needed to be done. There was therefore an expectation that working should permeate almost every moment of a placement, regardless of whether there was work that genuinely needed doing or not. This process of constantly 'creating' new work indicates that employers are determined to exploit this system to their advantage even when they don't need the labour. After all, this is *free* labour. But this process also indicates the way that the principle of absolute management control is embedded within workfare. Failure to complete or start a work placement can lead to the person on workfare having their benefits sanctioned.

The government has repeatedly downplayed and denied the harshness of its sanctions regime, yet as David Webster of Glasgow University has pointed out, over a million sanctions are now imposed on claimants every year.[3] It is the threat of further impoverishment or destitution that hangs over every single claimant that is forced to participate in a workfare scheme.

The testimonies indicate that employers exploited the fear that the sanctions regime generates (see Chapters 1 by Mary O'Hara and Chapter 3 by John Pring) and used this fear to make claimants work harder. As one claimant in our sample pointed out:

> The employer states any breaks or lunch break will not be taken off the 30-hour week required. All of the claimants there were afraid of losing their JSA entitlement and so did what was asked of them in cold and freezing conditions.

We also found that such threats are deliberately used to ensure people acquiesce to unsafe working practices. Another claimant who attempted to challenge an employer in relation to dangerous working conditions reported:

> [I] [a]m now facing a 6-month sanction due to [the fact I] got 'sacked' and failed to complete [the placement]. When I kept complaining about health and safety I was told I have a 'bad attitude'.

Another claimant described their placement in similar terms:

> [I] [w]ent to work as a volunteer. Made to feel like a slave. Unsafe working conditions i.e. H and S [health and safety] and Fire regulations breached. Told to leave because I complained and took pictures of the unsafe conditions.

And this is where we get to some of the most disturbing evidence in the testimonies we analysed. Not only does workfare as a forced labour programme rest upon the fear of sanction for compliance, but that the fear of sanction can intensify and generate yet more unreasonable demands from employers. Workfare thus contains within it the seeds of a further abuse of power: the power to force people to do *dangerous* work that threatens their health. It is the violence of this process that we now discuss.

Our analysis of the testimonies of claimants went deeper into the detail of the nature of their reported experiences in order to establish the *seriousness* of the risks they faced. One way to measure the seriousness of health and safety risks is by applying legal standards. And this is what we did: we undertook a detailed reading of claimants' accounts to establish any allegations that, if they were true, would constitute a breach of workplace health and safety law. Following this analysis, we found a total of 64 concrete allegations of breaches of health and safety law at 43 different workplaces. Table 4.2 sets out each of those potential breaches and the frequency with which they took place.

Table 4.2 Evidence of health and safety offences by employers

Law/regulation breached	No. of breaches
Personal Protective Equipment at Work Regulations 1992	12
Workplace (Health, Safety and Welfare) Regulations 1992	12
Control of Substances Hazardous to Health Regulations 2002	5
Manual Handling Operations Regulations 1992	7
The Management of Health and Safety at Work Regulations 1999	21
The Construction (Design and Management) Regulations 2007	1
Road Traffic Act 1988, Section 40A	1
The Working Time Regulations (1998)	4
The Confined Spaces Regulations 1997	1

The most common potential breaches related to a failure to provide personal protective safety equipment (such as gloves for sorting waste material, or masks for working in an enclosed 'dust room'), and conducting heavy lifting and manual handling tasks without proper risk or health assessment. One person reported that his job was to 'remove waste paper ... covered with bird droppings', with no gloves provided. Another noted how, under conditions described as 'sickening', claimants forced to work on a gardening project were given 'mandatory [labouring] duties with the wrong equipment and no PPE [personal protection equipment]'. In terms of the latter point, a number of claimants reporting heavy lifting risks after existing medical conditions were brought to the attention of assessors and/or employers but were not adequately assessed. One described his experience at length:

> They made me work without safety boots for the first week and without a protective jacket. All day was hard labour 9–5 pm. All day I either had to move wood or clean their place. Or they would send me with other people to places to clean houses and back-gardens which they would get money for. They claim to be a community place but I didn't see them help anyone. I told them of my back pain and they just ignored it, they didn't care. Also another business these people had was to charge local people money to pick up their rubbish and then sell it at their place. We were the ones who had to go to pick up the rubbish and there were many hazards. The truck we went on had no seat belts ... Just disgusting practice.

Reports of extreme physical pain were also common in those accounts:

> I can't stand or walk for more than 10 minutes and have severe stomach illness that means when I eat I'm in agony half an hour until 4 hrs after. They may as well have sent me a death sentence.

It was reported in only one case that the existence of pre-existing health problems was acknowledged, and that action was then taken to change the type of work being required of the claimant. Many of those claimants described their experience as an explicitly violent one. Indeed, two stated they had contemplated suicide as a result of the humiliation and physical stress they faced.

As the testimonies here indicate, workfare placements in practice can mean being coerced into working long hours at the whim of an employer. This can mean backbreaking work, exposure to chemicals and dust, and the denial of protective equipment. In extreme cases, it can mean the refusal of access to food or water while at work. Moreover, the evidence provided here indicates that workfare placements constitute a dangerous – and very often illegal – threat to the safety of claimants.

If being employed in workfare schemes can be read as a forced and therefore violent process in itself, it should also be read as a process that contains the potential for a different type of violence: the violence that confronts workers when they are told to stand in the cold, to lift heavy loads that they physically cannot lift, or to endure other forms of physical and psychological degradation. Moreover, the testimonies analysed in this chapter reveal how workfare, as a form of forced labour, effectively permits employers to breach health and safety laws with impunity. The threat of sanctions that underpins the arbitrary power of employers is used as an economic force that compels claimants to comply with such violent working conditions.

In addition to being forced to work for no wage, the breaches of health and safety law that we have uncovered indicate profound attacks on the civil and political status of claimants when they become workers. Benefit claimants, just like all workers and members of the public, are, in law, entitled to the same basic health and safety protections as regular workers.[4]

The sheer brutality of the experience reported in the testimonies documented in this chapter should be a national scandal. The fact that the proliferation of those schemes, conducted under the same conditions that we have reported here, remains a priority of government welfare strategy beggars belief, particularly in the context of a prime ministerial drive to end 'modern slavery' with the appointment of a new Anti-Slavery Commissioner. Although the government does not publish statistics revealing how many people precisely are being forced on to workfare, it is likely to be in excess of 100,00 per year.[5] As Theresa May's government wages a fake war on modern slavery, the government's forced work scheme goes on injuring and killing an unknown and unrecognised number of compulsory, unpaid workers.

ACKNOWLEDGEMENT

Thanks go to Boycott Workfare that we collaborated closely with on this chapter.[6]

NOTES

Websites were last accessed 2 December 2016.
1. D. Fletcher, 'Workfare – a blast for the past? Contemporary conditionality for the unemployed in historical perspective', *Social Policy and Society*, 14, 2015, 329–39.
2. See www.redpepper.org.uk/workfare-a-policy-on-the-brink/
3. D. Webster, 'Benefit sanctions: Britain's secret penal system', Centre for Crime and Justice Studies, 26 January 2015, available at: www.crimeandjustice.org.uk/resources/benefit-sanctions-britains-secret-penal-system
4. J. Burnett and D. Whyte, *The Wages of Fear: Risk, Safety and Undocumented Work*, Leeds and Liverpool: Positive Action for Refugees and Asylum Seekers and University of Liverpool, 2010.
5. See Freedom of Information request documented by the National Archive at: http://anotherangryvoice.blogspot.co.uk/2013/03/workfare-duking-labour-stats.html; and T. Clark, 'Workfare: junking the employment stats', 1 March 2013, available at: http://anotherangryvoice.blogspot.co.uk/2013/03/workfare-duking-labour-stats.html
6. More details on Boycott Workfare's campaigning work can be found at: www.boycottworkfare.org/

5

The Multiple Forms of Violence in the Asylum System

Victoria Canning

People seeking asylum under international refugee laws have often experienced disproportionately violent histories. The nature of asylum places abuses such as torture, sexual violence, and familial death or killing central to claims for refugee status and, as such, signatories to the Refugee Convention are obligated to provide safety. But rather than consistently providing safety and security for those who might require it most, British governments have worked hard to deter people from seeking asylum and deflect from these international obligations. Moreover, as this chapter will argue, measures implemented since the onslaught of so-called austerity measures have both facilitated and inflicted violence, structurally and directly.

It can be difficult to pinpoint what violence actually means in the everyday lives of people seeking asylum. Women and Lesbian, Gay, Bisexual, Transgender and Queer (LGBTQ) people seeking asylum in particular often experience trajectories of violence: in a home country, during migration, in detention camps, and as I focus on here, while waiting to be granted asylum. The period between when an application for asylum is made and a decision has been reached to grant refugee status can be long, drawn out and full of uncertainty. It is also, however, a time when violence can be simultaneously facilitated by state decisions and deliberately inflicted by the state. To begin to unpack this argument in the context of austerity, it is best to start at its foundations: the infliction of economic violence.

People seeking asylum do not have the right to work, and are instead forced into a period of state dependence. This financial dependence affects people's autonomy over their life choices, ability to develop a career or even friendship networks. Importantly, people are forced to live in destitution: asylum applicants now receive half the welfare income of citizens receiving Job Seeker's Allowance, which is itself on the poverty line. Currently, people seeking asylum in Britain receive £36.95 per week in cash (£5.28 per day), but those who are awaiting asylum appeals (some for incorrect or inadequate case decision-making, as we shall see) receive £35.39 per week on a prepayment Azure[1] card.

Considering that people seeking asylum received around £5 per day in 2008, at the beginning of the so-called 'economic crisis', and that inflation has increased on average 2.6 per cent each year[2] since then, the end result of the infliction of such poverty is clearly foreseeable. Evidencing the harmful effects of this meagre entitlement, in 2014 Refugee Action found that:

> Half of asylum-seekers surveyed couldn't buy enough food to feed themselves or their families. [Our] research also found that 43 per cent of asylum-seekers miss a meal because they can't afford to eat while a shocking 88 per cent don't have enough money to buy clothes.[3]

There are two forms of violence visible here. The first is structural: policies allow for poverty, and poverty allows for social exclusion. An 'us and them' mentality has been forged by representations of the 'immigrant other' as benefit scrounger, while non-immigrant groups also suffer poverty under the British government's erosion of welfare under the guise of austerity. Austerity is thus further used as a tool to divide not only the 'haves and have nots' in welfare terms but also, in the case of citizens and non-citizens, the 'should haves and should have nots' (see Chapter 24 by Jon Burnett). This, alongside an increasingly xenophobic climate, encourages exclusionary nationalist sentiment and justifies more borders. As discussed later in the chapter, increased borders means decreased rights to safe passage, which in turn leads to border-related deaths.

The second violence is deliberate and, working with women seeking asylum, is easier to see. It is hunger, malnutrition and the physical pains that arise from these. Women who are pregnant or experience prolonged menstrual bleeding (which can be common for survivors of sexual violence or sexual torture) suffer iron deficiency, fatigue and constant abdominal pain. People with already limited belongings or who have recently arrived from warmer climates face freezing conditions, fuel poverty and the subsequent illnesses that arise from these (see also Chapter 9 by Ruth London). State and council decisions to house otherwise unwanted guests in some of the poorest areas of Britain,[4] regularly in uninhabitable housing conditions, surely know the potential for people to fall ill through respiratory problems caused by damp, spores or pollution. They are not simply complicit in violence: they inflict it.

As many other chapters in this book evidence, poverty and destitution are experienced by multiple groups in society; it is not only people seeking asylum who face hunger and malnutrition. There are, however, precarious conditions specific to seeking asylum. People seeking asylum face significant barriers to gaining safe entry to many countries in Europe – even reaching the UK has become a dangerous feat for many. Opportunities for safe travel have been diminishing since the 1980s, when carrier sanctions[5] were introduced to reduce the possibility of irregular travel for those without visas or documents – a common issue for refugees. As the decades moved on, the UK increased its own border presence across other countries, effectively meaning that people were refused entry to Britain without actually leaving their own country, even if they may have the right to refugee status.

Now, as the crisis at Europe's borders continues to take hold and more people require sanctuary than ever before, the deliberate nature of these efforts to stem asylum claims has come to fruition for Britain: fewer claims are made than many European counterparts, and there are high rates of asylum refusals. Furthermore, as Figure 5.1 indicates, asylum applications have been heavily reduced throughout the past two decades.

By 2015, the UK showed a yearly increase of only 20 per cent in applications for asylum, rising from 32,344 in 2014 to 38,878.

While the drive towards reductions in applications has indeed been based on anti-immigrant sentiment, it has also been justified by the language of austerity. As with other aspects of welfare or support, the British public are told that we cannot afford to offer asylum to everyone and instead require the 'brightest and best', as though people seeking asylum are somehow inherently unskilled. But the myth that Britain cannot afford to support those seeking sanctuary can be easily derailed by three points: the cost paid to detain people in Immigration Removal Centres (IRCs); the money afforded to building external borders; and the

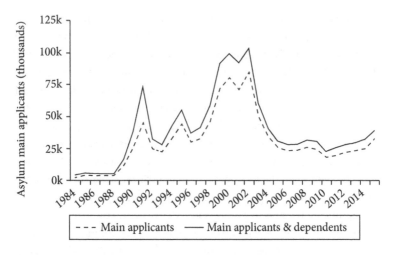

Figure 5.1 Asylum applications and estimated inflows, 1984–2015
(reproduced by permission of the Migration Observatory)

increased expenditure to provide 'humanitarian assistance' elsewhere to deal with the crisis of deaths in the Mediterranean.

To the first of these points, we can argue against cost saving: detaining people costs around £97 per person per day, with around 3200 people at any given time. To the second, since 2015 the British state has pledged £25 million to build a prison in Jamaica for returnees from British prisons, offered an undisclosed amount for a reception centre for Nigerian returnees in Lagos, and made an £80 million offer to commission corporations for the private securitisation of the Calais/Britain border.[6] Lastly, where costs might be placed in support of people seeking asylum in the UK, the government has instead paid to place responsibility elsewhere. When critiqued over Britain's lack of response to the deaths at Europe's borders, for example, the Home Office defended its position by arguing that the government had pledged £2.3 billion in humanitarian aid to Syria and neighbouring countries and was providing nearly £70 million in response to the Mediterranean migration crisis. The ideology of 'should haves and should have nots' has therefore legitimated increased border spending, with decreased welfare entitlement and – as we shall soon see – access to refugee rights.

This brings us back to the question of violence. As the number of people entering Europe increases, so too has the number of people who have died trying. Between January 2015 and October 2016, over 7000 lives were lost in the Mediterranean Sea alone. As documented by Leanne Weber and Sharon Pickering in 2011,[7] the more that borders become militarised, the more dangerous routes people take to reach safety. European states, Britain included, know this but instead deliberately expand border militarisation to keep people out. The results are death at sea or, as a 14-year-old experienced trying to reach Britain from Calais in September 2016, death by lorry.

If and when people do make it to Britain, safety is still not absolute. The immigration detention estate in itself is an extension of violence: holding people for undetermined periods of time in confinement, with no knowledge of if or when one might be deported or released. Instances of sexual and physical violence are reported on regular bases, with potential for severe impacts on people's mental and physical wellbeing. Rather than advocating detention centre closures, the IRC estate continues to expand and profit is made from those forced to live within its walls. The infliction of violence through confinement clearly costs money, but austerity justifies quick removals to avoid long-term welfare dependency or legal fees. Moreover, and as Monish Bhatia and I have argued,[8] profit is easily made elsewhere from the confinement of irregularised immigrants.

This brings me to a final point: that sanctuary in Britain is up for sale, based on the premise of austerity. Sanctuary for survivors of violence should mean support, access to healthcare and the capacity to live free of violence. For survivors of sexual violence, domestic violence or torture, it may mean the potential to access specialist mechanisms of support or access to domestic violence refuges. As the impacts of austerity creep into the everyday functioning of specialist services such as asylum advocacy and sexual violence support, organisations working with some of the most structurally oppressed groups in society are increasingly expected to devise ever more innovative ways of saving money while increasing outputs. Services close, and the very mechanisms used for survival continue to dwindle in the aftermath of violent austerity measures.

Alongside this, endemic cuts to legal aid introduced in the aftermath of the financial crash mean that only those with a perceived greater than 50 per cent chance of success in appealing asylum refusals are able to gain publicly funded representation.[9] For applicants with complex cases, or where poor judgements have been made, this means adequate legal review is out of reach. Recently, the judiciary system was set to charge appellants substantial sums of money for decisions, oral hearings and permission to appeal beyond a first-tier tribunal.[10] Drawing from the language of austerity, the Ministry of Justice claimed that 'in light of the current financial circumstances, it was no longer justifiable that the taxpayer should be responsible for funding the majority of the costs of administering these cases'.[11] The rise was so substantial – a fee increase of 500 per cent for a first-tier hearing – that political and legal outrage led to a decision reversal. Resistance was not futile, but the future remains uncertain so long as the myth of austerity justifies the unaffordable price for legal support. For those who cannot afford this, the Immigration Act 2016 introduced a 'Deport Now, Appeal Later' policy, sending immigration appellants to their country of origin before their case is even fully reviewed.[12]

This creates a very clear trajectory for people whose claims are refused: detention, forced removal and, for those facing return to their country of origin, the potential for violence. If and when people flee conflict or persecution, the minimum risk on return is stigma, shame or social ostracism. The maximum is death. Women fleeing violent relations or husbands cannot be guaranteed safety in countries where violence against women is endemic. LGBTQ people seeking asylum on the basis of homophobic or transphobic violence can face severe penalties on return, including the death penalty in their country of origin. The erosion of the legal right to appeal is an obvious effort to increase deportations: the possible outcome of which is already obvious to those who inflict such precarious conditions.

People who cannot afford to travel safely, or who are legally unable to travel due to carrier sanctions or outsourced visa checks imposed by Western European countries such as Britain, are literally dying at Europe's borders. For those who *do* survive the journey, other forms of destitution and deprivation are enforced in the name of austerity. With reduced access to health, welfare and specialist services, which are crucial for some survivors of persecution, immigrants face a different type of violence that can easily be described as institutional. Indeed, in austerity Britain the social conditions for those seeking asylum are seriously deteriorating, and multiple forms of violence have become everyday for some.

For practitioners working with some of the most oppressed and unsupported groups in society, ongoing reductions in service provision are a travesty. As advocacy and pressure groups such as Sisters Uncut, Imkaan and Safety 4 Sisters can attest, cuts to specialist services have the capacity to effectively facilitate deaths (see the Introduction to this book). If women cannot escape cycles of violence, gain access to refuges and receive emotional support – if they are depressed or feeling suicidal – some women will die. Just as the value of specialist services – BAMER women's refuges, HIV support services, asylum support and advocacy all included – have begun to reach fruition, the capacity for these to exist or be run with sufficient funds has been structurally diminished (see also Chapter 11 by Akwugo Emejulu and Leah Bassel).

The past seven years of austerity have eroded aspects of services that have otherwise taken 30 years of research, trial and error to develop. Reductions in legal aid make for poor standards of asylum appeals and case review, and will inevitably (perhaps deliberately) result in wrongful deportations. Indeed, as financial decisions continue to cut and border controls continue to bite, those seeking asylum are increasingly persecuted by the states in which they seek sanctuary.

NOTES

Websites were last accessed 15 June 2016.

1. The Azure card is run by the French corporation Sodexo. It can be used in some supermarkets but cannot be exchanged for cash or used to buy cigarettes, alcohol or fuel.
2. As calculated using the Bank of England Inflation Calculator, available at: www.bankofengland.co.uk/education/Pages/resources/inflationtools/calculator/flash/default.aspx.
3. Refugee Action, quoted by O. Bowcott, 'Asylum seeker subsistence payments defeat for government in high-court', *Guardian*, 9 April 2014, available at: www.theguardian.com/politics/2014/apr/09/asylum-seeker-subsistence-payments-defeat-government-theresa-may
4. V. Canning, 'International conflict, sexual violence and asylum policy: Merseyside as a case study', *Critical Social Policy*, 34 (1), 2014, 23–45.
5. Carrier sanctions enforce civil or criminal penalties (such as fines or prison) for the carrying of an illegal immigrant on boats, lorries or aircraft.
6. Corporate Watch, 'Home Office quietly advertises £80 million privatisation of Calais border security', 13 September 2016, available at: https://corporatewatch.org/news/2016/sep/13/home-office-quietly-advertises-%C2%A380-million-privatisation-calais-border-security
7. L. Weber and S. Pickering, *Globalisation and Borders: Death at the Global Frontier*, Basingstoke: Palgrave Macmillan, 2011.

8. V. Canning and M. Bhatia, 'Immigration detention: what's the problem with privatisation?', *Society Matters*, 25 April 2016, available at: www.open. edu/openlearn/people-politics-law/immigration-detention-whats-the-problem-privatisation

9. Asylum Aid, 'Appeal rights', n.d., available at: www.asylumaid.org.uk/the-asylum-process-made-simple/#Appeal

10. Ministry of Justice, *Tribunal Fees: The Government Response to Consultation on Proposals for the First-tier Tribunal (Immigration and Asylum Chamber) and Upper Tribunal (Immigration and Asylum Chamber)*, London, 2016, available at: www.gov.uk/government/uploads/system/uploads/attachment_data/file/553387/proposals-imm-asylum-chamber-consultation-response. pdf

11. Ibid., p. 9.

12. Full details of the Immigration Act 2016 are available at: www.legislation. gov.uk/ukpga/2016/19/contents/enacted/data.htm

6

The Degradation and Humiliation of Young People

Emma Bond and Simon Hallsworth

Youth-related violence has long provoked sensational coverage among the media. Fears played out currently, for example, in the sensational and disproportionate coverage given to urban street gangs, now blamed for everything from riots to destroying urban life as we know it. What rarely commands public attention, however, are the forms of violence young disadvantaged people are themselves subject to. Symbolic violence embedded, for example, in the stigmatised way they are positioned in dominant discourse as an underclass devoid of a work ethic and addicted to benefits; or through institutional violence that emanates through government policies shaped by this way of thinking: a violence that manifests itself through various degradation rituals that young disadvantaged people today are forced to undergo in their struggle to survive on diminishing benefits in this post-crash climate.

In this chapter we explore the impact of this rarely seen violence by exploring its catastrophic impact on the lives of young, multiply disadvantaged people in the de-industrialised coastal town of Lowestoft in Suffolk. We consider in particular the impact on these young people's lives of recent changes to welfare provision introduced by the Conservative Party under David Cameron in its Welfare Reform and Work Bill, implemented in 2012 – changes that would dramatically scale back access to benefits for young people, including entitlements to housing benefit; while also mandating a range of sanctions designed to compel young unemployed people back into the world of work as part of a wider attack on 'benefit culture'.

In a speech announcing those welfare reforms and changes, David Cameron made clear what this would mean:

We're finally going to make work pay – especially for the poorest people in society. And we're going to provide much greater support for unemployed people to find work – and stay in work ... So if you're unemployed and refuse to take either a reasonable job or to do some work in your community in return for your unemployment benefit you will lose your benefits for three months. Do it again, you'll lose it for 6 months. Refuse a third time and you'll lose your unemployment benefits for three years.[1]

Using interviews conducted with 51 long-term unemployed and sometimes homeless young people in the coastal town of Lowestoft, we will consider how this violence embedded in the austerity-driven reforms bears down on their lives. Far from providing 'unprecedented support' to those who are 'vulnerable and in need',[2] these policies reinforce and exacerbate the desperate situation that young unemployed people now face. Far from providing them with access to work, the current workfare regime has helped to drive them further into poverty and for some homelessness, crime and drug use. Rather than secure employment in the formal economy, this regime has driven many into the informal drug economy.

We begin by providing some context. Geographically, Lowestoft is the UK's most easterly point. Situated in the county of Suffolk, it is adjacent to Great Yarmouth and to the south sit the prosperous resorts of Southwold and Aldeburgh. While Lowestoft has faced sustained and continuing economic decline since the destruction of its fishing industries, and is home to the region's poorest and most disadvantaged communities, Southwold and Aldeburgh remain affluent millionaires' playgrounds, boasting holiday homes for the very wealthy.

In Lowestoft, one in five children live in poverty (on child poverty in austerity Britain, see Chapter 7 by Joanna Mack) and approximately 10 per cent of young people aged 16–18 in Lowestoft are not in education, employment or training (NEET). According to the index of multiple deprivation, Lowestoft sits within the poorest fifth towns nationally and in terms of the index of multiple child poverty index, six wards in Lowestoft are in the most deprived quintile.[3] There are few high skill professions in the town, which means opportunities for upward mobility are very limited. Instead, the town has far higher rates of occupations that are precarious, low waged, seasonal and low skilled.

While there are new developing industries in the region, such as offshore renewables, agro-tech and nuclear power, most young people in Lowestoft do not possess even the minimum qualifications required to get any meaningful foothold in these industries. Uptake into STEM subjects (science, technology, engineering and mathematics) in local schools is low, as are pass rates, which disqualifies most young people (and at an early age) from participation in the developing economies in the region. Likewise, uptake into higher education in Lowestoft is far lower than the national average.[4]

The difficulties that young people in Lowestoft face are also impacted by factors very specific to the locality. The lack of a comprehensive, reliable public transport system has reinforced geographical isolation and confinement. In its privatised form, public transport is prohibitively expensive for those on Income Support or in low paid work. Drawing directly on the testimonies taken from the very constituency Cameron's governmental policies have targeted – long-term unemployed young people and young homeless people – we explore how these welfare reforms and the underclass thinking that informs them bear down on their lives.

We asked young people what kind of work they were looking for. Everyone we spoke to wanted to work, indeed it would be fair to say they desperately wanted to work – so much so, they did not care what the work entailed as long as it was a job. Unemployment among this population appeared less driven by absence of a work ethic, a key trope in the underclass thinking that informs government policy, but because there simply were not enough job opportunities in the region. As one of the young people we asked put it, there is 'nothing for young people in Lowestoft', 'no hope of getting a job'. David had applied for over 30 jobs in the previous two weeks and most participants spoke of giving out 'hundreds of CVs'. Another, Jadine, handed out 200 CVs to shops and only received two responses.

The experience of failing to gain work left these young people frustrated and pessimistic about their future. They recognised that failure to gain paid work meant they had little work experience to offer employers (which compounded their inability to get into work). Many were aware of the stigma that went hand in hand with being unemployed, which manifests in a sense of being made to feel worthless and useless.

According to Sam, another young person we spoke to,

One of the reasons we can't find work is because we have been unemployed for so long we are a waste of space. No one wants us because we have nothing. No experience nothing. People think there must be something wrong with you if you have been unemployed for so long but they don't see how hard you tried, the shit you have been through and the sacrifices you have made. I've gone hungry many times. People just look at you like you are worthless and shit and half the time they are the people that should be helping you.

Holly, has been trying to find work for over a year and described the consequences:

It's shit, it's hard – you go out and give CVs to any shop and fish and chips and that but you never hear anything back – not one person got back to me, not one. And if you live on your own and don't have a family and that is really hard and you have to pay your bills and there is never anything left its hard ... it's lonely and there is no hope. No hope of a job because there aren't any. I don't know how to explain it but it makes me feel stressed worried and sad – I'm on income support and I have no money but if I could get a job I know income support take money off you but it would be nice to have a job and have a little bit more so I can afford food and that.

When work came, it was rarely permanent and typically low paid. Often it was seasonal work, which for the participants we interviewed meant they were left moving between intermittent jobs in a precarious labour market and the coercive and punitive workfare system created to 'help' them. We asked about their experiences in attempting to obtain welfare at their local JobCentre when there was no work. Our participants were scathing in their testimonies about an institution that offered them no practical support in getting a job; made them spend hours sitting in front of computers looking for work that simply did not exist; and whose staff would sanction them (remove entitlement to benefits) for the most trivial of infractions. Below we outline some of the young people's experiences of engaging with what we consider a highly coercive workfare regime.

When you do see your adviser they can only see you for 5 minutes and they are not interested in you and the JobCentre is too busy and they tell you that they are under-staffed and too busy to help you. If you are not doing enough to meet your job seekers' agreement they won't help you they just tell you that you aren't doing enough – get out! They don't help you and then you just get sanctioned. (Tom)

The way that it feels walking into the JobCentre is that you are there to do what you are told to do and that's it and then you leave. They are not there to actually help you it is just like, you have to do this and if you don't do this or you won't get no money. (Julie)

If you physically walk around and try to look for work by handing in your CV the JobCentre are like 'That's not good enough, you have to look online.' But you know there is nothing available online because you have looked and let's face it if you have a shop or a fish and chip place or that would you advertise a job? Online? No fucking way. You would put a notice in the window or employ someone that you know, not online. But the JobCentre say that is not good enough and you can't look for work that way. So they make you just sit and look online like a fucking idiot just because there is physical proof that you have done it. They are the fucking idiots. (Joshua)

What came powerfully across in these testimonies was of a system not there to enable people to gain employment but a degradation ritual designed to further humiliate and alienate this desperately vulnerable population (see Chapter 4 by Jon Burnett and David Whyte). Though wasting their time appeared a constant, the real violence of this workfare system was mobilised through the ability of staff to cut benefits often for minor infractions.

I am sanctioned at the moment because I was at college and I missed an appointment – so they stopped my money. It went to head office but they did not accept it but I was at Lowestoft doing a charity thing – a Princes Trust event setting up a youth centre for younger kids. (Tom)

Having been sanctioned several times, many young people literally gave up on the JobCentre. As a result of the sanctions imposed, many had gone hungry, some were made homeless and consequently forced to live in cheap, dirty flea-ridden hostels, which is where we interviewed many. Some had been evicted and lived on the street. One way some of our participants confronted their destitution was through drug use and working in the informal economy. For some, it was a way of coping with their desperate situation, while at the same time compounding it. For others, dealing in Crystal Meth became a way of making a living in a town where career opportunities in the formal economy simply did not exist.

Far from helping the long-term disadvantaged young people seek secure work opportunities, reforms introduced under the Welfare Reform and Work Act 2016 will compound their disadvantage, throwing them ever more deeply into debt, poverty, misery and helplessness. And this is why it is appropriate to study such reforms as an exercise in violence. The violent consequences of these welfare reforms is manifested in loss of financial income, increased drug use, eviction, homelessness and working in the informal and illegal economy. But the violence does not stop there and the effects of these welfare changes are drawn out over time, creating deeper, more internal violent thoughts.

We conclude this chapter with Bridget's testimony. It summarises in a heart-rending way precisely the level of 'unprecedented support' the 'vulnerable and the needy' receive in austerity UK today.

> I am ashamed to admit it but I did feel suicidal at one point. I felt so down after I was made redundant that I felt that there was no point. I had worked really hard at school and I got good grades but for what? I was happy when I got my job, it wasn't that well paid but it had prospects and a career path – or so the recruitment agency told me – I had my flat and that and I thought I was OK. But when it [the redundancy] happened I felt like I had been hit by a brick wall. I got really down especially when I went to the JobCentre and they would not help me. I felt so depressed. I could not afford my rent, I lost my flat and the few things I had saved up for. I did not know where to turn. I took drugs for the first time in my life – I felt so wretched, I wanted to die. I was too ashamed to tell my parents that I had lost my job.

NOTES

Websites were last accessed 18 November 2016.

1. David Cameron's full speech on the Welfare Reform Bill is available at: www.gov.uk/government/speeches/pms-speech-on-welfare-reform-bill

2. Cabinet Office, Press release, Hancock, 'Every young person should be earning or learning from April 2017', 17 August 2015.
3. Health and Wellbeing, Suffolk, *Joint Strategic Needs Assessment*, 2015, available at: www.suffolk.gov.uk/assets/suffolk.gov.uk/Your%20Council/Consultations%20and%20EOI/Addressing%20Poverty/2015-07-31-Poverty-Strategy-Booklet-LR-v3.pdf
4. HM Government, *Review of Post-16 Provision in North East Norfolk and North Suffolk: A High Level Summary Report*, 2015.

PART II

Poverty Amplification

7

Child Maltreatment and Child Mortality

Joanna Mack

In the summer of 2016, the United Nations issued their latest report on the UK's progress in meeting the internationally agreed targets on the Rights of the Child. Concentrating on the period since 2008, the report provides an independent assessment of the impact of the financial crash and, in particular, the first stage of the austerity policies that followed. Its verdict is damning. 'Recent fiscal policies and allocation of resources', the report concluded, were 'disproportionately affecting children in disadvantaged situations'.[1] Policies such as the 'household benefit cap', 'the bedroom tax' and limitations to entitlements to child tax credits were highlighted as particularly damaging. The high rates of child poverty were seen as a matter of 'serious concern'. In conclusion, the UN Committee on the Rights of the Child called for the re-establishment of the child poverty reduction targets, which the government repealed in 2016, the provision for 'clear and accountable mechanisms for the eradication of child poverty' and the revision of recent benefit reforms.

This is a powerful condemnation of the violence inherent in the politics of austerity. Under the guise of deficit reduction, and with little political opposition, the government promoted an aggressive programme of welfare cuts. While the government presented these policies as fair and evenly spread, that we were 'all in it together',[2] the outcomes – increased levels of child deprivation and the accompanying higher likelihood of ill health and diminished life chances – were entirely predictable. The policies were designed[3] to hit the incomes and housing security of families who already had a hand to mouth existence, missing out on the most basic of contemporary needs.

In 2012, before the impact of current changes to the benefit system, the Poverty and Social Exclusion survey[4] found that over two and a half million children, around one in five, live in a home that is cold or damp (see Chapter 9 by Ruth London). Over a million children, just under one in ten, do not have an essential item of clothing. One in 20 households cannot afford to feed their children adequately, resulting in 600,000 children missing out on one or more of three meals a day, fresh fruit and vegetables each day, or meat, fish, or the equivalent, while 300,000 children go without two or more of these essential food items (see Chapter 8 by Rebecca O'Connell and Laura Hamilton).[5]

It is against this background that the Coalition government opted for a programme of progressively harsher cuts to welfare spending. On taking office, they froze the rate of child benefit and changed the inflation rate for upgrading benefits to the lower Consumer Price Index (rather than Retail Price Index). In 2013, a 'big bang' of benefit reforms – which, among other cuts, set working-age benefit increases to a maximum of 1 per cent, brought in a cap to individual benefit payments and introduced the 'bedroom tax' – was passed, with the target to cut around £20 billion a year by 2015/16 from working-age benefits. At the same time, council tax benefit was effectively strangled by passing responsibility to local councils, which – already facing slashed budgets – had no money spare to take it on.[6]

Including tax changes – which gave away money through increases to the personal allowance but took it through increases to VAT – the Coalition government took around £30 billion overall from household incomes. And the poorest families were the hardest hit.

Figure 7.1 shows that while middle income households without children saw an increase to their incomes as a result of these changes, households with children saw a decrease and of these households, those on low incomes fared the worst.[7] Prior to these cuts, adults in households with children were already over twice as likely to be in poverty as adults without children.[8]

Lone parents – of whom, prior to the cuts, two thirds were in poverty[9] – saw the severest percentage reductions with close to 10 per cent (around £2000) for those out of work and nearly 7 per cent for those in work.[10] These reductions in the incomes of the poorest families are a direct result of the government's benefit changes.

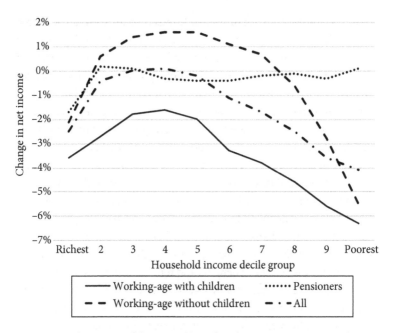

Figure 7.1 The impact of the tax and benefit reforms, May 2010 to April 2015

Existing on meagre incomes, such families already had nothing left to spare at the end of each week. As one lone parent from Birmingham explains:

> It's a struggle. It's an effort. I get up in the morning and it [money] is the first thing I think of and I go to bed at night and it is the last thing I think of. That's the impact it has.[11]

The consequence of such reductions in income is that the UK, which has long had a poor record on child poverty compared to many other nations with similar levels of economic development, has slipped further behind. Eurostat, which gathers comprehensive data from across Europe, reports that in 2014 over 22 per cent of children in the UK lived in deprived households, taken as being unable to afford three or more of a range of household items,[12] compared to 14 per cent in France, around 12 per cent in Germany and a mere 4 per cent in Norway and Sweden.[13] In 2007, before the austerity years, the UK's rate was 15 per cent well below the EU average – now it is above.

Many on low incomes report feeling 'stressed' or 'anxious' and for some the cumulative effect is that they end up suffering from depression.[14] Lone parents, in particular, were already facing additional levels of stress. Prior to 2008, lone parents whose youngest child was under sixteen didn't have to work and could claim Income Support but the then Labour government reduced that age to seven, forcing lone parents on to Job Seeker's Allowance with all the added pressure of benefits being conditional on having to look for work and suitable child care – and with the threat of sanctions for 'failing' to do so. Subsequently, the Coalition government reduced this to lone parents with five-year-olds and in 2014 sanctions were introduced for those with three- and four-year-olds on Income Support who failed to undertake 'work-related activities'.

As well as the sharp reduction in benefit levels, the Coalition government introduced a far more punitive regime with more restrictive conditions for the receipt of benefits and tougher sanctions (see Chapter 3 by John Pring and Chapter 4 by Jon Burnett and David Whyte). From 2012, penalties for claimants on Job Seeker's Allowance and for disabled people on Employment and Support Allowance were introduced for a wide range of supposed failures. These included missing an interview, non-attendance in a training scheme and not applying for as many jobs as specified. These sanctions came with a new set of fixed-period suspensions of benefits ranging from four weeks to three years. Claimants are not allowed to appeal until two weeks after the decision, leaving many penniless in the meantime.

Between October 2012 and the end of 2015, there were over 1.9 million decisions to sanction claimants.[15] More people suffer financial penalties through benefit sanctions than fines in the magistrate courts. It is a state administered penal system without any transparency or accountability.[16] This is institutional violence aimed at the poorest. Combined with administrative delays in processing applications through over-loaded benefit offices many people have been left desperate.

Gemma was four days away from giving birth when she ended up in a food bank in Stockton-on-Tees, dependent on an emergency food parcel for the next meal. She and her partner had had no money for three weeks as they waited for the Department of Work and Pensions (DWP) to process their Job Seeker's Allowance claim:

I was crying on the phone to them [the DWP] telling them I am pregnant. I don't want my baby coming home to a house with no gas or electric. We have laminated floor and it's so cold.[17]

The UK infant (0 to 1 years) mortality rate, at around four deaths per 1000 births in 2014, is higher than all but two of the nineteen Euro area member states.[18] About half of these deaths are linked to short gestation and low birth weight, both of which are highly associated with deprivation.[19] The result is that babies born into poorer families in deprived neighbourhoods are more likely to die than children from richer families.[20]

Allowing a pregnant woman to go without food in a cold, unheated home is to compromise her baby's life chances. The World Health Organization defines 'child maltreatment' as an action that in the context of a relationship of power results in 'actual or potential harm to the child's health, survival, development or dignity'.[21] If an individual takes such actions then they may be liable to prosecution. Yet if a political system results in such actions, it is seen as an inevitable, if unfortunate, by-product of economic necessity. This is not covert violence but overt violence.

Throughout childhood, poverty raises the risk of premature death. The progress that had been made in the 1980s and 1990s in reducing child mortality rates shuddered to a halt in this millennium with the result that the UK has fallen behind other European countries with similar levels of development. If the UK had the same all-cause death rate as Sweden, around 1900 children's lives could be saved each year.[22]

Poverty in childhood also leads to poor health. Children who live in damp and mouldy homes are up to three times more likely than those in dry homes to suffer from coughing, wheezing and respiratory illness.[23] Children living in overcrowded conditions – the numbers of which had risen sharply between 1999 and 2012 from 3 per cent of children to 11 per cent[24] – are more likely to catch infectious diseases.[25]

Children born in poor areas have, as is well and long established, a shorter life expectancy than those born in rich areas and a much shorter period of a life free of the limiting effects of illness and disability – inequalities that are increasing.[26] Much of this increased risk is the result of cumulative disadvantages across the adult years. Children from deprived backgrounds are more likely to have lower educational qualifications with lower long-term earnings and therefore to be deprived as adults (see Chapter 6 by Emma Bond and Simon Hallsworth). But there is growing scientific evidence that during the early years (and in the womb) there is a biological embedding of metabolic processes in the body that increases the risk of long-term illness and, with this, premature death – risks that are not completely removed even if there is subsequent upward social mobility.[27]

On winning the 2015 election, the Conservatives announced a further £12 billion cuts which included limiting tax credits to two children, a continued freezing of working-age benefits and a lowering of the level of the benefits cap. As Figure 7.2 shows, the poorest households are, again, the hardest hit and, in particular, poor households with children – who are set to lose up to 12 per cent of their income.[28]

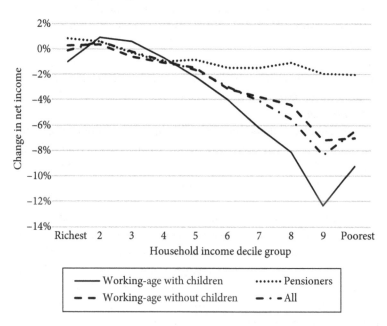

Figure 7.2   The projected impact of tax and benefit reforms, May 2015 to April 2019

Since 2010, the government – both Coalition and Conservative – have consistently downplayed the importance of lack of income as a cause of poverty. Instead, blame has been laid on the lifestyles of individual families and their parenting practice. David Cameron cast the problem as: 'Drug addiction. Alcohol abuse. Crime. A culture of disruption and irresponsibility that cascades through generations.'[29] A focus on personal inadequacies fitted much better the aim, for which austerity was providing cover, of rolling back welfare provision.

On becoming Prime Minister in July 2016, Theresa May tried to set a new tone, making bold promises about 'a country that works for everyone' and fighting the 'burning injustice' of those born poor dying earlier than others.[30] Yet for all the talk of an end to austerity, all of the planned benefits cuts will go ahead.[31] Largely as a direct result of these planned cuts, over half a million more children are set to fall below the 2010/11 poverty line in 2020/21 than did in 2015/16 while the percentage of children in relative income poverty[32] is predicted to rise from 18 per cent in 2015/16 to 26 per cent in 2020/21.[33] And these projections could prove optimistic given the economic uncertainties surrounding Brexit and the threats to turn the UK into a low-tax haven with its inevitable consequence of a further rolling back of the welfare state. There are warnings of sharp falls to come to the real-terms incomes of the poorest, particularly those with children.[34]

This makes a mockery of promises to fight the injustice of poverty. To do this, there would need to be a real commitment to the transfer of income and wealth from the rich to the poor. And that would challenge the very basis of the neoliberal ideology still underpinning the government – an ideology that embeds within it the violence of child poverty.

NOTES

Websites were last accessed 15 July 2016.

1. United Nations Committee on the Rights of the Child, *Concluding Observations on the Fifth Periodic Report of the United Kingdom of Great Britain and Northern Ireland*, CRC/C/GBR/CO/5, Geneva, 2016.
2. Full speech available at: www.theguardian.com/politics/2009/oct/08/david-cameron-speech-in-full
3. As admitted by the then deputy prime minister. See A. Asthana and S. Hattenstone, 'Clegg: Osborne casually cut welfare for poorest to boost Tory popularity', *Guardian*, 2 September 2016, available at: www.theguardian.com/politics/2016/sep/02/nick-clegg-george-osborne-cut-welfare-poorest-boost-tory-popularity
4. www.poverty.ac.uk
5. Stewart Lansley and Joanna Mack, *Breadline Britain: The Rise of Mass Poverty*, London, Oneworld, 2015.

6. www.theguardian.com/society/2016/aug/06/benefits-council-tax-poverty-families-liverpool
7. J. Browne and W. Elming, *The Effect of the Coalition's Tax and Benefit Changes on Household Incomes and Work Incentives*, BN 159, London: Institute for Fiscal Studies, 2015, available at: www.ifs.org.uk/uploads/publications/bns/BN159.pdf
8. G. Main and J. Bradshaw, *Child Poverty and Social Exclusion: Final Report of 2012 PSE Study*, 2014, available at: www.poverty.ac.uk/sites/default/files/attachments/PSE-Child-poverty-and-exclusion-final-report-2014.pdf
9. Lansley and Mack, *Breadline Britain*, p. 85.
10. Browne and Elming, *The Effect of the Coalition's Tax and Benefit Changes*.
11. S. Pemberton, E. Sutton, E. Fahmy and K. Bell, *Life on a Low Income in Austere Times*, Report published by Poverty and Social Exclusion in the UK, 2014, available at: www.poverty.ac.uk/sites/default/files/attachments/Life%20on%20a%20low%20income%20in%20austere%20times_final_report.pdf
12. The household items covered are available at: http://ec.europa.eu/eurostat/statistics-explained/index.php/Glossary:Material_deprivation
13. These figures are taken from Eurostat data tables, available at: http://ec.europa.eu/eurostat/web/income-and-living-conditions/data/database
14. Pemberton et al., *Life on a Low Income*.
15. Department for Work and Pensions, *Quarterly Statistical Summary, May 2016*, Newcastle-Upon Tyne, 2016, available at: www.gov.uk/government/statistics/dwp-statistical-summaries-2016
16. D. Webster, 'Benefit sanctions: Britain's secret penal system', Centre for Crime and Justice, 26 January 2015, available at: www.crimeandjustice.org.uk/resources/benefit-sanctions-britains-secret-penal-system; also see D. Webster, 'Benefit sanctions have failed: a comprehensive review is needed', London School of Economics, 5 January 2016, available at: http://blogs.lse.ac.uk/politicsandpolicy/benefit-sanctions-have-failed-a-comprehensive-review-is-needed/
17. Quoted in K. Garthwaite, *Hunger Pains – Life Inside Foodbank Britain*, Bristol: Policy Press, 2016, p. 1.
18. These figures are taken from Eurostat data tables, available at: http://appsso.eurostat.ec.europa.eu/nui/show.do?dataset=demo_minfind&lang=en
19. E. Rough, P. Goldblatt, M. Marmot and V. Nathanson, 'Inequalities in child health', in British Medical Association (ed.), *Growing up in the UK*, London: BMA Board of Science, 2013, pp. 37–55.
20. J. Roberts and R. Bell, *Social Inequalities in the Leading Causes of Early Death*, London: Institute of Health Equity, University College London, 2015.
21. World Health Organization, 'Child maltreatment', September 2016, available at: www.who.int/mediacentre/factsheets/fs150/en/
22. Ingrid Woolfe, 'Setting the scene', in British Medical Association (ed.), *Growing up in the UK*, London: BMA Board of Science, 2013, pp. 13–36.

23. The Marmot Review Team, *The Health Impacts of Cold Homes and Fuel Poverty*, London: Friends of the Earth, 2011.

24, Lansley and Mack, *Breadline Britain*, p. 45.

25. L. Harker, *Chance of a Lifetime: The Impact of Bad Housing on Children's Lives*, London: Shelter, 2006.

26. M. Marmot, Fairer Society, Healthy Lives, London: Institute of Health Equity, University College London, Marmot Review, 2010. Office for National Statistics, Life Expectancy at Birth and at Age 65 by Local Areas in England and Wales: 2012 to 2014, 2016, available at: www.ons.gov.uk/people populationandcommunity/birthsdeathsandmarriages/lifeexpectancies/ bulletins/lifeexpectancyatbirthandatage65bylocalareasinenglandand wales/2015-11-04#local-area-life-expectancy-at-birth

27. Gary Evans, E. Chen, G. Miller and T, Seeman, 'How poverty gets under the skin', in V. Maholmes and R.B. King (eds), *The Oxford Handbook of Poverty and Child Development*, Oxford: Oxford University Press, 2012, pp. 13–36. Also see D. Barker, 'Fetal origins of adult diseases', in British Medical Association (ed.), *Growing up in the UK*, London: BMA Board of Science, 2013, pp. 149–81.

28. W. Elming and A. Hood, *Distributional Analysis*, London: Institute for Fiscal Studies, 2016, available at: www.ifs.org.uk/publications/8206

29. Full speech is available at: www.gov.uk/government/speeches/troubled-families-speech

30. Full speech is available at: www.gov.uk/government/speeches/statement-from-the-new-prime-minister-theresa-may

31. J. Elgot, 'No more welfare cuts to come under Theresa May, says minister', *Guardian*, 18 September 2016, available at: www.theguardian.com/politics/ 2016/sep/18/no-more-welfare-cuts-under-theresa-may-says-minister-damian-green-end-to-austerity

32. The percentage falling below 60 per cent of median household income before housing costs.

33. James Browne and Andrew Hood, *Living Standards, Poverty and Inequality in the UK: 2015–16 to 2020–21*, R114, London: Institute for Fiscal Studies, February 2016 available at: www.ifs.org.uk/uploads/publications/ comms/R114.pdf. These projections, made pre-Brexit, use the Office for Budget Responsibility's forecast for earnings and employment as well as incorporating the planned tax and benefit changes.

34. Adam Corlett and Stephen Clarke, *Living Standards 2017*, London: The Resolution Foundation, February 2017 available at: www.resolution foundation.org/app/uploads/2017/01/Audit-2017.pdf

8

Hunger and Food Poverty

Rebecca O'Connell and Laura Hamilton

Britain is the world's fifth richest country,[1] but food poverty is a national concern. The UK media report an increase in the number of children arriving at school hungry, a marked growth in food banks handing out food parcels to families and households being forced to choose 'between heating and eating'. While the UK government has repeatedly denied responsibility, evidence shows that rising levels of food poverty and insecurity in the UK are linked to reduced affordability of food in the context of food price rises, stagnant incomes and so-called austerity measures. Given that food is fundamental to health and social participation, food poverty has violent consequences for individuals, households and society itself.

Emergency food provision has been used as an indicator of the scale of food poverty in the UK. As the Fabian Commission on Food and Poverty noted in 2015, the Trussell Trust, the largest emergency food provider, 'has seen the number of people referred for emergency food rise by 38 per cent in the last year'.[2] Oxfam and Church Action on Poverty calculate that 20,247,042 meals were given to 'people in food poverty' in 2013/14.[3] While these are shocking statistics, they are likely to underestimate the numbers in food poverty in Britain: not all people who are hungry go to food banks and not all food banks collect data in a systematic way. The Poverty and Social Exclusion UK (PSE UK) 2012 study found that the proportion of households unable to afford two adult meals a day in 2012 stood at 3 per cent, 'back to levels found thirty years earlier having dropped to negligible levels in the intervening period'.[4] In addition, well over half a million children live in families who cannot afford to feed them properly, that is, provide at least one of the following: three meals a day; fresh fruit and vegetables every day; or meat, fish or a vegetarian equivalent at least once a day.[5] If many parents were not cutting back on their own food intake to protect their children, the number would be much higher.[6]

Reports of rising food poverty and food bank use have largely been ignored or dismissed by the UK government, with politicians suggesting that supply is fuelling demand and blaming the poor for lacking budgeting skills, making poor food 'choices' and being unable to cook.[7] In contrast to government discourse, however, research shows that the cost of food relative to disposable income (affordability) is crucial[8] and that in the wake of the financial crisis and subsequent policies of economic austerity, the affordability of food was severely reduced.

Global food price rises in 2007 marked 'the end of cheap food'.[9] In the UK, a country which imported half of the food it consumed in 2007,[10] food prices increased by 11.5 per cent in real terms between 2007 and 2012 (when prices peaked), and even higher for fresh fruit (23 per cent) and vegetables (24 per cent).[11] Such increases reflect a more general rise in the cost of living in Britain over the same period, with households finding it more difficult to maintain or reach an acceptable standard of living, as defined by the Joseph Rowntree's Minimum Income Standard.[12] At the same time, real earnings remained stagnant or fell. For instance, a recent report by the Institute for Fiscal Studies[13] states that income from employment 'is on average still lower than before the recession, driven by the lower earnings of those in work'.[14] While overall incomes are higher, this is due to 'lower average tax payments, higher (pensioner) benefits and higher incomes from savings, investments and private pensions';[15] economic resources unlikely to be accessible to low income households. Precarious employment that has increased with the growth of zero-hours contracts, and high levels of debt, also leave households vulnerable to economic shocks. Since the food budget is relatively 'elastic' compared to other essential costs that have also risen, people can and do cut back on food to meet competing demands. Households seeking to economise may 'trade down' to cheaper versions of the same product or change what they buy and consume, although 'those in the lowest income group are not trading down because they have less opportunity to do so, being already on the most basic of diets'.[16]

Analysis by the UK government's Department for Environment, Food and Rural Affairs shows that falling incomes and rising living costs mean that food is now over 20 per cent less affordable for the poorest 10 per cent of people in the UK compared to 2003. In 2012, when the proportion of the household budget spent on food peaked in the UK, those in the lowest income decile spent 22 per cent more on food than in 2007 and purchased 5.7 per cent less, buying significantly fewer portions of fruit and vegetables than previously.[17] Further, the number of UK adults who have reported being unable to afford meat, fish or vegetarian equivalent every other day (a measure of adequate protein in the diet) has increased between 2004 and 2012, that is, in the context of economic austerity and rising food prices.[18] The PSE UK study noted above found that the proportion of adults going without meat or equivalent every second day because they could not afford it rose from 2 per cent in 1999 to 5 per cent in 2012. In addition, 3 per cent of children went without adequate protein and the same proportion did not eat fresh fruit or vegetables every day because their families could not afford it.[19] Reduced afford-ability of food therefore generally leads to a reduction in nutrient quality of food consumed and, in a growing number of cases, to hunger and reliance on emergency food provision.

There is a clear association between so-called austerity measures, implemented in Britain from 2011, and food poverty, something the UK government has repeatedly denied.[20] Evidence shows a clear correlation between increasing conditionality, benefits sanctions and the distribution of food parcels. Rachel Loopstra and colleagues[21] found that Trussell Trust food banks were more likely to open in areas with greater unemployment and welfare sanctions and reductions in local and central government spending (e.g. austerity measures). Although food bank parcel distribution was greater in areas with more and better established food banks, higher distribution was still significantly associated with government cuts, welfare sanctions and unemployment rates, contra-dicting the government's claims that supply is fuelling demand and signifying the consequences of austerity measures on those already living in precarious economic circumstances. Qualitative research supports the finding that benefits sanctions and delays are a main reason that people turn to food banks, and crucially considers the implications for individuals' and households' lived experiences[22] which are unlikely to improve in the near future due to further austerity and planned cuts to government spending and benefits.

The deleterious consequences of poor diet intake and malnutrition, particularly for children, are well established and have long-term implications (see Chapter 7 by Joanna Mack). The profound effects of health inequalities that are associated with poor dietary intakes and meal patterns include increasing incidence of coronary heart disease, type II diabetes and cancer.[23] Indeed, the UK Faculty of Public Health has argued that recent evidence of increasing malnutrition and hunger constitutes a 'public health emergency'.[24] Sub-optimal diet and food practices such as skipping meals are also associated with poor cognition and lower academic achievement[25] as children's ability to concentrate and study is damaged by insufficient food or food of poor nutritious value. In the UK, as elsewhere, food poverty and being overweight and obesity are closely connected, a trend partly explained by the relative cheapness and wide availability of unhealthy foods that are high in saturated fat and non-milk extrinsic sugars.[26]

But food is more than simply fuel or nutrition. It is fundamentally meaningful, intimately linked with identity, and an important medium of social relations, inclusion and exclusion. Exercising choice in the marketplace, including what food to buy and eat, is also one means of enacting agency in a consumer society. Individuals and households experiencing food poverty may be forced to procure foods in socially unacceptable ways (such as from food banks) and be unable to participate in ordinary social activities involving food, like eating out or offering and receiving hospitality. Although there is evidence of adapted preferences (reduced expectations) in the context of austerity, these 'social' dimensions of food and eating are widely included as part of a consensually determined minimum socially acceptable standard of living.[27] However, evidence from the PSE UK[28] suggests that 11 per cent of households could not afford to have friends or family around for a meal or drink at least once a month in 2012 compared to 6 per cent in 1999. Furthermore, the proportion who could not afford to have a friend's child around for tea or a snack once a fortnight doubled between 1999 and 2012, from 4 per cent to 8 per cent, representing 1,000,000 children.[29] Given that social relationships between children and their peers are an integral aspect of their development and well-being, the consequences are likely to be highly damaging and include increasing social exclusion and societal fragmentation.

Finally, the psychological dimensions of food poverty include not only worrying about whether there will be enough money for food but the shame of being unable to feed oneself and one's family in a society in which this is constructed as an individual responsibility (on the impact of poverty on mental health, see Chapter 1 by Mary O'Hara). Since the right to food is an entitlement, food charity is not the solution to food poverty.[30] Qualitative research reports the violent and harmful effects of stigma and shame experienced by those using food banks[31] both from staff in some settings and from 'othering' media discourses.[32] Suggestions that the poor are unable to budget or cook are forms of symbolic violence that serve to further stigmatise and marginalise those already suffering material deprivation and social exclusion.

The growth in emergency food provision has been 'the most visible symptom of the rise of food insecurity in the UK'[33] and food banks may be seen as a metonym for the impoverishment of Britain. Because food is fundamental to health and social participation, hunger and food poverty that have risen in austerity Britain have violent implications for individuals and households and for society itself.

NOTES

Websites were last 30 November 2016.

1. The World Bank, GDP at market prices (current US$), 2016, available at: http://data.worldbank.org/indicator/NY.GDP.MKTP.CD?order=wbapi_data_value_2012+wbapi_data_value+wbapi_data_value-last&sort=desc

2. Fabian Commission on Food and Poverty, *A Recipe for Inequality: Why Our Food System is Leaving Low-income Households Behind*, London: Fabian Society, 2015.

3. N. Cooper., S. Purcell and R. Jackson, *Below the Breadline*, Oxford: Church Action on Poverty and Oxfam, 2014.

4. S. Lansley and J. Mack, *Breadline Britain: The Rise of Mass Poverty*, London: Oneworld Publications, 2015, p. 38.

5. D. Gordon, J. Mack, S. Lansley et al., 'The impoverishment of the UK', Poverty and Social Exclusion UK, first results: Living Standards, 2013.

6. Lansley and Mack, *Breadline Britain*, p. 39.

7. L. Berger, 'People don't visit food banks because they're "unable to manage their finances", Mr Gove', *Independent*, 12 September 2013, available at: www.independent.co.uk/voices/comment/people-dont-visit-food-banks-because-theyre-unable-to-manage-their-finances-mr-gove-8810005.html; Patrick Butler, 'Food poverty: Panorama, Edwina Currie and the missing ministers', *Guardian*, 3 March 2014, available at: www.theguardian.com/society/patrick-butler-cuts-blog/2014/mar/03/food-poverty-panorama-edwina-currie-and-the-missing-ministers-food-banks; P. Butler, 'Tory peer says poor people go hungry because they do not know how to cook', *Guardian*,

8 December 2014, available at: www.theguardian.com/society/2014/dec/08/ tory-peer-apologises-poor-hungry-do-not-know-cook; R. Mason, 'Lord Tebbit scorns food bank demand', *Guardian*, 20 March 2014, available at: www.theguardian.com/politics/2014/mar/20/lord-tebbit-scorns-food-bank-demand

8. For example, K. Roberts, N. Cavill, C. Hancock and H. Rutter, *Social and Economic Inequalities in Diet and Physical Activity*, London: Public Health England, 2013; E. Dowler, 'Food and health inequalities: the challenge for sustaining just consumption', *Local Environment*, 13 (8), 2008, 759–72.

9. *The Economist*, 'The end of cheap food', 6 December 2007.

10. Defra, *Food Statistics Pocketbook 2009*, London: Department for Environment, Food and Rural Affairs, 2009.

11. Defra, *Food Statistics Pocketbook 2016*, London: Department for Environment, Food and Rural Affairs, 2016.

12. Joseph Rowntree Foundation, *A Minimum Income Standard for the UK in 2012*, York, 2012.

13. Chris Belfield, J. Cribb, A. Hood and R. Joyce, *Living Standards, Poverty & Inequality in the UK: 2016*, London: Institute for Fiscal Studies, 2016.

14. Ibid., p. 14.

15. Ibid.

16. E. Dowler, 'Food banks and food justice in "Austerity Britain"', in G. Riches and T. Silvasti (eds), *First World Hunger Revisited*, Basingstoke: Palgrave Macmillan, 2014, pp. 160–75, p. 167.

17. Defra, *Food Statistics Pocketbook 2012*, London: Department for Environment, Food and Rural Affairs, 2013.

18. Rachel Loopstra, A. Reeves, M. McKee and D. Stuckler, 'Food insecurity and social protection in Europe: quasi-natural experiment of Europe' great recessions 2004–2012', *Preventative Medicine*, 89, 2016, 44–50.

19. Lansley and Mack, *Breadline Britain*, p. 39.

20. For example, Zoe Williams, 'To Lord Freud, a food bank is an excuse for a free lunch', *Guardian*, 4 July 2013, available at: www.theguardian.com/commentisfree/2013/jul/04/lord-freud-food-banks

21. Rachel Loopstra, A. Reeves, D. Taylor-Robinson, B. Barr, M. McKee and D. Stuckler, 'Austerity, sanctions, and the rise of food banks in the UK', *British Medical Journal*, 350, 2015, h1775.

22. For example, J. Perry, M. Williams, T. Sefton and M. Haddad, *Emergency Use Only: Understanding and Reducing the Use of Food Banks in the UK*, Oxford: CPAG, CoE, Trussell Trust, 2014.

23. Debbie A. Lawlor, 'The Vienna Declaration on nutrition and non-communicable diseases', *British Medical Journal*, 347, 2013, f4417.

24. The UK Faculty of Public Health, 'UK Faculty of Public Health Public health experts call on PM to take action on nutrition and hunger', 2014, available at: www.fph.org.uk/public_health_experts_call_on_pm_to_take_action_on_nutrition_and_hunger

25. A. Hoyland, L. Dye and C.L. Lawton, 'A systematic review of the effect of breakfast on the cognitive performance of children and adolescents', *Nutritional Research Reviews*, 22 (2), 2009, 220–43.
26. S. Vandevijvere, C.C. Chow, K.D. Hall, E. Umali and B.A. Swinburn 'Increased food energy supply as a major driver of the obesity epidemic: a global analysis', *Bulletin of the World Health Organization*, 93, 2015, 446–56.
27. A. Davis, D. Hirsch, N. Smith, J. Beckhelling and M. Padley, *A Minimum Income Standard for the UK in 2012: Keeping Up in Hard Times*, York: Joseph Rowntree Foundation, 2012.
28. Poverty and Social Exclusion UK, *Households Going Without in 2012 and 1999: Britain, 2012*, available at: www.poverty.ac.uk/pse-research/households-going-without-1999-and-2012-britain
29. Ibid.
30. G. Riches and T. Silvasti, *First World Hunger Revisited: Food Charity or the Right to Food?* Basingstoke: Palgrave Macmillan, 2014.
31. K. Garthwaite, 2016, *Hunger Pains: Life Inside Foodbank Britain*, Bristol: Policy Press, 2016.
32. R. Wells, and M. Caraher, 'UK print media coverage of the food bank phenomenon: from food welfare to food charity?', *British Food Journal*, 116 (9), 2014, 1426–45.
33. Dowler, 'Food banks and food justice', p. 4.

9

The Deadly Impact of Fuel Poverty

Ruth London

On 25 November 2015 a crowd of pensioners, single mothers, asylum seekers and others were ejected from the lobby of the House of Commons. Fuel Poverty Action, a self-help and campaigning group, had come to 'warm up' and speak out about fuel poverty: it was announced that day that 15,000 people had died the previous winter because they could not afford to heat their homes.[1]

While the 'excess winter death' toll can rise and fall, reflecting many different factors, fuel poverty itself has dramatically increased under austerity. This crisis has been concealed. Households used to be defined as fuel poor if they had to spend more than 10 per cent of their income on fuel (itself an inadequate measure). But in 2013, the government changed the definition.[2] The new 'Low Income High Costs' definition counts only households whose fuel costs to keep warm put them below the official poverty line, and are also above average.

The 'above average' component of the new definition means the statistic hardly changes from year to year. It also means that any action now is targeted only at the most vulnerable households. Much money and time are spent on identifying the 'fuel poor' to ensure that help is not wasted on those who are just about managing.[3]

Fuel poverty costs the NHS £3.6 million per day, £27,000 for each local health trust.[4] And that is on top of the cost to the patients, who suffer from strokes, pneumonia and depression as a result of fuel poverty, and the cost to the people who care for them, unpaid. Meanwhile, children, ill half the winter in cold damp homes, miss school (or go in, sick, to keep warm) and fall behind (see Chapter 7 by Joanna Mack). Adults miss work or lose jobs. Students drop out of college. Relationships break up.

In this chapter we examine just a few examples of the violence we see, and point to how people are fighting the energy suppliers, the government and landlords who perpetrate it.

Anthony Waters, aged 48, committed suicide after British Gas workmen turned up at his family shop with a warrant to disconnect his energy supply. Warrant officer David Pickard told the inquest:

> He clearly felt he should have been given more time to pay. He said 'You will have to do it', referring to us de-energising the electricity supply. But he was getting more anxious and said 'I will hang myself'. I thought it was just a throw away comment, an idle threat. In my line of work I hear people say it quite regularly and think nothing of it.

Talking to the *Daily Mirror*, Mr Waters' father Keith, 87, said:

> I'm sure they could have arranged for another payment scheme if things were getting that bad. I don't understand why British Gas had to send three men to his shop without any warning. Where is their humanity?[5]

Where, indeed? David Pickard, a worker doing his – horrible – job, probably had sleepless nights, along with the lady in the office who gave 'the final say on whether we de-energise or walk away' after Mr Waters had phoned his friends and come up with just £1000. It speaks volumes that such desperation is normal in Britain: 'I hear people say it quite regularly'. In time, perhaps, some frontline workers will follow the example of members of the Utility Workers Union of Southern California, who in 1980 organised against being forced to commit violence, and established that they would not cut customers off if anyone on the property was sick, elderly or a young child. In France, 'Robin Hood' EDF engineers and electricians will often refuse company instructions to cut vulnerable people off, or return to a home to re-connect a disconnected supply.

Behind the violence of those frontline workers stands the violence of the corporations themselves, in particular the Big Six energy companies which still hold 80–90 per cent of the UK fuel market. Centrica, the owner of British Gas, recorded profits of £1 billion the year Anthony Waters died. The corporation's purpose is profit, and its executives' legal duty is to its shareholders. In a world where regulation is a dirty word and 'austerity' trumps 'humanity', energy prices have soared. The Competition and Markets Authority (CMA) reports that between 2004 and 2014 'Average domestic electricity prices rose by around 75% in real terms, and average domestic gas prices rose by around 125%.'[6] It further points out that '[i]n 2015, the upwards trend halted, with electricity prices roughly flat and gas prices falling nearly 5%'[7] – but this occurred during a period when the price of oil, a major component of the company's costs, was plunging, at one point by 70 per cent. The CMA found that customers had been paying £1.4 billion a year more than they would in a fully competitive market.[8]

In 2016 a woman – let's call her Sandra Blackstock – wrote to us,

> I was awoken today by two British Gas meter fitters. They had a warrant to put a gas meter OUTSIDE my bungalow. They could plainly see that I had a walker and a crutch and a wheelchair. They started asking the neighbours if I could walk ok and telling them I how much I owed ... they left me screaming and crying and having an asthma attack. When the gas goes I will have no gas at all. I haven't got a card to get any more and I can't go outside to put any in or see if I have any credit ... Is there anything I can do? They have frauded the court because they never informed the judge that I was disabled and ill.

A Fuel Poverty Action British Gas shareholder read out Ms Blackstock's letter at Centrica's Annual General Meeting.[9]

It is common for a prepayment meter (PPM) to be forced on customers who go into arrears.[10] It is illegal to disconnect vulnerable customers in winter. This applies to pensioners living alone or families with young children. But with a PPM you 'self-disconnect': with a quiet little click, the money runs out and everything goes dead. This violence is compounded by the misappropriation of hundreds of millions of pounds from PPM customers. In 2015 and 2016, the CMA acknowledged that the 4 million households on prepayment meters – usually the poorest customers – were paying £260–£320 more for fuel per year than people with bank orders for direct debit.[11]

Without fuel you can't cook,[12] bathe, watch TV, go online or charge your phone. You can't even keep the lights on. Nor the freezer, or even the fridge.

David Clapson, an unemployed ex-soldier, was diabetic, and used his fridge to keep his insulin chilled (if insulin gets warm it denatures and cannot be used). He had worked 29 years, had been a carer for his mother, and was training and applying for work, when in July 2013, he died. His sister, Gill Thompson, brought his case to Leigh Day solicitors, who wrote in a press release:

> David died ... from fatal diabetic ketoacidosis which occurs when [there is] a severe lack of insulin ... The Department for Work and Pensions had sanctioned him for a month, leaving him unable to afford to top up his electricity key and unable to afford food ... after he failed to attend two appointments. In a letter to David's MP, the DWP stated they were 'aware Mr Clapson was insulin dependent' ... We hope that these submissions will show the Coroner that there is a reason to suspect that David died an unnatural death and that an investigation should be opened with a view to holding a full Inquest into the circumstances of David's death.[13]

This is urgent: like the utility companies, the DWP, and their employees, hold the power of life and death over vulnerable people.

Nowhere has the sheer perverseness of UK government policy been more apparent than in their policy on energy. The good news is that, worldwide, renewable energy – using free and limitless power from the sun, wind, waves and tides – is rapidly taking hold. Renewables, and the huge potential savings in energy efficiency, mean that in the future we should all be able to heat our homes at low cost both to ourselves and to the climate. There are determined battles going on, on many fronts, which could dramatically reduce, or eliminate, fuel poverty.

The best long-term way of keeping homes warm is by insulation and other energy saving measures, which also protect the climate. But state programmes like the popular Warm Front, which provided insulation to approximately 2.3 million homes,[14] were replaced by a money-lending scheme, the Green Deal, which never got off the ground.[15] New, much smaller schemes to reduce demand for energy have been handed over to the firms that sell energy. Unsurprisingly, in 2015 the Association for Conservation of Energy documented an 80 per cent cut since 2012 in help to make cold homes more energy efficient.[16] Tighter energy efficiency requirements for new build homes were scrapped in 2015 and developers then redrew plans, already in the pipeline, to save themselves a bit of money. Yet, with the new insulation schemes paid for by a charge passed on to customers,[17] 'green measures' are blamed for high bills.

Meanwhile, the cost of renewable energy is plummeting. The UK has some of the best access to wind, waves and tide of any country in the world, and a strong renewables industry was developing, when the government – in the name of cutting costs to 'hard-working families' – pulled the rug out from beneath it with £5–600 million worth of cuts.[18] David Cameron called it 'green crap'.[19]

Instead, state support has promoted nuclear power, with its huge costs and huge risks; the consumer – and the tax payer – are expected to pick up the tab.[20] Electricity prices promised to potential investors in Hinkley C nuclear power station are double what electricity will cost from other sources, and opposition is intense.

The government's other favoured energy source is fracking, touted as an economic boon, but known to release not only carbon dioxide but the still more potent greenhouse gas methane, as well as polluting air and the water table. Fuel poverty is often used as an argument for fracking – but both the government and the companies hoping to frack have had to acknowledge that it would not significantly dent the price of UK fuel. Local and national popular opposition to fracking has been determined (see Chapter 16 by Will Jackson, Helen Monk and Joanna Gilmore) and after six years is still undefeated, leading the government to abolish the need for local planning consent.[21]

Government polling in April 2016 showed public support for fracking at 19 per cent.[22] In stark contrast, renewable power was supported by 81 per cent of the public, with only 4 per cent opposing it. And 68 per cent of the UK public say energy companies should be publicly owned[23] – a preference that is now giving birth to new non-profit municipal energy suppliers.

Housing policies that force more and more tenants into cold, damp, mouldy flats, with private landlords they do not dare to challenge, are another key cause of fuel poverty. We are now seeing, in addition, major problems with schemes in social housing, and privately owned homes on regenerated estates, where communal or district heating is replacing individual boilers or heaters. New 'Heat Networks', heavily promoted and subsidised by the government,[24] have the potential to bring down both bills and carbon emissions – but they are currently unregulated monopolies. Unable to switch suppliers, residents can face horrendous bills and unreliable service; many are going cold as a result.

Even renewables, when installed and run without accountability to consumers, can lead to a similar situation. In Cumbria, Longtown Action for Heat has for years been confronting Riverside Housing Association which in 2012 imposed solar power on their tenants, with no escape clause. At the launch of Fuel Poverty Action's Energy Bill of Rights in the House of Commons (October 2014), Paul Dill described how solar panels had been placed on a north-facing roof, boilers were too big for the flats, with no room for essential components, and other major failings of design and installation. All the profit from the solar panels goes to the housing association, despite them having been funded by a government grant, while tenants' bills doubled or in some cases quadrupled.[25]

Public outrage at being deprived of heat, or going hungry to pay the bills, runs deep in the UK. A change in government policies, at no net cost, could save or transform lives. Instead, austerity governments since 2010 have overseen the expansion of low waged, insecure employment and benefit cuts, and have cut the libraries and day centres where people go to keep warm and the advice centres and legal aid which defended their entitlements. They have legislated to sell off social housing in favour of private landlords, and have organised energy policy around profit instead of survival. As we write, Theresa May is questioning the justice of energy prices, and poll-scarred governments worldwide are jettisoning the rhetoric of austerity itself. But only the rhetoric. The reversal of austerity's lethal priorities is long overdue.

NOTES

Websites were last accessed 4 November 2016.

1. Office of National Statistics provide yearly 'Excess Winter Deaths'; the World Health Organization estimates that one third of these are due to cold homes. Fuel Poverty Action has pioneered the 'Warm Up' as a gentle form of direct action based on the principle that if you can't afford to heat your home, you have a right to go into any public building and collectively get warm there.
2. In March 2016, analysis carried out for Panorama suggested that about 13 million people would be classed as fuel poor if the definition had stayed the same. Under the new definition, the number was around 5 million.
3. For example, the Energy Company Obligation (ECO) which obliges the larger energy suppliers to help lower income households insulate their homes and otherwise improve their energy efficiency is to be changed in

2017 to a scheme focusing on the fuel poor, see www.energy-uk.org.uk/policy/energy-efficiency/energy-companies-obligation.html

4. In 2014, a pilot project in Sunderland offered people insulation, double glazing and efficient boilers – on prescription. Following the pilot, GP visits and outpatient appointments plummeted, see www.independent.co.uk/money/four-million-childen-in-fuel-poverty-which-costs-the-nhs-27000-a-day-a6896906.html

5. Jessica Best, 'Desperate shopkeeper facing huge energy bill hanged himself moments after British Gas cut electricity supply', *Mirror*, 30 September 2014, available at: www.mirror.co.uk/news/uk-news/desperate-shopkeeper-facing-huge-energy-4348990

6. Competition and Markets Authority, *Energy Market Investigation: Summary of Final Report*, London: CMA, 2016, available at: https://assets.publishing.service.gov.uk/media/576c23e4ed915d622c000087/Energy-final-report-summary.pdf. In 2015, the CMA found that 95 per cent of customers were overpaying for their energy, and that earnings at the Big Six increased tenfold in the years from 2007 to 2013, with higher margins taken from loyal customers on standard tariffs. The final 2016 report marked a retreat from its expected conclusions and recommendations. The *Guardian*, 23 June 2016 commented: 'The CMA launched its inquiry amid widespread anger that the large power companies were overcharging customers by £1.7 bn a year. There were calls for the owner of British Gas, Centrica, and the rest of the big six to be forcibly broken up and energy prices capped. But in the subsequent 24 months the market watchdog has been in almost constant retreat, under relentless pressure from the big six and after a significant fall in commodity costs filtered through to lower household energy bills.'

7. Competition and Markets Authority, *Energy Market Investigation*, p. 5.

8. Competition and Markets Authority, 'CMA publishes final energy market reforms', Press release, 24 June 2016, available at: www.gov.uk/government/news/cma-publishes-final-energy-market-reforms

9. Video at www.youtube.com/watch?v=oRgbjf8djlo&feature=youtu.be

10. In fear of debt, some people want a PPM, but most do not. With a court warrant, your home can be broken into and a meter forcibly installed. With determination and good advice, it is usually possible to avoid this. See Fuel Poverty Action, *In Trouble with Your Energy Company? A Mini-guide to Your Rights*, 2nd edn 2017, available at: fuelpovertyaction.org.uk

11. Ofgem's Standard Licence Condition 27.2A says any extra charge must reflect additional costs – but this is ignored. In 2016, the CMA capped the extra charge on PPM users, but these customers – who pay in advance, guaranteed – will still pay much more than customers who pay by direct debit (see Fuel Poverty Action's consultation response at www.gov.uk/cma-cases/energy-market-investigation).

12. 'Kettle packs' are now given out at food banks for people who can't afford to cook a hot meal. But some can't boil a kettle. And many have times when they cannot even choose between heating and eating: they can do neither.

13. Leigh Day, 'Submissions from lawyers call for inquest into death of ex-soldier who died following benefits sanction', 31 October 2016, available at: www. leighday.co.uk/News/News-2016/October-2016/Submissions-from-lawyers-call-for-inquest-into-dea

14. C. Watson, and P. Bolton, *Warm Front Scheme*, House of Commons Library Science and Environment Social and General Statistics Series, London: House of Commons, 2015.

15. A very useful history of this field is available at: www.nea.org.uk/the-challenge/fuel-poverty-energy-efficiency-timeline/

16. From 1.74 million a year to 340,000 now. See Association for the Conservation of Energy, 'Home energy efficiency 2010 2020', Briefing note 1, March 2016, London, available at: www.ukace.org/wp-content/uploads/2016/03/ACE-briefing-note-2016-03-Home-energy-efficiency-delivery-2010-to-2020.pdf

17. Notably ECO, see endnote 3.

18. Department of Energy and Climate Change, 'Changes to renewables subsidies', Press release, 17 December 2015, available at: www.gov.uk/government/news/changes-to-renewables-subsidies

19. George Eaton, 'No. 10 refuses to deny Cameron call to "get rid of all the green crap"', *New Statesman*, 21 November 2013, available at: www.newstatesman.com/politics/2013/11/no-10-refuses-deny-cameron-call-get-rid-all-green-crap

20. In January 2012, the campaign group Energy Fair, and others, filed a formal complaint with the European Commission over alleged unlawful state aid in the form of subsidies for the nuclear power industry, in breach of EU competition law. A summary of the case is available at: www.mng.org.uk/gh/private/forms_of_support_for_nuclear_power.pdf

21. Adam Vaughn, 'Government will step in if councils don't fast-track fracking applications', *Guardian*, 13 August 2013, available at: www.theguardian.com/environment/2015/aug/13/government-will-step-in-if-councils-dont-fast-track-fracking-applications

22. Adam Vaughn, 'UK support for fracking hits new low', *Guardian*, 28 April 2016, available at: www.theguardian.com/environment/2016/apr/28/uk-support-for-fracking-hits-new-low

23. Details of the poll are published on the YouGove site at: https://yougov.co.uk/news/2013/11/04/nationalise-energy-and-rail-companies-say-public/

24. Through the Heat Networks Investment Project and the Renewable Heat Incentive.

25. A report by Avoca consulting engineers in December 2013 found 'inherent design issues that contradict the requirement for providing efficient, effective and economical heating to the properties' and 'it is evident that the energy costs for each of the properties surveyed has increased

over and above the normal expected rate'. See Jenny Brown, 'Major flaws found in heating systems at homes in Cumbrian town', *The Cumberland News*, 18 July 2014, available at: www.cumberlandnews.co.uk/news/ Major-flaws-found-in-heating-systems-at-homes-in-Cumbrian-town-7a01a312-b85a-4502-97b0-c5322c9ae3f2-ds

10

The Violence of the Debtfare State

David Ellis

Debt can have devastating impacts upon individuals and families. To be trapped in a cycle of debt is an all-consuming torment for some. Constant demands for payment or the threat of bailiffs banging on the door to remove property produces an internalised, almost siege-like existence for debtors in what can seem a hopeless war of attrition. At the heart of the typical creditor/debtor relationship lies an unequal distribution of power. Creditors may enforce a claim upon debtors that is legitimated by the weight of the law, compelling payment in one form or another. An inability by a debtor to therefore fulfil their obligation will potentially see them incur a myriad of punitive sanctions enforced by the legal mechanisms of the state, including court action, the removal of property, eviction, home repossession and the arrestment of a debtor's bank account. Notwithstanding such threats of violent coercion, unmanageable debts can also lead to fear, guilt, shame and the feeling of personal failure to provide for one's family. Such relations therefore necessarily possess an insidious quality, 'since debt has long been a way for relations based on exploitation and even violence to be seen as moral in the eyes of those living inside them'.[1]

As this chapter argues, the everyday violence experienced by debtors has been exacerbated by the politics of austerity. Indeed, one of the key features of this period of 'austerity' is that the welfare state is progressively being displaced by a system more appropriately characterised as a debtfare state.[2] Collective welfare provisions have come under sustained political attack by successive UK governments over the last three decades, either by restricting access or through numerous privatisations. Simultaneously, the active suppression of wage-led inflation has reduced the value of earned income against the cost of living (see Vickie

Cooper and David Whyte's Introduction to this book). Those same governments have also taken a dogmatic approach to the liberalisation of financial services, enabling the provision of an almost inexhaustible supply of debt by banks, building societies and other credit providers. Taken together, these measures have contributed to the normalisation of pervasive debt as a means of replacing the living wage and sufficient welfare provisions. The 2007/08 global financial crises laid bare some of the worst excesses and instabilities that this approach had produced. However, the UK government's response of imposing austerity measures has served to not only perpetuate an intractable reliance on debt but is actively exacerbating the situation, with particularly tragic consequences for the most vulnerable members of society.

Debt is ultimately the lifeblood of the economy – it sustains retail markets, property markets, and the financial system generally – and has increasingly been so for the last 35 years. Since 1980, total UK personal indebtedness increased from less than £50 billion to over £1.4 trillion by 2015, which amounts to an average debt of approximately £55,000 per UK household.[3] Debt is required for accessing the housing market and opportunities in higher education. It feeds consumption in an acquisitive world and, for the very poorest in society, debt is too often the only means to attain the bare essentials of life. Nevertheless, the rise of the 'debt society' cannot be thought of as a spontaneous transformation or the result of market forces alone. Rather, the shift from welfare to debtfare represents the product of a political movement that has undermined collective provisions and endorsed a more individualistic conception of welfare based on the provision of debt. To this end, debt has increasingly become an indispensable part of daily life, with more and more people facing economic uncertainty as a consequence. This trend has only intensified since the introduction of government-imposed austerity.

Downward pressures on household incomes mean that 15 million people are now using credit to pay for basic living costs, with nearly 3 million using credit to finance existing credit commitments.[4] Since 2012, a leading debt charity has seen the number of people coming to them for advice almost triple to well over half a million, with households in arrears on essential household bills increasing every year.[5] Over the same period, creditors increasingly sought to enforce debts owed to them through legal redress, to the extent that the number of County Court Judgements (CCJs) issued against individual debtors is now higher than at any point since the peak of the financial crisis.[6] There has long been an acknowledgement that there is a relationship between indebtedness and mental health problems, with estimates suggesting that half of British adults with problem debt also have mental health problems,[7] including stress, anxiety, depression and even suicide attempts.

In 2013, Kane Sparham-Price committed suicide after the Payday lender, Wonga, emptied his bank account, leaving him with zero money. Kane was 18 years old and suffered mental health problems. The coroner at his inquest, John Pollard, explicitly raised the concern that payday lenders are 'legally entitled to clear-out someone's bank account if money is owing to them'.[8] Pollard sent his report to the Financial Conduct Authority (FCA) and suggested that there ought to be a 'statutory minimum' amount of £10 that Payday lenders must leave in the consumer's bank account. The FCA replied that such measures are likely to be harmful to insurers since they 'face the prospect of incurring additional fees for failed payments, if payments are blocked to protect a residual amount'.[9] Put simply, the FCA failed to see how protecting a small sum of money in a person's bank account may help to prevent future similar deaths.

Indeed, cases like those discussed above are indicative of a trend of increasing rates of suicide since 2010, particularly among young males, which should come as no surprise given that financial difficulties and debt are known to increase the risks of both mental health problems and suicidal tendencies (see Chapter 1 by Mary O'Hara).

FROM FINANCIAL CRISES TO AUSTERITY

While the root causes of the 2007/08 financial crises were many and varied, there can be no doubt that the protracted years of debt-fuelled economic growth not only contributed to the initial crisis but left the UK economy extremely vulnerable to its effects. Such instabilities were in fact foreshadowed in the 1980s when the Conservative governments of that era established the foundations of the debtfare state. Under the 'right-to-buy scheme', the mass privatisation of council housing initially stimulated the housing market, leading to a boom in mortgage lending and property values (see also Chapter 17 by Kirsteen Paton and Vickie Cooper on the withdrawal of the social housing 'buffer'). The consumer boom that followed, hailed as an 'economic miracle', only ended when a surge in inflation prompted the government to raise interest rates sharply. Unable to maintain mortgage payments, homeowners quickly found themselves in arrears, as housing repossessions reached record levels in 1991.[10] The impact of deteriorating property values on household wealth had devastating consequences for the wider economy, triggering a prolonged recession throughout the 1990s.

When New Labour came into government in 1997, growth had already returned to the economy. As well as accepting the public spending plans inherited from the previous Tory government, Labour went much further by extending financial market liberalisation, privatisation and welfare reforms. As in the 1980s, the promotion of homeownership loomed large over the economy again. A sustained period of housing market inflation pushed property values increasingly higher to the point that mortgage-lending requirements were relaxed in order for new homeowners to enter the market. Confident that property values would continue to grow, lenders even began offering 'subprime' mortgages in excess of 100 per cent of a property's value to those who could not afford to save for a deposit. By 2007, another 'economic miracle' was proclaimed following 11 years of continuous growth in which household wealth was reported to have increased by 88 per cent since 2000.[11]

During the summer of 2007, a collapse within global financial markets quickly spread to the retail banking sector, which, as it later emerged, had invested heavily in risky asset speculation. As banks saw the value of their assets plunge, their ability to lend became severely restricted. The subsequent 'credit crunch' inevitably had severe repercussions for an economy sustained and maintained predominantly through debt. Facing the prospect of a systemic banking collapse, the UK government effectively 'bailed out' the banks by underwriting their balance sheets with billions of pounds of taxpayers' money. But rather than indict the banking sector over its recklessness, the legitimacy for government intervention was predicated on the necessity of defending housing market wealth that had accumulated prior to the crises.[12] Public consent was therefore achieved for the restoration of the banking sector by aligning the interests of banks with those of 'responsible mortgage borrowers' who were represented as deserving of government assistance.

Despite further government measures to provide economic stimulus, the economy nevertheless slipped into recession. Scrutiny quickly shifted to government deficits as reduced economic activity and the expectation of falling tax revenues brought into question the ability of the government to service outstanding public debt.[13] As a consequence, the financial crisis gave way to a government debt crisis. This shift meant that the economic downturn was successfully framed by subsequent governments as an outcome of Labour's public spending profligacy while in government. A consensus soon emerged that the remedy to the crisis was to implement cuts in public expenditure 'as a necessary, responsible mode of managing the consequences of shameful, reckless excess'.[14] And so, the election of the Coalition government in 2010 brought with it the 'age of austerity'.

Debt has obscured growing wage and wealth inequalities that have emerged in the UK over the last 30 years.[15] The age of austerity has only served to intensify a regressive transfer of wealth from the asset-poor to the asset-rich (see also Vickie Cooper and David Whyte's Introduction to this book). Those areas worst affected by government-imposed funding cuts also have the highest proportion of people struggling with debt, with over 40 per cent of the total population in some of these areas classified as over-indebted.[16] Households receiving working tax credits and housing benefits have seen their entitlements slashed dramatically. People reliant on out-of-work benefits, including those on disability living allowances, face losing their entitlement altogether due to stringent eligibility criteria. Swingeing cuts in central government funding to Local Authorities puts pressure on council budgets leading to the closure of vital frontline services and restricted access to council tax relief. In addition, the uncertain economic climate increases the insecurity of paid employment, with the growing incidence of casual and part-time work adding yet another layer of unpredictability to household budgeting.

For low income households, the loss of essential welfare entitlements means that it is no longer a question of whether they are *in* debt, but how they are able to cope with debt, just to get by. Redirecting government funding from the poorest members of society to the wealthiest has therefore forced those most in need of assistance into exploitative debt relations. Despite stringent regulation of the debt collection industry, the inherent asymmetries of power provide creditors with a measure of threat in their dealings with debtors. At a state level, the continuing austerity agenda has also incorporated debt collection as a priority of government welfare reforms.[17] To this end, the number of people with debt problems related to national and local government has more than doubled since 2010. Debt charities have noted the rise of such incidences, with demands from government agencies often compounding existing hardship in vulnerable families. The Citizens Advice Bureau provide one example:

> A woman approached her local Citizens Advice for help with a child tax credit overpayment of over £1,000 which HMRC alleged had arisen because she had not told them that her child had left school. The woman disputed this as her child was studying for A Levels during the period in question. HMRC had taken over five months to investigate and had passed the account to a debt collector. The woman and her husband were not working due to illness and could not afford to make payments while the matter was investigated.[18]

With such an imperative placed upon debt recovery, public bodies and government departments, particularly the DWP and HMRC, are now among the worst offenders of 'aggressive enforcement' practices, wherein 'the legal violence of the state ultimately plays the same role as the freelance violence of the "debt enforcer"'.[19]

The dynamics of debtfare entail an individualising conception of citizens, at once responsible for repaying their debts and therefore 'justifiable' targets for enforcement. For those struggling with debt, enforcement implies the indeterminate prospect of impending violence in the shape of domestic intrusion or the forcible seizure of property.[20] The debtfare state therefore necessarily involves a highly intimate form of coercion, where the lingering threat of potential violence remains a constant feature of everyday life for the indebted.

NOTES

1. David Graeber, 'Debt, violence and impersonal markets: Polanyian meditations', in C. Hann and K. Hart (eds), *Market Society: The Great Transformation Today*, Cambridge: Cambridge University Press, 2011, p. 112.
2. Susanne Soederberg, *Debtfare States and the Poverty Industry: Money, Discipline and the Surplus Population*, Oxon: Routledge, 2014.
3. Figures are derived from the Bank of England and The Money Charity relating to secured and unsecured borrowing. Not included are other forms

of debt such as short-term loans, student loans, consumer finance or arrears on household bills, like council tax, rent and utilities.

4. StepChange, *Life on the Edge: Towards More Resilient Family Finances*, Leeds: Foundation for Credit Counselling, 2014.

5. StepChange, *Personal Debt 2015: Statistics Yearbook*, Leeds: Foundation for Credit Counselling, 2016.

6. The annual figures of CCJs issued for the last four years are as follows: 2012: 468,115; 2013: 499,610; 2014: 671,305; 2015: 694,680. All figures relate to consumer CCJs derived from Registry Trust Limited.

7. Merlyn Holkar and Polly Mackenzie, *Money on Your Mind*, Bristol: Money and Mental Health Policy Institute, 2016.

8. Report of the Coroner's Inquiry into the death of Kane Sparham-Price, 5 September 2014, Ref: 2014-0463, available at: www.judiciary.gov.uk/wp-content/uploads/2015/03/Sparham-Price-2014-0463.pdf (accessed 2 October 2016).

9. The FCA's response is also available at: www.judiciary.gov.uk/wp-content/uploads/2014/09/2014-0463-Response-by-Financial-Conduct-Authority.pdf (accessed 2 October 2016).

10. Janet Ford, Rob Burrows and Sarah Nettleton, *Homeownership in a Risk Society: A Social Analysis of Mortgage Arrears and Possessions*, Bristol: Policy Press, 2001.

11. Department for Business Enterprise and Regulatory Reform, *Tackling Over-indebtedness: Annual Report 2007*, London: HMSO, 2007.

12. Matthew Watson, 'Headlong into the Polanyian dilemma: the impact of the middle-class moral panic on the British government's response to the sub-prime crisis', *British Journal of Politics and International Relations*, 11 (3), 2009, 422–37.

13. Adair Turner, *Between Debt and the Devil: Money, Credit and Fixing Global Finance*, Princeton, NJ: Princeton University Press, 2016.

14. Rebecca Bramall, *The Cultural Politics of Austerity: Past and Present in Austere Times*, Basingstoke: Palgrave Macmillan, 2013, p. 20.

15. Mark Blyth, *Austerity: The History of a Dangerous Idea*, Oxford: Oxford University Press, 2013.

16. The Money Advice Service, *Indebted Lives: The Complexities of Life in Debt*, London, 2013.

17. HM Government, *Tackling Fraud, Error and Debt in Benefits and Tax Credits System*, 2015.

18. Citizens Advice Bureau, *The State of Debt Collection: The Case for Fairness in Government Debt Collection Practices*, 2016, London, p. 22.

19. Costas Lapavitsas, *Social Foundations of Market, Money and Credit*, Oxon: Routledge, 2003, p. 76.

20. Joe Deville, *Lived Economies of Default: Consumer Credit, Debt Collection and the Capture of Affect*, Oxon: Routledge, 2015.

11

Women of Colour's Anti-Austerity Activism

Akwugo Emejulu and Leah Bassel

Sisters Uncut, the feminist collective fighting against budget cuts to domestic and sexual violence organisations and services in Britain, succinctly and powerfully captures the violence that austerity wreaks on women of colour with protest slogans like 'Austerity is state violence against women' and 'They cut, we bleed'. In this chapter, we discuss how austerity, as both a political frame for this time of economic uncertainty and as a programme of asymmetrical and devastating cuts to social welfare provision, represents a form of epistemic violence that women of colour activists are compelled to confront and resist. By 'epistemic violence' we follow Kristie Dotson and refer to the 'persistent epistemic exclusion that hinders one's contribution to knowledge production'.[1] We argue that this exclusion from knowledge production is a kind of violence that renders the Other, and in our case, women of colour and their experiences, invisible and inaudible to both policy-makers and ostensible social movement 'allies'.[2] We argue that there is little attention paid or action to combat women of colour's poverty and inequality because there is a widespread assumption that poverty is an endemic feature of the experience of the racialised Other and can thus be ignored. Rather than treating austerity as a 'new' phenomenon, we argue that the concept of austerity is but the latest example of violently erasing women of colour's persistent, institutionalised but unremarkable economic and social inequalities. What is 'new' under Britain's austerity regime is the further undermining of women of colour's economic security through the unprecedented roll back of the welfare state and its social protections.[3] Thus, the epistemic violence of austerity represents both a discursive and material challenge to the agency and dignity of women of colour.

However, women of colour are not passive objects at the mercy of Britain's austerity regime. They are undertaking creative resistance to austerity in order to advance intersectional social justice claims derived from their race, class, gender and legal status. In the first half of this chapter, we offer a snapshot of austerity debate in Britain and how it misrecognises women of colour and their precarity. We then discuss the ways in which women of colour are resisting the epistemic violence of austerity through counter-hegemonic knowledge production and activism derived from their lived experiences, perspectives and agency.

As highlighted by Cooper and Whyte in the Introduction to this book, the asymmetrical, racialised, gendered and classed effects of austerity are devastating – especially for women of colour. However, starting our analysis with austerity measures introduced by the 2010 Conservative-Liberal Democratic Coalition government is, in fact, very misleading. Charting the deterioration of women of colour's economic security using the frame of austerity actually misrecognises the nature of women of colour's experiences of poverty and economic inequality. Well before the 2008 crisis, women of colour, on the whole, were already living in an almost permanent state of austerity. As the All Party Parliamentary Group for Race and Community[4] noted in its inquiry into the labour market experiences of Black, Pakistani and Bangladeshi women in Britain: 'For all groups except for Indian men, ethnic minority unemployment has consistently remained higher than the rate for white people since records began.' African and Caribbean women have an unemployment rate of 17.7 per cent, for Pakistani and Bangladeshi women it is 20.5 per cent, compared to 6.8 per cent for white women.[5] Women of colour who are employed are more likely to be concentrated in low skilled, low paid and temporary work – regardless of their educational qualifications. These unequal experiences in the labour market, unsurprisingly, translate into high levels of household poverty with poverty rates for minority groups at 40 per cent – double the rate of the white population in 2007.[6] These shockingly high levels of poverty and unemployment, which predate the crisis and have persisted throughout it, however, do not feature in popular or policy discussions about the crisis. We ask: *whose* crisis counts and *whose* crisis is being named and legitimated?

Austerity causes further immiseration due to its uneven effects.[7] Because women of colour are more likely to be employed in the public sector in feminised professions such as teaching, nursing and social work; because women of colour and migrant women in particular are more likely to be subcontracted to the state via private sector organisations in low skilled, low paid and temporary work as carers, cleaners and caterers; and because women of colour are more likely to use public services because they are typically the primary care givers of children and/or older adults, austerity measures clearly increase women of colour's unemployment while simultaneously reducing the scope, coverage and access to public services (see Chapter 5 by Victoria Canning).[8] We ask: why doesn't austerity's asymmetrical impacts on women of colour feature in the dominant understandings of austerity?

To understand why women of colour are so often omitted from dominant constructions of austerity requires an understanding of how epistemic violence operates. The very real state violence experienced by women of colour through austerity is made possible by and necessitates the misrecognition of women of colour's experiences of poverty and inequality. Austerity is a kind of knowledge production that generates policy attention and social movement action on the deteriorating economic prospects of white middle class and working class groups.[9] Austerity functions as an exclusive category that only names and legitimises some groups' experiences, while subjugating others. The knowledge produced by austerity is not inconsequential but rather reinforces common sense understandings of economic inequality which assume a racialised social order of white supremacy. In other words, there is little attention or action to combat women of colour's poverty and inequality because there is a widespread assumption that poverty is a central feature of the racialised Other and can thus be ignored.

However, women of colour are not passive victims of the epistemic violence of austerity. Centering women of colour's institutionalised crises can help us legitimise and make visible the particularities of their inequalities and help to authorise their resistances. It is to this issue that we now turn.

To recognise women of colour as political agents and authors of their lives requires critical considerations of how British policymakers and many social movement allies uphold the racialised social order. To counter the epistemic violence of austerity requires a commitment to dismantling the identities, ideologies and social relations that legitimise and reproduce women of colour's erasure and exclusion.

There is an urgent need to highlight and take seriously women of colour's knowledge production about the diverse, contradictory and competing notions of what justice and equality might mean. There is an urgent need, therefore, for epistemic justice about austerity which centres the lived experiences of women of colour. By 'epistemic justice' we mean the ability of women of colour to 'participate in knowledge production'[10] in an 'ecology of knowledges'[11] engaged in debate. There is a need for dialogue: speaking with and listening to women of colour – especially for those women who are too often deliberatively silenced and unheard – in order to develop knowledge and actions for rethinking equality, freedom and solidarity. There is also a need for recognizing the lived experiences of women of colour. By 'lived experience' we mean the knowledge acquired and produced through living life and the collective understandings and resistance that arise from being constructed as a subordinate and alien Other. As Patricia Hill Collins argues:

> Living life as Black women requires wisdom because knowledge about the dynamics of intersecting oppressions has been essential to ... Black women's survival ... Black women cannot afford to be fools of any type for our objectification as the Other denies us protections that white skin, maleness and wealth confer.[12]

Centering the lived experiences of women of colour is radical politics because these experiences, as we have demonstrated, are denied and erased in austerity politics. Focusing on lived experience makes women of colour visible political actors in a context that asserts their passivity, absence and/or subordination. Epistemic justice can be achieved under austerity when women of colour produce counter-hegemonic knowledge for and about themselves.

As we have documented elsewhere,[13] women of colour anti-austerity activists are organising and mobilising in creative ways for epistemic justice that challenges white supremacy. As one of our research participants, a British Asian woman activist in Edinburgh, argues, a crucial part of activism is listening and collectively imagining a different world with women of colour:

> The pressures are higher on women to get out of the welfare system ... I think they are talking to each other a lot more about how they're

managing financially or managing their goals and ambitions ... it's about ways of supporting [each other] and surviving, ... So I think when they speak to each other they are beginning to dream a little bit more, have a lot more ambition and finding ways of working together.

It is only when women of colour assert control over how they are defined, what their experiences mean to them and how they might collectively imagine radical new futures – beyond the constraints of the British austerity regime – that epistemic justice can be achieved. It is through collective understandings and resistance learned through lived experiences and critical dialogue that we might problematise and subvert the dominant ways of knowing and resisting austerity in Britain.

In this chapter we have examined how austerity measures violently erase the experiences of women of colour in Britain. Ironically, even though women of colour are more likely to live precarious lives and are dispro-portionately disadvantaged by austerity measures, their experiences and perspectives are silenced in the dominant understandings of austerity. We name this erasure as a form of epistemic violence. Counteracting this violence necessitates taking women of colour seriously by centering their institutionalised crises and resistance. Epistemic justice for women of colour is possible under austerity through women of colour's counter-hegemonic knowledge production that informs their activism for social justice.

NOTES

Websites were last accessed 7 September 2016.

1. K. Dotson, 'Conceptualizing epistemic oppression', *Social Epistemology*, 28 (2), 2014, 115.

2. See, for example, C.W. Mills, *The Racial Contract*, Ithaca, NY: Cornell University Press, 1997; G.C. Spivak, 'Can the subaltern speak?', in C. Nelson and L. Grossberg (eds), *Marxism and the Interpretation of Culture*, Urbana, IL: University of Illinois Press, 1998, pp. 271–313.

3. L. Bassel and A. Emejulu, *The Politics of Survival: Minority Women, Activism and Austerity in France and Britain*, Bristol: Policy Press, 2017.

4. All Party Parliamentary Group on Race and Community (APPG), *Ethnic Minority Female Unemployment: Black, Pakistani and Bangladeshi Heritage Women First Report of Session 2012–2013*, London: The Runnymede Trust, 2013, available at: www.runnymedetrust.org/uploads/publications/pdfs/APPGfemaleunemploymentReport-2012.pdf

5. Ibid.
6. L. Platt, *Poverty and Ethnicity in the UK*, Bristol: Policy Press, 2007.
7. P. Taylor-Gooby and G. Stoeker, 'The Coalition programme: a new vision for Britain or politics as usual?', *The Political Quarterly*, 82 (1), 2010, 4–15; P. Taylor-Gooby, 'Root and branch restructuring to achieve major cuts: the social policy programme of the 2010 UK Coalition government', *Social Policy and Administration*, 46 (1), 2011, 1–22; Paul Whiteley, Harold Clarke, David Sanders and Marianne Stewart, 'The economic and electoral consequences of austerity in Britain', *Parliamentary Affairs*, 68 (1), 2014, 4–24; N. Yeats, T. Haux, R. Jawad and M. Kilkey (eds), *In Defence of Welfare*, Social Policy Association, available at: www.social-policy.org.uk/downloads/idow.pdf
8. Women's Budget Group, *The Impact on Women of the Autumn Statement and Comprehensive Spending Review 2015: Still Failing to Invest in Women's Security*, London, 2015, available at: http://wbg.org.uk/wp-content/uploads/2015/12/WBG_CSR_FullResponse_final_8Dec15.pdf
9. D.Z. Strolovitch, 'Of mancessions and hecoveries: race, gender, and the political construction of economic crises and recoveries', *Perspectives on Politics*, 11 (1), 2013, 167–76; A. Emejulu and L. Bassel, 'Minority women, activism and austerity', *Race & Class*, 57 (2), 2015, 86–95.
10. Dotson, 'Conceptualizing epistemic oppression', p. 115.
11. Boaventura de Souza Santos (ed.), *Another Knowledge is Possible: Beyond Northern Epistemologies*, London: Verso, 2008.
12. Patricia Hill Collins, *Black Feminist Thought: Knowledge, Consciousness and the Politics of Empowerment*, New York: Routledge, 2000, p. 257.
13. Emejulu and Bassel, 'Minority women, activism and austerity'; Bassel and Emejulu, *The Politics of Survival*.

12

Dismantling the Irish Peace Process

Daniel Holder

There is little doubt that many of the poorest in Northern Ireland live in areas which have suffered greatly during the long years of inter-community strife and conflict. Many would accept that the poverty and disadvantage endemic within such communities has led to a sense of limited opportunity and limited investment in the future. In such an environment it is easy to see why so many young people were drawn into violence and paramilitarism.[1]

'Lifetime Opportunities' – UK Government
Anti-Poverty Strategy for Northern Ireland, 2006

The dangers of the imposition of inequality and poverty are compounded in a divided society where they fuel and facilitate conflict. Discrimination and general assaults on economic and social rights were a root cause of the violent conflict that ensued from the late 1960s following the suppression of civil rights protests. The 1998 Good Friday Agreement and its implementation agreements at least recognised that reversing long-standing patterns of inequality were a premise for a lasting peace. A coach and horses is now being driven through this premise by the imposition of austerity and the sidelining of the equality agenda. Austerity threatens to deepen poverty and widen the inequalities that the UK government itself argued needed to be tackled to stifle the attraction of paramilitarism. It does so in a context in particular where there is a sense within loyalist communities of a loss of dominant position, and the involvement of sections of loyalist paramilitarism in orchestrated racist violence.

This chapter examines these developments culminating in the institutional crisis created by the imposition of austerity that led to the structural adjustment-type 2014 Stormont House and 2015 Fresh Start Agreements.

Northern Ireland was created by the partition of Ireland in the 1920s. Fifty years into the majoritarian Stormont Parliament the polity slipped into conflict and collapsed. The British government set up the 'Cameron Commission' to ascertain just what were the 'immediate causes and nature of the violence and civil disturbance in Northern Ireland on and since 5th October 1968'. The Commission conclusions list the first cause as the 'rising sense of continuing injustice and grievance among large sections of the Catholic population' over the inadequacy of housing provision, unfair methods of allocating houses and misuse of discretionary powers by some Local Authorities. It was followed by complaints that it considered to be 'now well documented in fact' of 'discrimination in the making of local government appointments, at all levels but especially in senior posts, to the prejudice of non-Unionists and especially Catholic members of the community, in some Unionist controlled authorities'. It also recorded 'Fears and apprehensions among Protestants of a threat to Unionist domination and control of Government by increase of Catholic population and powers.'[2]

Following the removal of the then Stormont Parliament in 1972, decades of 'direct-rule' from London ensued which were characterised by attempts at reform, in particular by the introduction of 'fair employment' anti-discrimination legislation and the removal of housing powers from local government to an independent authority duty bound to allocate housing on the basis of objective need.

This was unfinished business at the time of the 1998 Good Friday Agreement. The agreement provided for a new statutory equality duty that obliged all new or revised policies to be assessed for their impact on equality; enhanced fair employment legislation; measures to tackle the unemployment differential on the basis of objective need; 'affirmed' (but provided no framework for) the full and equal political participation of women; guaranteed the incorporation of the European Convention on Human Rights (ECHR) into Northern Ireland law; and provided for a binding ECHR+ Bill of Rights for meeting the particular circumstances of the jurisdiction. Provisions which were properly implemented enjoyed a degree of success, for example, in tackling the unemployment differential between Catholics and Protestants. Other measures were, however, rolled back or not implemented at all. In 2008 the Northern Ireland Human Rights Commission, itself a product of the Good Friday Agreement, issued its final advice to the UK government on the content of the Bill of Rights, urging the inclusion of economic and social rights. The following year a UN Committee appealed to the UK to enact a Bill of Rights 'without delay'.

Years of delays to this process have, however, followed. The regular crises threatening to collapse the political process led to further UK-Ireland Agreements, including the 2006 St Andrews Agreement, which foresaw a single equality bill, an Irish Language Act and an anti-poverty strategy based on the principle of objective need. Although the power-sharing institutions of the 1998 Good Friday Agreement had been regularly suspended, the period immediately following the 2006 St Andrews Agreement was one of relative stability.

This period of stability was all to change with the imposition of austerity and particularly the political demands for similar social security cuts to those imposed in Britain. The power-sharing government has been destabilised and at some points seemed likely to implode.

Following weeks of crisis talks on 23 December 2014 the then Secretary of State for Northern Ireland Office (NIO), Theresa Villiers MP, published the 'Stormont House' Agreement. Its first section essentially contains a Structural Adjustment Programme (SAP) for the jurisdiction providing for: a 'balanced budget' (i.e. cuts to public spending); 'Public Sector Reform and Restructuring' including a 'Voluntary Exit Scheme' for up to 20,000 public sector jobs to be funded by borrowing of up to £700 million and an OECD review; implementing the cuts to the welfare state introduced in Britain, but with a top up mitigation fund for existing claimants; powers over Corporation (profits) Tax with a view to lowering the rate to 12.5 per cent and consideration of privatisation of public assets. In publishing the Agreement, the Secretary of State described it as 'historic', providing a 'new approach to some of the most difficult issues left over from Northern Ireland's past'.

The two Irish nationalist parties – Sinn Féin and the Social Democratic and Labour Party (SDLP), had resisted the imposition of social security cuts and other austerity policies and along with the Greens voted down the passage through the Northern Ireland Assembly of legislation equivalent to Britain's Welfare Reform Act 2012. The response from Whitehall was belligerent: economic sanctions against the power-sharing administration to the tune of £2 million a week were imposed. There was no legal basis for these officially termed fines or penalties. London simply decided to cut that amount from the block grant the Northern

Ireland Executive receives from the UK Treasury each year. Austerity led to the institutions regularly teetering on the brink of collapse. The Executive at one stage passed a 'fantasy' budget which balanced the books by overlooking a £600 million hole created by both the sanctions and other cuts. The Stormont House deal was ultimately struck to stave off the collapse of the institutions, yet as quickly as the ink had dried it unravelled with disagreements over the terms of a transitional fund to mitigate against the worst impacts of welfare 'reform'. Further cuts imposed by Chancellor George Osborne following the May 2015 election meant that even Stormont House would no longer balance the books. After further months of crisis talks an implementation deal dubbed the 2015 'Fresh Start Agreement' was concluded, an Agreement which sets out that £3.7 billion of 'savings' had already been imposed on the Stormont budget.

This raised alarm bells amongst public sector institutions already burdened by the harmful austerity effects. At an anti-austerity conference, one UNISON researcher warned that nearly half of the 'savings' proposed by health Trusts were being vetoed by the Public Health Agency as they put patient safety at risk.[3] The same conference heard evidence that one in five children could expect to be living in poverty for most of their childhood (twice the rate in Britain; see also Chapter 7 by Joanna Mack). It is worth noting the uneven geographical concentration of these poverty levels: the most severe geographical concentrations of this poverty can be found in the same areas that bore the brunt of a conflict rooted partly in legacies of discrimination and deprivation.[4]

Unofficial research into the implications of the deal on sectarian inequality commissioned by non-governmental organisations (NGOs) and trade unions found that:

> the economic model made explicit in the financial annex of the Stormont House Agreement is likely to deepen and widen inequality – both generally (between richer and poorer people) and in terms of the differences between Protestants and Catholics.

The authors go on to warn that if care is not taken in implementing the Agreement

> there is a risk that a carefully established political settlement which aimed to move Northern Ireland from a less to a more inclusive

society could be unravelled with a very clear financial and social cost to nearly two decades of peace-building.[5]

As evident in the 1960s, people can only put up with certain levels of inequality and poverty before something breaks. In the post-peace process context, the lessons of history are being set aside for austerity.

The impacts of elements of the Stormont House Agreement are predictable. The elephant-in-the-room impact of welfare cuts is that, by definition, the cuts will hit persons most in need. In Northern Ireland this means that they will exacerbate existing inequalities and disproportionately affect Catholics. While the cutting of public sector jobs with a view to shift employment in the private sector has gender implications for equal pay, it also has 'fair employment' implications. Equality Commission data shows that there are still 267 firms with less than 30 per cent of Catholic employees and 161 firms with less than 30 per cent of Protestant employees in the private sector, which compares unfavourably with the public sector where the comparative figures are 16 and 7, respectively (and only two of these bodies are major employers).[6] Couple this with the reality that areas of high deprivation, which bore the brunt of the conflict, tend to be areas that do not benefit from private sector investment and are more reliant on public sector employment. The risks of structural adjustment exacerbating and regressing long-term patterns of inequality which were meant to be dealt with as part of the peace settlement are plain.

The 'structural adjustment' measures were, however, to be introduced in the context where all new policies are to be subject to legally binding duties to assess their impacts on equality. Such processes have too often been sidestepped. There has been no overarching assessment of the impacts of the voluntary exit scheme or the Stormont House Agreement itself. In relation to the Welfare Reform Bill, the equality impact assessment managed to miss out four of the nine discrimination categories (namely, religious belief, racial group, political opinion and sexual orientation), thus duly disguising equality impacts across those four categories.

This is occurring in a context whereby ten years on key equality provisions committed to in the 2006 St Andrews Agreement have not been delivered, including the adoption of an anti-poverty strategy on the basis of objective need, a matter subject to a successful judicial review by the Belfast-based human rights NGO, the Committee on the Administration of Justice (CAJ) in 2015.[7] Meanwhile the Northern Ireland Poverty and Social Exclusion Survey found that in 2012, 32.5 per cent of Catholic families were in poverty compared to 18.5 per cent of Protestants, and that the gap had in fact widened in the preceding decade.[8]

Austerity can be used as cover to unravel peace settlement safeguards in other ways. In 2015, as part of the programme of public sector cuts, there was a push to dispense with the entire function of an independent human rights scrutiniser for the Policing Board. In general, austerity is a key vehicle for the opponents of accountability to quietly dismantle key safeguards that have been built up as part of the process of institutional reform.

Paramilitary involvement in orchestrated racist violence predates austerity, yet in recent years it has certainly fed off the effects of austerity. In a 2011 report to the UN anti-racism committee, the Northern Ireland Human Rights Commission – itself a product of the Good Friday Agreement – raised continued concerns regarding evidence of orchestrated racist violence involving elements of loyalist paramilitarism. Their report describes the then 'Independent Monitoring Commission' on paramiliatary activity in rather understated terms, declaring it would be an 'important step' for loyalist paramilitaries to 'stop targeting [Irish] nationalists and members of ethnic minorities'. The practice of burning things that represent Catholics on some loyalist bonfires has been augmented by similar attacks on migrant communities, with incidences of Portuguese and Polish flags being burned alongside Irish tricolours.

In April 2014 the Police Service of Northern Ireland (PSNI) expressed concern at a 70 per cent increase in hate crime in the city of Belfast, and when asked whether an organisation was behind the attacks, Assistant Chief Constable Will Kerr told the Policing Board, 'yes', elaborating,

> we think that the [loyalist paramilitary] UVF at least in south Belfast are undoubtedly behind orchestrating some of these racist attacks. Some of the motivation behind that is social housing based which worries us because it has a deeply unpleasant taste of ethnic cleansing in parts of Belfast that could cause us all some concern.[9]

The human stories that lie behind the statistics provide a stark illustration. In June 2014 a Nigerian man, the victim of a racist attack in

2011 where stones and bottles were hurled at him, was allocated social housing in East Belfast, only to find a racist picket on the doorstep and the unfurling of 'Houses 4 local people' and 'We need homes 2' banners. The response from the then MP Naomi Long of the centrist Alliance Party in describing the incident as 'blatantly racist behaviour' was not universal across the political establishment. The then Democratic Unionist Party (DUP) First Minister, Peter Robinson, supported the protestors and maintained their actions were neither racist nor intimidating. Later in 2014, when the Ulster Unionist Mayor of Portadown praised migrant workers for their contribution to the town, a DUP councillor responded in the media that the town had been 'swamped' by foreign nationals, that local infrastructure had been 'stretched to the limit', implying migrants were a 'drain on the health service' and local schools, and claiming the matter was 'the hottest topic in Portadown'. Soon after this a loyalist political party closely associated with the paramilitary UVF issued its own press release demonising migrants. Shortly afterwards there were attacks on Roma groups in the town. Some families fled. Graffiti then appeared in a prominent signboard announcing, 'Roma out – last night was only the start'.[10]

The phenomenon of migrants being violently scapegoated for the slide in living standards of significant sections of the population in recent years has been energised by the context of the 'Brexit' referendum campaign. While this mix of legitimised anti-migrant racism and attacks provoked by austerity-fuelled inequality (see also Chapter 24 by Jon Burnett) is not leading us back to the type of armed conflict that existed before the 1994 ceasefires, it is creating a new lease of life for paramilitarism. Austerity has therefore fuelled the re-emergence of a violence that cannot hope to sustain the vision of a fully peaceful society.

NOTES

Websites were last accessed 30 September 2016.
1. Office of the First Minister and the Deputy First Minister, *Lifetime Opportunities: The UK Government's Anti-poverty and Social Inclusion Strategy for Northern Ireland*, Belfast: Northern Ireland Department Central Anti-Poverty Unit, 2006, para. 28.
2. Government of Northern Ireland, *Disturbances in Northern Ireland: Report of the Commission Appointed by the Governor of Northern Ireland (Cameron*

Commission), *Cmd 532*, Belfast: HMSO, 1969, available at: http://cain.ulst. ac.uk/hmso/cameron.htm#contents

3. Jonathon Swallow, 'Cuts to the health sector', in *Austerity and Inequality: A Threat to Peace? Conference Report*, Belfast: Equality Coalition, October 2015, pp. 71–2.

4. Goretti Horgan, Northern Ireland Child Poverty Alliance and Ulster University, 'Child poverty', in *Austerity and Inequality: A Threat to Peace? Conference Report*, Belfast: Equality Coalition, October 2015, pp. 73–4.

5. Christine Bell and Robbie McVeigh, 'A fresh start for equality?' *The Equality Impacts of the Stormont House Agreement on the 'Two Main Communities'*, Belfast: Equality Coalition, 2016, para. 10 executive summary and p. 11.

6. Ibid., pp. 32–3.

7. The Committee on the Administration of Justice (CAJ) and Brian Gormally's Application [2015] NIQB 59.

8. Gabi Kent, 'Shattering the silence: the power of purposeful storytelling in challenging social security policy discourses of "blame and shame" in Northern Ireland', *Critical Social Policy*, 36 (1), 2016, 124–41.

9. See 'UVF "behind racist attacks in south and east Belfast": loyalist paramilitary group behind attacks says PSNI', *Belfast Telegraph*, 3 April 2014; Robbie McVeigh, 'Living the Peace Process in reverse: racist violence and British nationalism in Northern Ireland', *Race & Class*, 56 (4), 2015, 12.

10. Ibid., p. 9.

PART III

State Regulation

13

Undoing Social Protection

Steve Tombs

In his classic book *The Condition of the Working Class in England*, Friedrich Engels describes 'social murder' – the systematic, routine deaths of workers and citizens in the horror of the emergence of industrial capitalism.[1] It was these conditions which generated inter- and intra-class struggle for laws to regulate business and to mitigate their profit-driven, harmful effects. And so it is no coincidence that a system of social protection through regulation was put into place in Britain during the 1800s. As this chapter indicates, that system is now being thoroughly undermined. The chapter explores evidence for the undermining of social protections in three categories of 'social murder': deaths caused by environmental pollution; deaths caused by foodborne illnesses; and deaths caused by working.

There is good reason to be concerned about the undermining of protections in this 'era of austerity', since the scale of contemporary harm caused in those categories in contemporary Britain remains significant.

- An April 2016 House of Commons report on air quality estimated that up to 50,000 deaths every year are 'brought forward' by pollution.[2]
- According to the FSA, its 'best estimate suggests that there are around a million cases of foodborne illness in the UK each year, resulting in 20,000 hospital admissions and 500 deaths'.[3] Even these estimates of food-related illness are likely to understate the scale of the problem.
- There is now strong evidence that around 50,000 or so deaths in Britain *per annum* are caused by working.[4]

The chapter demonstrates that the system of regulation designed ostensibly to mitigate social violence has, in recent years, come under sustained political attack (see also Chapter 14 by Hilda Palmer and David Whyte). Initially, this was justified by neoliberal ideas – whereby regulation and enforcement were seen as a burden on business, and therefore to be minimised. More latterly, however, the sustained political attack on regulatory bodies has been ratcheted up in the context of austerity. Under state-imposed austerity, not only have regulation and enforcement been cut as part of the claimed need to shrink the state but they have become ever more counter-productive: if private business is to be the vehicle of recovery from recession or stagnation, then it must be ever freer of burdensome 'red tape'.

This chapter provides an overview of enforcement trends in three fields of social protection: food safety, pollution control and worker health and safety. The declining levels of enforcement across these three regulatory functions are creating the conditions where social violence is less and less subject to challenge. As we shall see, this unfolding reality is the product of a policy choice for 'better regulation' coupled with the opportunism of austerity.

In 2004, Sir Phillip Hampton was appointed by Chancellor Gordon Brown to oversee a review of 63 major regulatory bodies as well as 468 Local Authorities. His subsequent report[5] proved to be a watershed in the trajectory of business regulation and enforcement across Britain. The report formally established a concept of 'better regulation' in British government; a policy shift from enforcement to advice and education, a concentration of formal enforcement resources away from the majority of businesses on to so-called high risk areas, and consistent efforts to do what it called 'more with less'. Then Chancellor Gordon Brown summed up this new approach to regulation and enforcement pithily: 'Not just a light touch but a limited touch.'[6]

The following presents data, mostly generated from Freedom of Information requests, on two indices of enforcement – inspections and prosecutions. The time period covered was deliberately chosen – 2003/04 marks the rolling out of the Better Regulation agenda, 2014/15 is generally the year for which the most recent data is available. But this period is also marked by the 2007 financial crisis which was used, by the Coalition government from 2010 onwards, to justify austerity – so, as this chapter will show, there is concrete evidence of how both 'better regulation' and austerity have undermined regulation, and have done so in mutually reinforcing ways.

Between 2003/04 and 2014/15 food hygiene and food standards inspections fell by 15 per cent and 35 per cent, respectively, while there were 35 per cent fewer food prosecutions. In relation to occupational health and safety, between 2003/04 and 2014/15, inspections by both the national regulator, the Health and Safety Executive, and local health and safety inspectors[7] fell by 69 per cent; and national prosecutions fell by 35 per cent, while local prosecutions fell by 60 per cent. Meanwhile, in the same period, Local Environmental Health Officers enforcing local pollution control law undertook 55 per cent fewer 'Part B' inspection visits (to 2013/14) and issued 30 per cent fewer enforcement notices.

The trends in enforcement are staggering in that they all point in the same direction – enforcement across these three areas is in rapid decline. These are, I have argued elsewhere, effects of 'better regulation' (see also Chapter 15 by Charlotte Burns and Paul Tobin).[8] But they are also effects of austerity policies, imposed by the UK government since 2008/09.

In order to assess what this combination of the politics of better regulation overlain by austerity have meant on the ground, I interviewed 35 Local Authority frontline inspectors across five Local Authority areas in Merseyside (Knowsley, Liverpool, Wirral, St Helens and Sefton) during 2014 and 2015 as a way of examining the state of their enforcement capacities across food, pollution control and occupational health and safety.

In the context of business regulation and enforcement, Local Authorities are a particularly appropriate site of analysis – in the three spheres of social protection at issue here, the vast bulk of enforcement occurs at this level. Meanwhile, this is also the place where funding for regulation and enforcement has been reduced the most. Thus, from 2009/10, local government funding from Westminster came under pressure. Indeed, of all the cuts to government departments between 2010 and 2016, the Department for Communities and Local Government has been impacted most of all. Moreover, analyses of the distribution and impacts of these cuts indicate overwhelmingly that they impact most heavily upon poorer Local Authorities.[9]

Perhaps the clearest finding in my interviews across five Local Authorities was that each experienced significant reductions in staffing, notably in the latter part of the period under scrutiny. In every Local

Authority, the numbers of frontline inspectors had fallen significantly between April 2010 and April 2015. Overall, total numbers across the three functions fell by over 52 per cent – from 90.65 FTEs to 47.78 FTEs (full-time equivalents). The declines were across all functions and authorities, with health and safety inspectors falling most starkly; indeed, in two authorities, Liverpool and Sefton, by 2015 there were no dedicated health and safety inspectors, while at the same date there were no pollution control inspectors in Knowsley.

Inspectors were in no doubt what these cuts in staffing meant. As one told me:

It's going to come to the point where it's going to affect the residents, the local population, in many ways we are at that point now, public health and protection is being eroded.

That view was mirrored almost exactly by another who told me:

We're at the point where there is no flesh left, this is starting to get dangerous, a danger to public health.

With fewer staff, it is hardly surprising that the inspectors I interviewed raised the issues of a long-term decline in inspection, a long-term decline in the use of formal enforcement tools, and a decreasing use of prosecution. Time and time again, inspectors told me of increasing obstacles to the ability to prosecute. These obstacles included: a lack of staff time; fear of losing cases; lack of support from Legal Services departments to prosecute; and an increased political risk ('flak') in prosecuting. Moreover, these types of responses are indicative of a political context for regulatory enforcement where the idea of regulation is under attack, and are a powerful illustration of how discourses and policies at the national level can translate into barriers to enforcement at local levels.

While all of the Local Authorities had seen reductions in staff, this did not just mean a loss of overall resource, but the loss of a *particular* kind of resource, that is, expertise and experience: redundancies did not only mean that staff were not replaced but a loss of specialist expertise, alongside pressures for regulators to become generalists. As one inspector put it, 'it's the experienced staff who have gone, so we have lost numbers and expertise'. In fact, the shift from regulators being specialists to generalists was one consistent theme across the interviews, referred to by numerous respondents and in every authority: 'People have had to become generalists'; 'most of them are just thankful they've still got a job'.

The transformation of social protection is not simply about non-enforcement, which has longer-term origins. More latterly, under the political opportunity generated by 'austerity', it has involved a concerted effort to change the relationship between the state, the private sector and regulation. A paradigmatic instance of this transformation is the Primary Authority (PA) scheme. The PA scheme was originally introduced by the Labour government in 2009 – but given considerable impetus by the Coalition government from 2010 when it created the Better Regulation Delivery Office (BRDO) in 2012 to oversee its implementation.

The scheme has mushroomed in recent years. In April 2014, 1500 businesses had established PA relationships across 120 Local Authorities; by 3 October 2016, there were 16,757 'partnerships' across 179 different Local Authorities. Moreover, PA now applies across a vast swathe of areas of regulation, including food safety, occupational health and safety and pollution control, and a wide range of regulators, from environmental health and trading standards departments to fire and rescue services and port authorities.

PA allows a company – and, since April 2014, franchises and businesses in trade associations – operating across more than one Local Authority area to enter an agreement with one specific Local Authority to regulate all of its sites, nationally. Thus, for example, a supermarket like Tesco may have stores in every one of the Local Authorities in England and Wales. Under the PA scheme, it can reach an agreement with one Local Authority to regulate its systems across all of its stores in every Local Authority for complying with a relevant body of law – occupational health and safety or food hygiene, for example. The company makes a payment to the Local Authority nominated as 'PA' and agreed through contract. The benefit for the company, of course, is the absence of effective oversight in the vast majority of its outlets. These can be visited in other areas, but any enforcement action needs to be undertaken through the Local Authority which is the PA. Should a Local Authority wish to prosecute a company in a PA agreement, for example, it can only do so with the permission of the Local Authority which is party to that agreement. Then, under the scheme, any consideration of a potential prosecution must entail prior notice being given to the company; the company can then request that the matter be referred to the BRDO for determination.[10]

PA is a classic Better Regulation initiative – and, at the local level, its key formal initiative. It places regulation in a market context: Local Authorities compete with each other to sign up large companies to the scheme, seeking to conclude contracts based upon monetary exchange. It is clear, however, that the scheme is proving highly problematic for local regulators. As one inspector put it, while 'in theory it could work well, in practice it protects large companies from Local Authority enforcement'. Other inspectors elaborated upon these, and two clear problems emerged: first, that the scheme is largely paper based – 'under PA they [companies] only have to demonstrate the existence of systems'; the second, then, is that PA schemes 'protect companies from inspection and enforcement'. Notwithstanding these widely articulated concerns, however, many Local Authorities continue to compete for PA agreements in order to generate much-needed income.

While the PA is instituting marketised regulation across Local Authorities, some have taken this process even further. A handful have now formally privatised their environmental health regulatory functions. In October 2012, North Tyneside Council announced the transfer of 800 employees to Balfour Beatty and Capita Symonds as part of a privatisation deal; the transfer included environmental services. In August 2013, the 'One Barnet' model was unveiled. This entailed 'business services' being outsourced to Capita in a ten-year contract worth £350 million, with other services – including regulatory services – contracted to Capita Symonds, in a £130 million contract, also for ten years. And in January 2016, Burnley Council's environmental health services were outsourced as part of a major privatisation package to another private company, Liberata.

Meanwhile, councils in Bromley, Chester West, Cheshire and Wandsworth have all publicly considered wholesale privatisation of regulatory services. Alongside full-scale privatisation, outsourcing of services is becoming increasingly common; outsourcing is an umbrella term which includes diverse arrangements such as the use of Strategic Service Partnerships (SSPs), Joint Venture Companies (JVCs), shared services and collaborative outsourcing.

Taken together, the trends set out above may mark the beginning of the end of the state's commitment to, and ability to deliver, social protection. What began as a neoliberal policy turn to 'better regulation' then became turbo-charged under conditions of austerity, where the state claims it cannot afford to enforce law, and where business must be left to generate recovery. The subsequent institutionalisation of the non-enforcement of law sends a green light to business that its routine, systematic, widespread social violence is to be tolerated, allowing private business to externalise the costs of its activities on to workers, consumers, communities, the environment. It further diminishes the quality and longevity of the lives of those with the least choice about where they live, what they do for a living or where they buy foodstuffs. And it adds a further dimension to our understanding of the multi-dimensional violence of austerity – even if the story documented in this chapter is one which attracts little or no political attention. In short, we are witnessing the transformation of a system of regulation – *social protection* – which has existed since the 1830s. And, despite its political framing, this is not a story about rules, regulations, nor red tape, nor about the demands of austerity. It is a story about social inequality and avoidable business-generated, state-facilitated violence: that is, social murder.

NOTES

Websites were last accessed 5 August 2016.

1. Friedrich Engels, *The Condition of the Working Class in England*, Moscow: Panther, 1845, reprinted in 1969.
2. House of Commons Environment, Food and Rural Affairs Committee, *Air Quality*, London: House of Commons, 2016, p. 3.
3. Food Standards Agency, *Annual Report of the Chief Scientist, Food Standards Agency*, 2012, p.11, available at: www.food.gov.uk/multimedia/pdfs/publication/csar1112.pdf
4. Steve Tombs, 'Hard evidence: are work-related deaths in decline?', *The Conversation*, 29 October 2014, available at: https://theconversation.com/hard-evidence-are-work-related-deaths-in-decline-33553
5. Phillip Hampton, *Reducing Administrative Burdens: Effective Inspection and Enforcement*, London: HM Treasury/HMSO, 2005.
6. BBC News, 'Brown pledges law to cut red tape', May 2005, p. 24, available at: http://news.bbc.co.uk/1/hi/uk_politics/4574229.stm

7. Occupational health and safety regulation and enforcement is divided between a national regulator – the Health and Safety Executive (HSE) – and local regulators, Environmental Health Officers (EHOs).

8. Steve Tombs, 'Better regulation': better for whom?', *Centre for Crime and Justice Studies*, Briefing No. 14, London, 2016, available at: www.crimeandjustice.org.uk/publications/better-regulation-better-whom

9. Andrew Sparrow, 'Councils in poorest areas suffering biggest budget cuts, Labour says', *Guardian*, 25 August 2014, available at: www.theguardian.com/society/2014/aug/25/councils-poorest-areas-biggest-cuts-laboursays

10. Corin Williams, 'Tesco gave green light to prosecution', *Environmental Health News Online*, 10 April 2013, available at: www.ehn-online.com/news/article.aspx?id=8790

14

Health and Safety at the Frontline of Austerity

Hilda Palmer and David Whyte

The UK government is waging a punitive war on working people, from cradle to grave, in the name of 'austerity'. This war includes attacks on child care, education, wages and pensions; cutting public services, privatising them and slashing the welfare/social security safety net to shreds. Workers' rights and working conditions, including health and safety, are at the forefront of austerity cuts.

Across Europe, the EU's financial and economic crisis has been used to attack collective labour rights. Amendments to the Lisbon Treaty, changes in the EU's economic governance and austerity measures have led to national labour law reforms in a number of states which undermine the role of trade unions and workers' representatives, consultation and collective bargaining. As the European Trade Union Institute has noted: 'collective labour rights were identified as adjustment factors to counter the crisis'.[1]

In the UK, key attacks on workers' rights are at the core of the austerity agenda. Perhaps the high point of anti-labour opportunism has been the Trade Union Act 2016 that introduced a raft of measures that undermine the ability of unions to legally engage in strike action. As part of this attack on workers' rights, we are currently witnessing a series of attempts to weaken workplace health and safety regulation and enforcement that was hard won through collective action by workers and trade unions over the last 200 years. The aim of the current Conservative government is to pander to corporate power and the elite by removing regulation, restraint and scrutiny of employers so that 'UK PLC' can compete with countries with much lower standards (see Chapter 15 by Charlotte Burns and Paul Tobin). This government is therefore involved in a deliberate 'race to the bottom' with the aim of forcing those with jobs to accept any changes, however detrimental to their health, and forcing unemployed workers to take any job, at any conditions including low wages and poor health and safety, just to get by.

Under the mask of austerity-driven public sector cuts, the Health and Safety Executive (HSE), the regulatory watchdog charged with keeping workers safe and ensuring that employers keep within the law has had its funding cut by 47 per cent. The consequences for workers are clear: that employers are empowered to kill and injure workers with impunity. Thus, the physical violence that faces all of us in the workplace, and faces some workers on a day-to-day basis, is going unchecked and unrecorded.

Typically, the official 'headline figure' published by the HSE records between 140 and 240 deaths per year resulting from sudden injury and 13,000 deaths caused by occupational diseases and illnesses. Those figures, however, only reflect a small proportion of total deaths caused by work.[2] The first figure does not include key categories of deaths caused by work. The Hazards Campaign estimates that seven times more deaths are caused by work incidents than the figure officially cited by the HSE.[3] HSE figures exclude work-related road traffic deaths, the workplace deaths recorded in other industries that the HSE does not have formal responsibility for, like the maritime and civil aviation industries, or deaths to members of the public killed by a work activity, such as scaffold collapses or train crashes. A more complete estimate would also include suicides attributed to work-related stress. There are approximately 6000 suicides involving working-age people in the UK each year, and a number of those involve workers driven to despair by work-related stress.[4] In Japan, where work-related suicides are officially recognised and compensated, it is estimated that 5 per cent of suicides are work-related. This estimate, if applied to the UK, would amount to roughly 300 people killed through work-related stress.[5]

In sum, a more complete figure of workplace deaths caused by sudden injury, which takes into account all of the above exclusions, would amount to between 1000 and 1400 death every year, or 3–4 deaths per day.

The second figure of deaths noted above, those caused by occupational diseases and illnesses, is revealed to be a gross underestimate when we consider some of the key academic studies of the main causes of those deaths. First, if we accept the estimates made by Richard Clapp, the author of a 2005 review of the causes of occupational and environmental cancer, the probable range of occupational deaths is 8–16 per cent of the total number of deaths caused by cancer.[6] Applying the mid-range of 12 per cent to all cancer deaths in Great Britain therefore gives an estimate of 18,000 work-related cancer deaths a year. Second, another major source of those deaths is pulmonary diseases. In 2005, a paper in the journal *Occupational and Environmental Medicine* suggests that 15–20 per cent of all chronic obstructive pulmonary disease (COPD) deaths could be work-related, which equates to around 6000 deaths per year. In addition to this figure, there is evidence that up to 20 per cent of all heart disease deaths have a work-related cause, including, for example, stress, long hours and shift work.[7] This figure adds up to about 20,000 deaths per year. Third, for all those diseases to which work can be a contributory cause, such as Parkinson's, Alzheimer's, motor neurone disease, rheumatoid arthritis, chemical neurotoxicity, auto-immune conditions and restrictive lung diseases, a further conservative estimate of about 6000 deaths a year can be made. All of this adds up to an overall estimate by the Hazards Campaign of up to 50,000 deaths from work-related illness every year – four times the typical HSE estimate of around 13,000 per year. Our contention, then, is that the HSE figures grossly underestimate the number of workers whose current working conditions expose them to both the well-known and the newer risk factors, that will produce the worker deaths of the future.

Indeed, it is likely that this toll is still rising. Deaths resulting from occupational diseases can be the cause of exposures that may have occurred up to 40 years ago. Cancers such as mesothelioma have up to 40-year latency periods, but many cancers and most other occupational illnesses have a much shorter latency. This suggests that we are going to see high rates of work-related cancers for many years to come. The EU's CAREX database of occupational exposure to carcinogens estimated that in the early 1990s, about 5 million workers (22 per cent of those employed) were exposed to carcinogens.[8] And there are additional dangers from new and emerging hazards such as nanoparticles, endocrine disrupting chemicals and the increase in shift and especially night work.[9]

Under current economic and labour market conditions, we also have an ever increasing number of workers subjected to long hours, bullying and harassment, and shift work. It is estimated that up to 5.5 million UK workers are now effectively on zero-hours contracts[10] and are therefore working under conditions of insecurity that are linked to higher levels of stress, heart and circulatory diseases. In addition, far too many workers are still routinely exposed to dusts and chemicals that cause respiratory illnesses and contribute to heart disease. Low paid work is proliferating under conditions of austerity. Badly paid work guarantees more than hardship: low pay goes hand in hand with low safety standards. Occupational injuries and diseases such as diabetes and cancer are directly linked to low paid jobs.

This toll of workplace violence – an annual total of up to 50,000 deaths and many times more deaths and injuries caused by working in the UK – should be a call to arms for any government, no matter its political allegiance. Yet successive governments have made it clear that they see workplace health and safety controls as an intolerable nuisance. When the business lobby brays for less safety regulation, this government has one response: to jump, to cut down on enforcement and health and safety inspections, despite the glaring evidence that 'red tape' is actually beneficial for workers, employers and the economy (see Chapter 15 by Charlotte Burns and Paul Tobin and Chapter 13 by Steve Tombs).

Academic Jamie Peck has argued the political purpose of austerity is that it seeks to force through a series of 'fiscal purges of the state'.[11] The parts of the state that guarantee social protections are always targeted by austerity measures as a political strategy (see Chapter 19 by Robert Knox and Vickie Cooper and David Whyte's Introduction to this book). Austerity therefore is a political, rather than an economic strategy in the sense that it promotes attacks on state provision that reveal deep-seated political prejudices. Neoliberal reformers use austerity as a means of denigrating and marginalising government services as a viable solution to social problems. It is within this context that we should understand the intensification of a political war on health and safety protections in the post-2008 period of austerity.

Since becoming prime minister in 2010, David Cameron made frequent public statements about 'killing off health and safety culture', 'waging war on red tape', 'removing the millstone' and the 'burden on business'. Under his governments there were regular calls to respond to a mythical 'compensation culture' and 'health and safety culture' that, they claimed, placed an unbearable burden on business.

One of the first moves of the Coalition government, in October 2010, was to appoint Lord Young, a former Cabinet minister under Margaret Thatcher, to deliver 'a Whitehall-wide review of the operation of health and safety laws and the growth of the compensation culture'. He found absolutely no evidence of this 'compensation culture', citing figures which actually showed a downward trend in legal claims, but still demanded action to deal with 'red tape'. Indeed, figures obtained by *Hazards Magazine* show that fewer than one in seven people suffering an occupational injury or disease ever receive compensation.[12] For occupational diseases alone, this drops to just one in twenty-six. For most occupational cancers, there is barely any prospect of compensation at all.

Regardless of the fact that the government assumptions about the existence of a 'compensation culture' turned out to be untrue, the Young Review set in train a David Cameron-championed, multi-pronged government assault that has dramatically curtailed access to compensation for work-related injuries and disease.[13] What followed was a long series of policy initiatives that generally sought to restrict official safety inspections to a small minority of 'high risk' workplaces.[14] Health and safety protections thus became part of the fiscal purge of the state.

Yet the government's definition of what constitutes 'low risk work' is highly dubious. It includes: low risk manufacturing (e.g. textiles, clothing, footwear, light engineering, electrical engineering), the transport sector (e.g. air, road haulage and docks), electricity generation and the postal and courier services. When *Hazards Magazine* investigated the hard figures, it found that 53 per cent of all deaths at work caused by sudden injury occurred in government-defined *low* risk activities.[15] In other words, the government's fiscal purge of health and safety enforcement has meant abandoning scrutiny of the workplaces where the majority of deaths occur.

Nonetheless, the consequence of this fantasy distinction between high and low risk work is that it has enabled the government to impose a rule barring unannounced inspections in most workplaces. Now, the majority of workplaces in the UK will never be inspected or visited by the HSE unless a major incident occurs. This is hardly the risk-averse, 'elf and safety gone mad' culture that successive prime ministers have railed against.

Other government policy reviews have resulted in what the Trades Union Congress (TUC) described as a 'stupid and dangerous' move to exempt many self-employed workers from health and safety laws.[16] One key review, published in 2013, assessed 'whether there is a continuing need for HSE's functions, as well as whether it is complying with the principles of good governance'.[17] At the time of the publication of this review, Minister for Employment Mark Hoban said ominously, '[i]n 2010 we acted to close down unnecessary public bodies and ensure that those that remained were fit to deliver public services efficiently and effectively'.[18] Rather than closing down the HSE, the government has simply decided to leave this threat hanging over the watchdog's head as it wages a war of attrition against it.

Instead of providing a wake-up call to the government about the perils of deregulating and allowing a powerful sector of business to effectively self-regulate, the financial crisis of 2007/08 has had the opposite effect. If anything, the austerity-driven cuts that followed the crash have been used by the UK government to undermine regulators and impose unprecedented budget cuts (see also Vickie Cooper and David Whyte's Introduction to this book). The HSE has been one of the agencies that has been targeted the most by those cuts.

This had an immediate effect on the capacity of the organisation to fulfil its function as the total number of HSE staff fell from 3702 in April 2010 to 2769 in December 2013.[19] The cuts have taken their toll on both inspection and enforcement. The HSE was already at a historically low ebb in activity, having halved its prosecution rate and cut inspection numbers by two thirds under the 1997–2010 Labour governments.[20] The austerity agenda has driven this activity to even lower levels. Government figures obtained by *Hazards Magazine* show unannounced HSE inspections overall have dropped by much more than a third since 2011 (see also Chapter 13 by Steve Tombs).

Wider cross-departmental government austerity-driven initiatives are putting additional pressure on the HSE. In 2015, a new legally binding duty introduced by the Deregulation Act (2015) stipulated that frontline inspectors across regulatory agencies must 'have regard to the desirability of promoting economic growth'. Thus, in one sweep of a politician's pen, HSE inspectors are now required to do what businesses always wanted them to do – to think twice before enforcing the law, lest it might harm profits.

The result of all this government activity, the constant sniping and attempts to denigrate worker safety and the safety watchdog have taken their toll on both the regulatory system and on workers' and trade unions' attempts to defend basic standards. Running through all of this is the presumption that safety requirements are burdensome, without acknowledging huge costs to the public and to workers themselves of sickening, maiming and killing working people. Little wonder, then, that the HSE has been so disciplined by public sector cuts and political attacks that it does not even consider asking, 'what's so wrong with red tape anyway?' The government's ideological obsession has left no room for argument or evidence that health and safety legislation doesn't burden business, while its absence carries a high cost to business, workers and the public purse.[21]

One lesson that the Hazards Campaign has learned over years of experience working to protect our workplaces is that all of this adds up to an unfathomable cost to countless workers: remove the red tape, and all you are left with is more bloody bandages.

NOTES

Websites were last accessed 2 December 2016.

1. I. Schömann, 'European Economic, Employment and Social Policy Collective labour law under attack: how anti-crisis measures dismantle workers' collective rights', European Trade Union Institute, No. 2, Brussels, 2014, available at: www.etui.org/Publications2/Policy-Briefs/European-Economic-Employment-and-Social-Policy/Collective-labour-law-under-attack-how-anti-crisis-measures-dismantle-workers-collective-rights

2. S. Tombs, 'Death and work in Britain', Sociological Review, 47 (2), 1999, 345–67; S. Tombs and D. Whyte, 'The crisis in enforcement: the decriminalisation of death and injury at work', Crime and Society Foundation, London, 2008, available at: www.crimeandjustice.org.uk/sites/crimeandjustice.org.uk/files/crisisenforcementweb.pdf

3. H. Palmer, 'Work related deaths – what is the true picture?', Safety and Health Practitioner Online, 10 December 2008, available at: www.shponline.co.uk/the-whole-story/

4. Ibid.

5. Hazards Magazine, 'Crying shame?', No. 101, January–March 2008, available at: www.hazards.org/suicide

6. R. Clapp, G. Howe and M. Jacobs, 'Environmental and occupational causes of cancer: a review of recent scientific literature', UMASS Lowell, 2005, available at: www.sustainableproduction.org/downloads/Causes%20of%20Cancer.pdf; see also Hazards Magazine, 'Burying the evidence', No. 92, October–December 2005, available at: www.hazards.org/cancer/index.htm

7. *Hazards Magazine*, 'Job to die for?', No. 92, October–December 2005, 18–19, available at: www.hazards.org/disease/index.htm

8. T. Kauppinen, J. Toikkanena, D. Petersenb et al., 'Occupational exposure to carcinogens in the European Union', *Occupational and Environmental Medicine*, 57 (1), 2000, 10–18, available at: http://oem.bmj.com/content/57/1/10.full

9. *Hazards Magazine*, 'Low paid work comes with high paid risks', No. 128, October–December 2014, available at: www.hazards.org/workingworld/lowblow.htm

10. Unite, 'Research uncovers growing zero hour subclass of insecure employment', 8 September 2013, available at: www.unitetheunion.org/news/research-uncovers-growing-zero-hour-subclass-of-insecure-employment/

11. J. Peck, 'Austerity urbanism', *City*, 16 (6), 2012, 626–55.

12. *Hazards Magazine*, 'Robbed! Bloody bandages but no bloody compensation', No. 122, April–June 2013, available at: www.hazards.org/votetodie/robbed.htm

13. Ibid.

14. *Hazards Magazine*, 'Dangerous li(v)es', No. 112, October–December 2010, available at: www.hazards.org/votetodie/dangerouslies.htm

15. *Hazards Magazine*, 'Low life: how the government has put a low price on your life', Special Online Report, January 2013, available at: www.hazards.org/votetodie/lowlife.htm

16. Ibid.

17. TUC Risks, 'Government questions HSE's existence', No. 603, 4 May 2013, available at: www.tuc.org.uk/workplace-issues/health-and-safety/risks-newsletter/risks-2013/risks-603-4-may-2013

18. Department for Work and Pensions, 'Review of Health and Safety Executive launched', Press release, 25 April 2013, available at: www.gov.uk/government/news/review-of-health-and-safety-executive-launched

19. Prospect, 'Reverse attacks on health and safety – TUC conference', 8 September 2014, available at: www.prospect.org.uk/news/id/2014/September/8/Reverse-attacks-on-health-safety-TUC

20. S. Tombs and D. Whyte, *Regulatory Surrender: Death, Injury and the Non-enforcement of law*, London, Institute of Employment Rights, 2010.

21. *Hazards Magazine*, 'You lie, we die', No. 118, April–June 2012, available at: www.hazards.org/votetodie/youliewedie.htm

15

Environmental Degradation

Charlotte Burns and Paul Tobin

We are at a critical stage in the planet's history. It has been suggested that our impact on the earth has become so extreme that we are entering a new geological era that should be named after human beings (the so-called 'Anthropocene'[1]). Environmental violence, taken here to mean the unsustainable use and extraction of natural resources in ways that push the planet past its carrying capacity and also damage human welfare,[2] will reverberate for decades and even centuries to come. Climate change, in particular, represents an issue of intergenerational violence.[3] Future generations will have done nothing to cause climate change – or its resultant droughts, floods and famines – but they will be forced to deal with its impacts. Environmental protection is similarly a question of international justice. Those states that are least able to adapt to climate change and have done the least to cause it – such as low-lying islands – will feel its effects most starkly. These effects are sure to impact upon developed states too, through mass migration pressures. If Europe has struggled to deal with the Syrian refugee crisis,[4] imagine the pressures of responding to even greater numbers of climate refugees. Finally, as well as intergenerational and international justice for humans, environmental neglect can wreak havoc on non-human species.[5] Due to air and water pollution, habitat destruction and temperature change, extreme biodiversity loss continues unabated. Protecting the environment is consequently vital for human and non-human life to be able to flourish. Yet in times of economic crisis and austerity, environmental policies are often first in line for cuts, as exemplified by former UK Prime Minister, David Cameron, apparently instructing policy-makers to 'get rid of all the green crap' in November 2013.[6] Austerity-led deregulation of environmental policies, to secure efficiency gains and cost minimisation for businesses at the expense of the protection of the environment, is a clear manifestation of state-led environmental violence.

In this chapter, we use two case studies, the EU and the UK, to trace the way in which austerity and the pursuit of deregulation, or so-called 'better regulation', has led to a downgrading of the environment (see also Chapter 13 by Steve Tombs). This deregulatory agenda is based upon streamlining legislation, to ensure that policies – including environmental protection – are not too burdensome for governments and business,[7] even if removing them risks environmental or social harm. We begin by analysing the ways in which the environment has fallen down the EU's list of priorities, as part of a broader focus on 'jobs and growth' and 'better regulation'.[8] These events demonstrate a significant shift in the EU's environmental trajectory, which had previously been described as inherently ambitious and expansionist in nature.[9] We then review how the UK has neglected and even rolled back climate change policies, as well as seeking to sell off much of the nation's forests, under the auspices of the austerity agenda. Finally, we conclude by touching upon 'Brexit', which is sure to shape environmental policy in the EU and UK alike for years to come. Throughout, we demonstrate that environmental protection has been stymied, at best, under austerity.

The EU increasingly positioned itself as a global environmental pioneer throughout the 1990s and 2000s, particularly regarding climate change,[10] providing the EU with a 'soft power' reputation with which to forge its global identity. Under Commission President José Manuel Barroso (2004–14), the win-win objective of 'green growth' dominated Commission thinking around the environment.[11] However, the narrative of the environment being a 'win-win' opportunity appears to have been replaced by a 'zero-sum' framing that prioritises the economy. In October 2014, in a context of austerity across Europe, Jean-Claude Juncker was selected as Commission President, having been the pro-austerity President of the EuroGroup between 2011 and 2014. One of Juncker's first acts was to reorganise the European Commission in ways that deprioritised environmental protection in favour of economic growth. Hence, he merged the Climate and Energy portfolios together,[12] and appointed a new vice-president responsible for Energy to whom the new Climate and Energy Commissioner would report, signalling that energy security was taking priority over climate change. The new Climate Commissioner, Miguel Arias Cañete, was also a controversial choice, due to his past as a director of two oil companies.[13] Meanwhile, the Environment brief was merged with Fisheries and Maritime Affairs[14] and the new Commissioner was given a clear remit to deregulate environmental policies.[15] The election of the European Parliament in May 2014 was also shaped by austerity politics in European states with a lurch towards more populist parties, such as the French Front National. In the UK, marginalised voters gave the Eurosceptic and climate-sceptic UK Independence Party (UKIP) the largest UK delegation.

The policy implications of these structural changes are already being felt. The Circular Economy package – designed to 'close the loop' of product life cycles – was postponed in December 2014. The revised package proposed in June 2016 featured weaker environmental targets than the previous version. For example, for municipal waste, the new target is to achieve a recycling level of 65 per cent by 2030, rather than 70 per cent, while for packaging it is 75 per cent rather than 80 per cent.[16] In addition, the EU appears to be reducing spending in certain environmental policy areas, for example, it will not ring-fence funds to pay for projects that boost energy efficiency in buildings,[17] instead encouraging the private sector to decide where funding should be allocated.

The Commission is also pursuing deregulation via its REFIT (Regulatory Fitness and Performance Programme) agenda, which seeks to reduce 'regulatory burdens' for businesses.[18] The assumptions underpinning the description of existing legislation as 'burdens' is clear; onerous regulations are inefficient and may hinder jobs and growth. Pieces of environmental legislation that do not appear to be particularly burdensome to the economy are included within the review, suggesting that a wide range of environmental policies may be affected by it. For instance, the Birds and Habitats Directives were evaluated by the Commission to determine whether they were 'fit for purpose'.[19] This process, although in its infancy, may indicate a new trajectory of European policy-making, in which existing pieces of legislation are weakened and rolled back.

In the UK, the Conservative-Liberal Democrat Coalition elected in 2010 claimed they would be the 'greenest government ever'. Yet we saw a range of policies that suggested the opposite. The first sign was the mooted possibility of selling 150,000 hectares of forest and woodland in England in 2010, in order to secure budget savings for the Department for Environment Food and Rural Affairs (Defra). Defra argued that the outcome would 'be a new approach to ownership and management of woodlands and forests, with a reducing role for the State and a growing role for the private sector and civil society'.[20] In doing so, the assumptions underpinning austerity – namely, a smaller state and a bigger role for the market – were outlined explicitly. However, due to significant popular opposition, the proposals were abandoned in July 2012, following the findings of an expert panel. The UK is also rolling back existing legislation – or undergoing 'policy dismantling'.[21] In particular, climate policy ambition appears to have fallen since a peak in 2008, when the UK created the world's first Climate Change Act.[22] Here, the election in 2015 of a Conservative government – freed from the constraints of coalition with the more environmentally inclined Liberal Democrats – was significant. In its first eight weeks of office, the new government rolled back a host of existing pro-climate policies.[23] Subsidies for onshore wind were ended entirely in June 2015, on the grounds that the technology was now mature enough to survive without state support.[24] Instead, the government has encouraged fracking (see Chapter 16 by Will Jackson, Helen Monk and Joanna Gilmore) and nuclear energy.[25] Even more explicitly linked to austerity were the decisions to remove the guaranteed level of subsidy for biomass conversions, and the launch of a consultation on controlling solar power subsidies. Both of these polices were rolled back 'to ensure [that] consumers are protected from higher energy bills'.[26] In 2014, 2.38 million households – or 10.6 per cent of all households – in England suffered from fuel poverty (see Chapter 9 by Ruth London). As such, rather than ensuring that citizens had enough money to cover heating costs, austerity has ensured that millions could not afford to stay warm, and the government's solution has been to weaken nascent renewable energy programmes.

The Conservative government also reined in existing policies for promoting more climate-friendly housing. Household energy consumption accounts for more than a quarter of UK carbon dioxide emissions.[27] A decade-long aspiration to ensure that all new homes would be carbon neutral by 2016 was axed in July 2015, leading the Liberal Democrat former Energy Secretary, Ed Davey, to suggest that the prime minister at the time, David Cameron, 'may as well hug a coal power station'.[28] The flagship Green Deal, launched in 2013, was also ended in July 2015. Although the scheme had struggled to garner much support from the public,[29] it provided a means for individuals to take out a government-supported loan in order to insulate their homes more efficiently. The dismantling of this policy therefore worsened both fuel poverty and climate change alike.

Moreover, in June 2016 the UK voted to leave the EU. Although the government moved quickly to adopt the fifth carbon budget (which sets targets for CO_2 up until 2032), once Theresa May became the new prime minister in July 2016, she rapidly disbanded the Department for Energy and Climate Change (DECC), replacing it instead with a Department for Energy, Business and Industrial Strategy. This departmental change was a clear indication that climate change had been downgraded on the UK's political agenda. The UK's exit from the EU has also raised fears amongst environmental campaigners that areas where the UK has been forced by the EU to take action, such as on air and water quality, now face the risk of weaker standards, with cost being used as an excuse for weaker policies. Here, we see an irony – on the one hand, the EU is clearly pursuing an austerity agenda. However, for those who work in this sector, the EU is clearly regarded as a vehicle for safeguarding minimum environmental standards in the UK. Indeed, some environmental campaigners are greeting Brexit with relief as the UK has been in the vanguard of efforts to block new EU regulation and push the deregulatory agenda at the European level, thus weakening Europe-wide standards. One consequence of Brexit may therefore be weaker domestic standards in the UK and the adoption of stronger standards in some areas in the EU. However, it is important not to overstate the latter likelihood, as the UK is not the only reluctant environmentalist within the EU.

In summary, since the rise of austerity, we have seen a clear shift away from previous policy trajectories that prioritised environmental protection. Regulation aimed at ensuring environmental outcomes has been increasingly seen as a burden, particularly on businesses, with the result that existing legislation has been postponed, reviewed or even dismantled. Brexit could exacerbate these trends still further, and may worsen the environmental performance of the UK. The result has been that environmental violence is tacitly encouraged by austerity-driven policies. In response, it is vital that this environmental violence is halted. One way is to reframe environmental protection as a means of providing jobs and growth, as well as being worthy of protection in its own right, as a matter of international justice and intergenerational survival.

NOTES

Websites were last accessed 23 December 2016.

1. Paul J. Crutzen, 'Geology of mankind', *Nature*, 415 (23), 2002, 23.
2. For example, Jürgen Zimmerer, 'Climate change, environmental violence and genocide', *International Journal of Human Rights*, 18.(3), 2014, 265–80.
3. Edward Page, 'Intergenerational justice and climate change', *Political Studies*, 47 (1), 199, 53–66.
4. Daniel Byman and Sloane Speakman, 'The Syrian refugee crisis: bad and worse options', *Washington Quarterly*, 39 (2), 2016, 45–60.
5. Julius Kapembwa and Joshua Wells, 'Climate justice for wildlife: a rights-based account', in Gabriel Trindade and Andrew Woodhall (eds), *Intervention or Protest: Acting for Non-human Animals*, Wilmington, NC: Vernon Press, 2016, pp. 359–90.
6. George Eaton, 'No. 10 refuses to deny Cameron call to "get rid of all the green crap"', *New Statesman*, 21 November 2013, available at: www.newstatesman. com/politics/2013/11/no-10-refuses-deny-cameron-call-get-rid-all-green-crap
7. European Council, 'Better regulation to strengthen competitiveness', 2016, available at: www.consilium.europa.eu/en/press/press-releases/2016/05/26-conclusions-better-regulation/
8. Sajjad Karim, 'All EU institutions must embrace "better" regulation', *EurActiv*, 2015, available at: www.euractiv.com/section/trade-society/opinion/all-eu-institutions-must-embrace-better-regulation/
9. Albert Weale, 'European environmental policy by stealth: the dysfunctionality of functionalism?', *Environment and Planning C: Government and Policy*, 17 (1), 1999, 37–51.
10. R. Daniel Kelemen, 'Globalizing European Union environmental policy'. *Journal of European Public Policy*, 17 (3), 2010, 335–49.
11. Ed King, 'EU chief Barroso eyes 40% emissions reduction target', *Climate Home*, 2013, available at: www.climatechangenews.com/2013/02/01/eu-chief-barroso-eyes-40-emissions-reductions-target/
12. Ecaterina Casinge, 'Parliament reacts to Juncker's plan to merge energy and climate portfolios', *Euractiv*, 2014, available at: www.euractiv.com/section/energy/news/parliament-reacts-to-juncker-s-plan-to-merge-energy-and-climate-portfolios/
13. See the *Guardian* report, available at: www.theguardian.com/environment/2014/oct/09/former-oil-mogul-confirmed-as-eu-climate-and-energy-commissioner
14. Beatrice Denis, 'Vella elusive on fisheries and environmental policy', *Euractiv*, 2014, available at: www.euractiv.com/section/sustainable-dev/news/vella-elusive-on-fisheries-and-environmental-policy/
15. Village, 'Eurout of line on the environment', 2014, available at: http://villagemagazine.ie/index.php/2014/10/eurout-of-line-on-the-environment/

16. European Parliament, 'Circular economy: revision of waste legislation', 2016, available at: www.europarl.europa.eu/RegData/etudes/BRIE/2016/573291/ EPRS_BRI(2016)573291_EN.pdf

17. James Crisp, 'Katainen: private sector will decide if EU money goes to energy efficiency', *Euractiv*, 2015, available at: www.euractiv.com/section/ europe-s-east/news/katainen-private-sector-will-decide-if-eu-money-goes-to-energy-efficiency/

18. European Commission, 'The need for better regulation', available at: http:// ec.europa.eu/info/strategy/better-regulation-why-and-how_en, undated

19. Ibid.

20. UK Government, 'Forestry in England: a new strategic approach', 2010, available at: www.gov.uk/government/news/forestry-in-england-a-new-strategic-approach/

21. Michael W. Bauer, Andrew Jordan, Christoffer Green-Pedersen and Adrienne Héritier (eds), *Dismantling Public Policy: Preferences, Strategies, and Effects*, Oxford: Oxford University Press, 2012.

22. Neil Carter, 'The politics of climate change in the UK', *Wiley Interdisciplinary Reviews: Climate Change*, 5 (3), 2014, 423–33.

23. Adam Vaughan and Terry Macalister, 'The nine green policies killed off by the Tory government', *Guardian*, 24 July 2015.

24. Amber Rudd, 'Statement on ending subsidies for onshore wind', 2015, available at: www.gov.uk/government/speeches/statement-on-ending-subsidies-for-onshore-wind

25. Adam Vaughan, 'Solar and wind "cheaper than new nuclear" by the time Hinkley is built', *Guardian*, 11 August 2016.

26. UK Government, 'Controlling the cost of renewable energy', 2015, available at: www.gov.uk/government/news/controlling-the-cost-of-renewable-energy

27. Jason Palmer and Ian Cooper, 'United Kingdom housing energy fact file', 2012, available at: www.gov.uk/government/uploads/system/uploads/ attachment_data/file/201167/uk_housing_fact_file_2012.pdf

28. Vaughan and Macalister, 'The nine green policies'.

29. UK Government, 'Green Deal and Energy Company Obligation (ECO): monthly statistics', 2015, available at: www.gov.uk/government/statistics/ green-deal-and-energy-company-obligation-eco-monthly-statistics-july-2015

16

Fracking and State Violence

Will Jackson, Helen Monk and Joanna Gilmore

Hydraulic fracturing, better known as 'fracking', is a central pillar of the UK government's strategy on energy security. The rise of fracking in the UK, encouraged by current and previous governments, is based on an attempt to replicate the fracking boom seen in the USA and, in the last decade, technological advancements developed in the USA – specifically the merger of hydraulic fracturing and horizontal drilling techniques – have been exported around the globe. Significant shale deposits have been identified in the UK and exploratory drilling has been actively encouraged by UK governments since 2007. However, at these new frontiers the developing onshore oil and gas industry has met resistance in the UK, just as the industry has in countries all around the world. New coalitions of local opponents and more established climate and social justice groups have focused on the risks of environmental degradation seemingly inherent in fracking, with campaigners pointing to the real environmental impacts already documented in the USA.

Evidence from fracking in the USA demonstrates the risk of groundwater contamination and the uncontrolled release of toxic fluids.[1] The US experience also illustrates the risk of seismic instability, a risk realised in the UK when the first test drilling was conducted in Lancashire in 2011. Considering environmental impacts more generally, fracking, as the extraction of unconventional fossil fuels, raises concerns about climate change and a declining commitment to renewable energy that appears to accompany an embrace of fracking.

Fracking involves the pumping of water, proppants (sand or similar manufactured granules) and assorted chemicals into the ground at high pressure, and opponents have highlighted the risks of land, air and water pollution, seismic instability, and the broader issue of maintaining a reliance on carbon-intensive fossil fuels in the face of global climate change. To understand how, and why, this form of fuel extraction is being so fervently supported by government and corporations in the face of both the apparent risks and growing popular opposition, we have to locate the development of fracking in historical, economic and political context. In doing so, the aims of this chapter are to explore the importance of fracking to contemporary capitalism, to demonstrate that fracking is an inherently violent process in terms of both its environmental and social impacts, and to illustrate why, in the UK, fracking has become an urgent government priority in the era of austerity.

Despite the environmental risks associated with fracking, its economic potential has been loudly championed by UK governments and the fracking industry as an essential component of a UK energy policy for the twenty-first century. Fracking was sold to the public by the then Prime Minister David Cameron as being 'good for the country' in 2014 and positioned as central to the government's long-term economic plan. In the UK, the development of fracking has been accelerated most significantly within the austerity agenda imposed since 2010 and has been promoted by both government and the onshore oil and gas industry through appeals to energy security *and* economic recovery. This is not a coincidence. Rather than seeing fracking and austerity as disconnected issues, it is more useful to consider their connections as contemporary strategies of accumulation. Fracking is, in this sense, part of economic policy and is bound up in a particular vision of contemporary capitalism developed by successive governments in the UK since 2007. Positioning fracking within the austerity agenda, and moreover, positioning it within the wider neoliberal project that defines the politics of austerity, helps us to draw out its place within contemporary capitalism.

Fracking and austerity are united in their status as contemporary, interconnected forms of what David Harvey has termed 'accumulation by dispossession'.[2] Accumulation by dispossession is the concept deployed by Harvey to help us to understand that the 'primitive' accumulation described by Marx in final chapters of *Capital* is a continuous, omnipresent and vital component of capitalism, as opposed to a historic phase situated at its origins. In this sense, the regime of accumulation based on the predation, fraud and violence described by Marx is constant, and lies at the core of contemporary capitalism. In focusing on dispossession, Harvey has sought to draw our attention to processes by which wealth and power are increasingly centralised in the hands of a small elite and that this is achieved, in no small part, by dispossessing the public of their wealth and/or land. Crucially, it is through the foundational process of dispossession that the privatisation, redistribution and deregulation central to austerity are connected to the enclosure, exploitation and degradation of land and energy resources inherent in fracking.

According to Harvey:

> contemporary forms of dispossession are now increasingly administered under the virtuous disguise of a politics of the austerity required to bring an ailing capitalism back into a supposed healthy state.[3]

The reliance on dispossession is key to neoliberalism's central aim to 'open up new fields for capital accumulation'[4] and austerity and fracking must be understood as connected in their contemporary importance to capitalism post financial crisis. While fracking has been championed, and actively encouraged, by UK governments, since 2007, it has assumed greater urgency under the conditions of austerity. It has been promoted through appeals to the new common sense in the age of austerity, promoted as a significant source of revenue that cannot be wasted in times of hardship. Fracking has been lauded, most notably from 2013, by both industry and key figures in government (including very vocal support from Cameron and Osborne and now by the May government) for its potential to reduce gas prices, create jobs, help 'hard workers', bring money into local communities and increase living standards for the next generation. These appeals have clearly tied into the dominant narrative on austerity and the pursuit of economic security. The most explicit attempts to 'sell' fracking to local communities have come in the form of a shale wealth fund established by ex-Chancellor George Osborne to allow a percentage of the proceeds from fracking to be given to councils or community trusts to spend. This policy has been revamped by Theresa May in a promise to give money instead directly to households in areas affected by fracking. While remaining a tiny proportion of the potential revenues from shale extraction, these proposed payments, described by critics as bribery, are clearly aimed at communities suffering the effects of austerity.

According to the political logic driving the fracking agenda, it would be foolish to fail to exploit the resources at 'our' disposal when communities are suffering from the unavoidable pain of austerity measures. But the call for the exploitation of natural resources for the benefit of the nation – where the relationship between the British public and fracking was explained by Cameron through the mantra of 'we're all in this together' (see Vickie Cooper and David Whyte's Introduction to this book) – is an attempt to conceal a process of dispossession. Fracking must be understood as a quintessentially neoliberal form of resource extraction, as it involves, at its core, advances in the commodification of nature into previously inaccessible zones. The basic form of fracking involves the physical enclosure and privatisation of land and resources, a process that in reality serves only the interests of corporations. The necessary industrial infrastructure, even for exploratory drilling, requires the establishment of a site licensed to a corporation and as opposition grows, the importance of barricading the drill site is heightened. We see here the importance of the 'fence', of the physical partition, in much the same way it was in the original formulation of the idea of private property.[5] The physical partition of the drill site is the tip of the iceberg. Fracking involves horizontal drilling technologies that have the capacity to extend up to 6000ft from the well site. Highlighting both the risks and realisation of the impacts of fracking has been central to resistance movements against fracking and other forms of fossil fuel extraction around the world in recent years. In various actions, protesters have focused on the physical enclosure of a site because it arguably heightens the potential for environmental damage, concealing the process from those communities who stand to suffer.

The potential for what Rob Nixon describes as the 'slow violence' of environmental damage[6] (see also Chapter 15 by Charlotte Burns and Paul Tobin) is inherent in the physical process of fracking and, crucially, runs far beyond the partitioned site above ground. It is the new technological fusion of hydraulic fracturing and horizontal drilling that has enabled the exploitation of previously inaccessible or unprofitable shale reserves, and as a result, this violent remaking of space has both a visible and invisible dimension. Many campaigners have pointed to the reach of fracking companies, in terms of the land they effectively colonise and their potential negative environmental impacts; opponents have argued that the violence visited on the natural environment has immediate and obvious consequences but also long-hidden ones as well.

In the contemporary era, states and corporations have a major problem in that accumulation by dispossession is central to the survival of capitalism, but it is in response to acts of dispossession that capitalism meets its most significant source of resistance. The strength of anti-globalisation and anti-austerity movements is a testament to the centrality of struggles around dispossession, but it is in response to the privatisation and degradation of the natural environment that neo-liberalism has met its most powerful sources of opposition and this is illustrated in the growing environmental movements around the world. It is here also that the importance of the state is further revealed in both facilitating acts of dispossession themselves through state-corporate alliances and in the policing of resistance.

While one of the key ideas of neoliberalism is that the state should 'roll back' and shrink in size, the reality is that states across the world have been restructured and reorganised in this context rather than reduced in size and importance. Cutting back the state's involvement in social provision and quality of life has of course been all too real, and intensified under austerity programmes, but in practice, state intervention, and more particularly the state's capacity for violence, is central to neoliber-alism. Capitalism requires the state to be 'an enforcer of austerity'[7] (see also Chapter 19 by Robert Knox), and in the same way the development of fracking in the UK has been reliant on state interventions that have included substantial tax breaks for the fracking industry, changes to property laws to disarm opponents, government-led opposition to EU regulation, the issuing of drilling licences in the face of local opposition, and the provision of government-funded boreholes. The importance of state intervention in this context is reinforced here, but it is arguably in the response to *dissent* that we see more clearly the significance of the capitalist state's monopoly over the means of violence. The two sides of state intervention – the regulation and organisation of privatisation and dispossession, and the repression of resistance – are as crucial to the onward march of onshore oil and gas extraction as they are to the endurance of austerity.

Since 2013, the UK has witnessed the exercise of police violence in response to community opposition to fracking. Mirroring community responses to fracking around the world, the attempt to privatise public resources, combined with an apparent disregard for the natural environment on behalf of states and corporations, has elicited opposition from established campaigners and local residents in each of the sites selected for exploratory drilling. The Network for Police Monitoring has documented policing of anti-fracking protest, observing strategies that have included:

> large-scale operations, inappropriate police powers and arrests, the disproportionate use of physical force and a reluctance to negotiate in good faith with protesters.[8]

The particular experience of the Barton Moss Community Protection Camp, in Salford, Greater Manchester between November 2013 and April 2014, is illustrative of the capacity of police to respond to protests against fracking. At Barton Moss, a coalition of social justice and climate activists, alongside local residents, established a protest camp and mounted a five-month campaign of disruption to delay the exploratory drilling operation and raise awareness about fracking. While seeking to disrupt the operation, the protesters maintained a committment to peaceful, non-violenct direct action in line with the principles of other anti-fracking protests in the UK and in keeping with the principles of the environmental movement more generally. These actions, however, elicited a tough response from Greater Manchester Police (GMP), who met the protest with a substantial police presence at almost every protest event and utilised a significant number of Tactical Aid Unit (public order) officers in the routine management of what were relatively small-scale daily protest marches (on over-policing of anti-austerity protestors, see Chapter 23 by Rizwaan Sabir). There were more than 200 arrests – including the detention of children, pregnant and elderly protesters, and the violent arrest of women – alongside many additional reports of police misconduct related to GMP's management of the protest. Bail and arrest powers were routinely abused in the management of the protest and research by the authors found that violent behaviour and harassment were central features of the policing operation including sexualised violence by GMP officers experienced by several women who were involved at Barton Moss.[9] In refusing to facilitate a peaceful protest, the police at Barton Moss did not simply fail to fulfil their obligations under the European Convention on Human Rights but mounted an operation predominantly concerned with stripping the protest of legitimacy and justifying its suppression. We saw at Barton Moss how, through an alliance between police and corporation, a non-violent protest was repressed, and the actions of the community affected were repeatedly presented as irrational and dangerous responses to an uncontroversial and necessary process.

In considering contemporary forms of accumulation by dispossession, Harvey stressed that these processes require the power of the state to impose them upon communities, by force if necessary.[10] As we saw at Barton Moss, and subsequent anti-fracking protests in the UK, as well as at protests against the slow violence of environmental degradation globally, the use of police power to pacify resistance illustrates the continued dependency of capital on state violence. Forms of protest approved, or at least tolerated, by the neoliberal state include only those that do not threaten the status quo. Any real attempt to disrupt or even bring into question the fundamental features of the current order fall outside the incredibly narrow definition of 'peaceful' protest and are thus defined as unacceptable, and responded to as such. The emphasis on respecting the right to peaceful protest enables police to justify the repression of protests that they can designate as outside of accepted parameters. This is as evident in police responses to environmental protests as it has been in response to anti-austerity protests around the world since the financial crisis.

A substantive opposition to fracking or austerity involves posing a threat to the reproduction of contemporary capitalism and these opponents are responded to by states and corporations in line with the threat that they pose. An effective opposition to any form of accumulation by dispossession is anti-capitalist. As the policing of those movements who seek to disrupt accumulation illustrates, states alongside private security forces continue to be willing and able to exercise violence in response to resistance movements. Recent experiences of fracking in the UK and across the globe have demonstrated both the environmental and social impacts that define the process. Those communities attempting to confront the slow violence of environmental damage are in turn being countered by the violence of the state. To seek a future that spares the planet and its protectors from this fate is to imagine, and begin to enact, an alternative to capitalism; those actively challenging the status of fossil fuels in our current order are already doing this, but they do so at great risk. Challenging the violence of neoliberalism involves us exposing the current role that dispossession plays in reproducing and exacerbating inequality. Here our task requires us to dismantle the common sense of austerity and to understand that in this context a process such as fracking is not simply peripheral to capitalism but central to its survival. Governments and corporations know this, and that's why they are, in the words of David Cameron, 'going all out for shale'.

NOTES

Websites were last accessed 2 November 2016.

1. Greenpeace, *Fracking's Environmental Impacts: Water*, n.d., available at: http://tinyurl.com/h9bekpb
2. David Harvey, 'The "new" imperialism: accumulation by dispossession', *Socialist Register*, 40, 2004, 63–87.
3. David Harvey, *Seventeen Contradictions and the End of Capitalism*, London: Profile, 2014, p. 58.
4. David Harvey, 'Neoliberalism as creative destruction', *Annals of the American Academy of Political and Social Science*, 610, 2006, 22–44, 35.
5. Mark Neocleous, *War Power, Police Power*, Edinburgh: Edinburgh University Press, 2014, pp. 68–9.
6. Rob Nixon, *Slow Violence and the Environmentalism of the Poor*, Cambridge, MA: Harvard University Press, 2011.
7. Craig Browne and Simon Susen, 'Austerity and its antitheses: practical negations of capitalist legitimacy', *South Atlantic Quarterly*, 113 (2), Spring, 2014, 220.
8. Netpol, 'Netpol secures funds until 2018 to campaign to change anti-fracking protest policing', 8 July 2016, available at: https://netpol.org/2016/07/08/new-jrrt-funding-fracking/
9. Joanna Gilmore, Will Jackson and Helen Monk, *Keep Moving! Report on the Policing of the Barton Moss Community Protection Camp*, Liverpool: Centre for Crime and Social Exclusion, Liverpool John Moores University and Centre for Urban Research, University of York, 2016.
10. Harvey, 'The "new" imperialism'.

17

Domicide, Eviction and Repossession

Kirsteen Paton and Vickie Cooper

Evictions and displacement are common and traumatic events in today's housing landscape. Evictions involve the forced removal of people from their home and since the financial crash in 2007/08, they have become everyday phenomena in a number of countries, including the USA, Spain, Ireland and Greece. In the UK, evictions have spiked with an estimated 170 evictions carried out each day in 2015.[1] The main drivers of these evictions are rent arrears that are due to recent and direct cuts in household income under austerity and welfare reforms; cuts that directly affect the ability of tenants to pay their rent. This chapter will argue that evictions constitute an everyday form of violence faced by people living in rented accommodation, a form of violence that we describe as 'domicide'.

First, the chapter will show how the violence of evictions, while not a new phenomenon, has been intensified by conditions of austerity. While Local Authorities have formally protected tenants from evictions by providing secure tenancies and housing subsidies, such as housing benefit payments, today the most common cause of evictions is rent arrears, mainly due to housing benefit cuts. The UK government has played a primary role in the enforcement of evictions through the provision of legislation that has enhanced powers and the role of bailiffs and enforcement companies whose practices are increasingly aggressive and violent. Second, the chapter will show how 'domicide' has directly affected the personal and everyday lives of its victims. Eviction – the forced removal of people from their homes – itself constitutes a primary act of violence. And evictions also generate a series of secondary effects that are also profoundly violent.

Until recently, social housing acted as an important buffer that protected people against the inequities of the housing market. In spite of the growing privatisation and commodification of housing since the

1980s, the political status quo maintained that 'housing benefit would take the strain'[2] and protect the poor against the marketisation of private sector rents. Today, 40 per cent of welfare recipients are living in private rented accommodation and the redistributive effects of this means that approximately £9 billion of the housing benefit budget is being spent on private tenancies per year.[3] Rather than tackling these growing costs through national rent controls, UK government policy individualises the cost by 'capping' the maximum amount households can receive in housing benefit payments.

Thus, the 'benefit cap' introduced under the Welfare Reform Act 2012 limited the total weekly income an individual or family can receive in welfare payments. These caps resulted in an estimated 58,700 households experiencing a reduction in housing benefit (45 per cent in London).[4] When a household exceeds the overall benefit cap (OBC), their housing benefit payments are reduced. Thus, the cap is administered primarily through housing benefit payments. It is estimated that 50,000 households have lost around £93 per week and 15 per cent are losing around £150 per week.[5] Given that the cap is administered primarily through housing benefit payments, it would be more accurate to reconceptualise the benefit cap as a 'rent cap' because it automatically reduces a person's rent income.[6] Another key change affecting rent was the introduction of the 'bedroom tax' in 2013 – a subsidy or tax on housing benefit levied at social housing tenants deemed to have a 'spare' bedroom. Housing benefit payments are reduced if tenants are assessed as having one or more spare rooms in their rental property. Tenants must themselves make up this rent shortfall. Ian Duncan Smith, the former Secretary of State for Work and Pensions, suggested that capping household rent would help 'keep rents under control',[7] and that landlords would lower their rents, exerting downward pressure on the market. But these welfare cuts had a very different impact. Private sector rents show no sign of falling and those in poverty and in receipt of welfare benefits now face the greatest risk of eviction.

Today, we see staggering levels of displacement in private and public rented housing, manifesting through debt (see Chapter 10 by David Ellis), rent arrears, eviction and repossession. Since the financial crash and subsequent cuts to welfare benefits, hundreds of thousands of households have fallen into debt, with rent arrears (in both the private and public sectors) increasing by 130 per cent from 2007 to 2013.[8] Local housing authorities have seen a 94 per cent increase in the number of households with rent arrears, and this trend is partly or wholly due to welfare reforms.[9] One year after its implementation in April 2014, two thirds of households in England affected by the bedroom tax had fallen into rent arrears, while one in seven families received eviction-risk letters and faced losing their homes. Around 6 per cent of benefit claimants affected by the bedroom tax have been forced to move home as a result.[10] Given such levels of household debt, it is hardly surprising that there has been an unparalleled rise in the numbers of evictions in the rented sector. In England and Wales, there were 42,000 evictions in the rented sector in 2015. This figure represents a 50 per cent increase in the past four years, and the highest level since records began in 2000.[11] All together, these changes in policies and legislation around welfare are tantamount to housing violence.

We use the term 'domicide' to describe the violent impact that austerity cuts and welfare reforms have on tenants.[12] Domicide describes 'the deliberate destruction of home by human agency in the pursuit of specific goals, which causes suffering to the victims';[13] in other words, domicide can be understood simply as 'the murder of home'.[14] At the extreme level, domicide involves the large-scale destruction of homes, settlements and neighbourhoods through war, conflict and national violence. At the everyday level, domicide involves the destruction of homes and neighbourhoods through 'normal, mundane operations of the world's political economy' which manifests through national and local level policy changes that affect housing.[15] Thus, the destruction of people's homes is not inevitable but the direct result of human intervention, where policy is as mighty as the bulldozer. We extend the understanding of everyday domicide to describe how austerity cuts have increased housing insecurity and rent arrears, with tenants in social and private rented accommodation now facing the greatest risk of eviction and being purged from their home communities.

The act of eviction involves forcibly removing people from their homes and communities. It is, in essence, a violent experience, involving techniques of forced entry and the physical removal of people from their homes carried out by bailiffs and enforcement agents. Bailiffs also have the power to call for police presence. Many tenants feel threatened by eviction practices, and some have been subject to aggressive and intimidating behaviour.[16] The government, acknowledging the use of aggressive practices, finally in 2014 introduced regulation aimed at barring bailiffs from using physical force against debtors.[17] Nonetheless, the violence practiced in evictions continue.

In one example of this process, in 2015, a private equity investment firm evicted 140 households from Sweets Way housing estate in North London. The eviction was done in order to free up valuable property and redevelop and build some 300 new 'affordable' homes. These evictions were facilitated by a major police operation, supported by High Court enforcement officers armed with heavy battering rams and sledgehammers. The final day of these evictions culminated in violent confrontations as enforcement agents forcibly removed tenants and activists, including a disabled wheelchair user. This form and scale of eviction, described by some as 'social cleansing', is not atypical, nor is it limited to London. In 2013, not long after the welfare reforms came into effect, 200 tenants, all of whom were in receipt of housing benefits, were evicted en masse from one landlord's pool of 1000 properties in Kent because the tenants 'failed to pay the rent'.[18]

These examples of eviction capture the level of violence involved at the enforcement stage. But the violence experienced by individuals and families facing eviction is more deep-seated and devastating and is less visible.

The violence of eviction not only concerns the point at which people are forcibly removed from their homes and the hardship they face thereafter. Violence also plays out in the build-up to the eviction, where the *threat* of being evicted induces much psychological stress and anxiety. One study in Sweden[19] found that tenants who face losing their homes are up to nine times more likely to commit suicide, compared to the general population. Such violent effects resonate with evidence emerging from the UK. Not long after the welfare reforms were implemented, Housing Associations were put on high alert regarding the impacts of the welfare reforms on their tenant groups. Housing Associations were on 'suicide watch', with 50 per cent of housing staff claiming they received at least one suicide threat from a tenant. As a response, housing officers were trained by the Samaritans charity to help tenants assuage harmful or suicidal thoughts.[20]

Despite these efforts, there are several cases where tenants have committed suicide. We are seeing daily reports about people inflicting bodily harm and committing suicide as a result of the Coalition welfare reforms, namely, reductions in housing benefits and subsequent increase in debt (see Chapter 1 by Mary O'Hara). One victim, a 53-year-old woman, Frances McCormack, committed suicide the day after the Housing Association served an eviction notice, due to non payment of rent arrears. Frances McCormack's arrears had accrued because of unpaid bedroom tax. Following the death of her son, she was instantly deemed eligible to pay bedroom tax and was then pursued by her Housing Association. The coroner concluded that Frances probably only intended to 'stage' her suicide and use it as 'persuasive ammunition' for 'dealing with her eviction'.[21] In another case, Nygell Firminger committed suicide in 2012 after he was evicted by his Housing Association for falling into rent arrears. Not long after he was evicted, Nygell returned to his home and committed suicide. The coroner, Andrew Walker, said that Nygell died 'as a direct consequence of his being evicted and the effect that the eviction had on his mental health'.[22]

As well as leading to 'inward' violence in which people harm themselves (see Chapter 1 by Mara O'Hara), eviction also triggers outward violence. Nothing else disturbs a sense of order more than being purged from one's own home and being displaced far away. The desperation not to lose one's home has resulted in violent outbursts of resistance from tenants against those trying to evict them.

In one incident in 2014, one tenant, Andrew Stephenson, opened fire and shot a bailiff and housing officer as those agencies tried to evict and remove him from his home. At the trial, the judge said of the tenant, '[i] t is alarming that you should go from being a man of good character to commit offences of this type'.[23] Andrew Stephenson was sentenced to 15 years in prison. This violent outburst occurred in the same area where the Local Authority, supported by police officers, had recently evicted several squatters to free up property for the private housing market.

In this chapter we have explored the increasing violence of evictions resulting from austerity cuts and welfare reforms. We have illuminated some of the state practices in these processes of evictions – from its causal role to enforcement role – where tenants in social and private rented housing are being purged from their homes and communities. We argue that the effects of violence are manifested first through the act of eviction itself as people are coercively removed from their homes and that this begets more violence as conflict escalates between enforcement agencies, the police and tenants. Second is the less documented violence experienced by individuals and families through the psychological impacts which result in grave, physical harm and even suicide.

The evidence set out in this chapter leaves no doubt that impacts of housing austerity – that we argue constitutes an everyday 'domicide' – not only continue to destroy homes but also lives in all of its violent consequences. As housing austerity continues, this violence will also continue.

NOTES

Websites were last accessed 16 December 2016.

1. Ministry of Justice, *Mortgage and Landlord Possession Statistics Quarterly, England and Wales October to December 2015*, London: Ministry of Justice, 2015.
2. Sarah Heath, *Rent Control in the Private Rented Sector (England) Standard Note Briefing papers SN06760*, London: House of Commons Library, 2014.
3. National Housing Federation, *Briefing: The Growing Housing Benefit Spend in the Private Rrented Sector*, London, 2016.
4. Steven Kennedy, Wendy Wilson, Vyara Apostolova and Richard Keen, *The Benefit Cap, Briefing Paper 06294*, London: House of Commons Library, 2016.
5. Shelter, National Housing Federation, Homeless Link and Crisis, 'Welfare Reform Bill – House of Lords Report Stage Joint briefing on Clause 94: the overall benefit cap', 2013, available at: https://england.shelter.org.uk/__data/assets/pdf_file/0019/410590/Welfare_Reform_Bill_Clause_94_briefing.pdf
6. Kirsteen Paton and Vickie Cooper, 'It's the state, stupid: 21st gentrification and state-led evictions', *Sociological Research Online*, 21 (3), 2016, 3.
7. Hansard, 28 June 2010, para. 512, pp. 608–9.
8. Money Advice Trust, 'Rent arrears the fastest growing UK debt problem', 2013, available at: www.moneyadvicetrust.org/media/news/Pages/Rent-arrears-the-fastest-growing-UK-debt-problem.aspx
9. Carl Brown, 'Rise in tenancy terminations', *Inside Housing*, 20 June 2014, available at: www.insidehousing.co.uk/rise-in-tenancy-terminations/7004223.article
10. BBC News, 'Housing benefits: changes "see 6% of tenants move"', 24 March 2014, available at: www.bbc.com/news/uk-26770727
11. Ministry of Justice, *Mortgage and Landlord Possession Statistics Quarterly*.
12. J. Douglas Porteous and Sandra E. Smith, *Domicide: The Global Destruction of Home*, Montreal and Kingston: McGill Queen's University Press, 2001.
13. Ibid., p. 12.
14. Ibid., p. 3.
15. Ibid., p. 106.

16. BBC News, 'Councils allow bailiff aggression, says Citizens Advice', 23 December 2013, available at: www.bbc.com/news/business-25469806

17. Ministry of Justice, *Taking Control of Goods: National Standards*, London: Ministry of Justice, 2014.

18. E. Dunkley, 'Britain's biggest landlord sells half his buy-to-let property empire', *Financial Times*, 11 September 2016.

19. Yerko Rojas and Sten-Åke Stenberg, 'Evictions and suicide: a follow-up study of almost 22 000 Swedish households in the wake of the global financial crisis', *Journal of Epidemiology and Community Health*, 4 November 2015, available at: http://jech.bmj.com/content/early/2015/11/04/jech-2015-206419.abstract

20. Straightforward and Northern Housing Consortium, *Impact of Welfare Reform on Housing Employees Research Project*, August 2013, available at: www.northern-consortium.org.uk/wp-content/uploads/2015/02/Impact-on-Housing-Staff-Research-Proposal.pdf

21. Ashitha Nagesh, 'Mum who faced bedroom tax eviction after son killed himself found hanged with note to David Cameron', 22 January 2016, available at: http://metro.co.uk/2016/01/22/mum-who-faced-bedroom-tax-eviction-after-son-killed-himself-found-hanged-with-note-to-david-cameron-5639229/

22. Heather Spurr, 'Coroner recommends social landlords are told about vulnerable patients', *Inside Housing*, 12 September 2013, available at: www.insidehousing.co.uk/nhs-trust-told-to-alert-landlords-after-suicide/6528523.article

23. Pete Apps, 'Brixton bailiff shooter jailed for 15 years', *Inside Housing*, 16 May 2014, available at: www.insidehousing.co.uk/brixton-bailiff-shooter-jailed-for-15- years/7003781.article

18

Austerity's Impact on Rough Sleeping and Violence

Daniel McCulloch

Rough sleeping is widely considered to be the most visible manifestation of poverty. Many people who sleep rough have encountered violence in their lives, either in the domestic or family sphere or within institutions such as the armed services, institutional care or prison. For those suffering from violence within the home, homelessness presents an opportunity to escape.[1] However, just being homeless is often a violent experience in and of itself. Examining homelessness in England in the early 2010s, when the full force of government austerity saw vast welfare reform coupled with drastic cuts across the homelessness sector,[2] this chapter explores how rough sleeping is a violent condition of poverty that is amplified by austerity.

Many people experience various forms of violence while homeless. Evidence suggests that people sleeping rough are up to 13 times more likely to experience violence than the general population.[3] Up to 45 per cent have been assaulted, 35 per cent victims of wounding and 29 per cent are victims of robbery while sleeping rough.[4] It is also common for people sleeping rough to experience sexual assault and rape, although incidents often go unreported to state agencies due to a sense of shame and stigma. Verbal abuse is often experienced while sleeping rough (often perpetrated by members of the public) and has profound psychological impacts, including the reinforcement of feelings of exclusion and stigma.[5] Even where violence is not enacted, rough sleepers still have to deal with the potential threat of violence, as 'Dangerousness exists as a constant issue in their lives'.[6]

Compounding physical, sexual and verbal forms of violence, people sleeping rough suffer the consequences of the state's structural violence on multiple levels. On a physical level, homeless people suffer significantly poorer health than the general population, with 73 per cent reporting a physical health problem, 80 per cent reporting a mental health need and 35 per cent eating less than two meals per day.[7] Individuals are also more likely to die younger than the housed population, with the average age of death at just 47 years old.[8] On an emotional and psychological level, state institutions require individuals to negotiate demeaning and excessively bureaucratic processes in order to gain access to basic statutory services. Such demands reinforce stigma, and perpetuate imagined distinctions between a 'deserving' and 'undeserving' poor.

These forms of violence interact and reinforce each another. Rough sleepers are victimised in multiple ways and criminalised through various street-level policing methods (see Chapter 22 by Steven Speed).[9] This begs questions about how homeless people protect themselves on a daily basis.

People sleeping rough use numerous strategies to deal with violence, but these strategies often have other consequences. For example, some individuals sleep in industrial bins to shelter from the vulnerabilities of sleeping rough, a method which can, at worst, result in death. Alternatively, carrying a weapon might provide self-protection but can lead to criminalisation. One way in which many people negotiate the complexities of being homeless is to seek support from local services, such as day centres and accommodation services, as well as related services such as citizens advice organisations, domestic violence charities and mental health groups. These services play an important role in dealing with the effects of violence, offering a place to sleep, wash, eat and rest, as well providing advice, counselling and support.

Despite the benefits of homelessness services, it is crucial to recognise their limitations, with services representing spaces of fear for many homeless people. Some service practices also reinforce notions of 'deservingness', prioritising limited resources towards support for those deemed most 'worthy'.[10] These issues notwithstanding, services provide support for many in dealing with the effects of violence and homelessness, offering a vital safety net for those who are not entitled to statutory support (see also Chapter 17 by Kirsteen Paton and Vickie Cooper).

Between 2010 and 2015, the estimated number of people sleeping rough in England more than doubled, increasing year-on-year. Notably, there is strong evidence that austerity has played a key role in this, with one study suggesting that 67 per cent of Local Authorities see the rise in rough sleeping as a direct outcome of welfare reforms.[11] There is growing evidence of the impact of increasingly punitive benefit sanctions, with one study noting that 'as well as exacerbating the problems homeless people face, sanctions may increase the risk of homelessness'.[12]

The increased number of people sleeping rough has resulted in more people being made disproportionately vulnerable to physical, sexual and verbal violence. There is also evidence of the impacts of state-imposed structural violence, enacted through austerity policies such as welfare reform. This exacerbates the difficulties that people have in dealing with the impacts of poverty, and reduces the chances that people can move out of homelessness, with services reporting that:

A reduction or loss of income attributed to sanctions, benefit reform and changes to eligibility were linked ... to food poverty, loss of or difficulty accessing accommodation, increased debt and use of credit loans ... People are also finding it harder to pay for the clothes and transport needed for job interviews.[13]

The impact of welfare reform affects not only accessing accommodation or employment. Evidence from frontline service workers highlights that 'these changes have caused stress among clients of homelessness services and led to an increase in harmful behaviours in order to cope, including alcohol and drug use'.[14] The violence of austerity is thus also manifested in the harmful ways that people cope with welfare changes, resulting in physical violence through detrimental health implications that are ultimately fatal for some and can prolong and exacerbate poor health for others.

Austerity measures have also affected a range of homelessness-related services,[15] with cuts to domestic violence refuges and mental health services threatening the existence of vital services dealing with the effects of both violence and austerity. Reduced funding has also affected day centres and accommodation services. Funding reductions have impacted both 'direct access' accommodation services for people sleeping rough and 'second-stage' services for those moving on to longer-term accommodation, with 14 per cent fewer accommodation services (Table 18.1), and a 16 per cent loss in bed spaces between 2010 and 2015 (Table 18.2).

Table 18.1 Losses in the number of accommodation services since 2010[16]

Type of service	Number lost since 2010	Percentage lost since 2010 (%)
All accommodation services 2010–15	208	14
Direct access accommodation services 2010–14	38	14
Second-stage accommodation services 2010–14	190	16

Cuts to these various services means that day centres are 'picking up clients who previously would have been able to access support elsewhere,'[17] in addition to an increased number of people sleeping rough. Services are thus under growing strain to meet ever increasing demand for support. Although the number of day centres increased by 11 per cent between 2010 and 2015,[18] in no way does this growth match the number of wider support services that have closed. In response to reduced funding and increasing demand, many services have rationed their provision. Specialist services are often only able to support those with the most acute needs, while mainstream services are so stretched that they are unable to provide specialist support, finding it difficult to support individuals with the highest needs. Thus, many whose needs are not acute enough for specialist support, but too specialist to be met by general services, are falling between the cracks. This changing service landscape has grave consequences for people sleeping rough. Individuals directly suffer greater psychological and emotional violence as well as detrimental health outcomes as a result of the state's austerity programme, and are less likely to gain access to services that might alleviate the violent conditions of homelessness.

In 2016, the Conservative government announced an 'investment' of £115 million in homelessness services. However, this 'investment' does little to address the impacts of austerity for homelessness services, with many services facing reduced funding and unable to meet increasing demand. This 'investment' committed the delivery of 2000 bed spaces in second-stage accommodation. However, this failed to compensate for the loss of beds across the sector, equating to less than half of the total reduction in second-stage bed spaces since 2010 (Table 18.2).

The government also announced funding for particular types of homelessness prevention schemes. However, like many centrally administered homelessness programmes, this funding is time-limited, relatively small in scale, and channels provision through narrow criteria which focus on particular types of service provision. Even where services have access to this funding, it is unlikely to compensate for the overall loss in funding.

Table 18.2 Losses in accommodation service bed spaces since 2010

Type of bed space	Number lost since 2010	Percentage lost since 2010 (%)
Bed spaces in all accommodation services 2010–15	7115	16
Direct access bed spaces 2010–14	1613	17
Second-stage bed spaces 2010–14	5121	15

'Investing' in homelessness services allows the government to utilise austerity to generate political legitimacy. Providing targeted funding for homelessness services signals that the government is responding to rough sleeping, while it actually exercises greater control over which services are supported through funding, with reduced general homelessness funding. This reinforces the legitimacy of particular forms of provision, while making it increasingly difficult for others to operate.[19] Many individuals who previously looked to such services as alcohol and drug support and benefits advice have found they no longer have access to adequate support. This reduces their chances of being able to cope with the violence of welfare reform, and increases the likelihood of harmful coping behaviours.

Furthermore, while these proclaimed 'investments' in homelessness services happen, the government has relentlessly pursued its welfare reform agenda, which continues to exacerbate the rate of rough sleeping and the structural violence forced upon people sleeping rough. Violence is a reoccurring reality for people sleeping rough. One way in which individuals deal with this is to engage with services; however, austerity has resulted in already stretched services rationing provision further, intensifying the marginalisation of those who are most excluded.

Austerity also serves as a political vehicle for the Conservative government, whose proclaimed 'investment' in homelessness services enables the government to reclaim political legitimacy about homelessness, while masking the violence of the wider austerity programme for people sleeping rough. This is epitomised by the simultaneous funding cuts to numerous services combined with an unrelenting welfare reform programme, which has resulted in more people sleeping rough, as well as detrimental psychological and health consequences.

The violence of austerity is thus multiple for people sleeping rough: first, in the increased incidence of people sleeping rough, making more people vulnerable to physical, verbal and sexual violence; second, in the psychological violence and poorer health outcomes as a result of changing access to welfare; and third, in reducing many key areas of support which aid rough sleepers in dealing with the effects of violence and austerity.

ACKNOWLEDGEMENTS

The author would like to thank Deborah Drake, Victoria Canning and the editors of this collection for their comments on earlier versions of this chapter.

NOTES

Websites were last accessed 8 October 2016.
1. A. Tomas and H. Dittmar, 'The experience of homeless women: an exploration of housing histories and meaning of home', *Housing Studies*, 10 (4), 1995, 493–515.
2. This includes accommodation and day services, and numerous organisations that tackle homelessness-related social issues, such as domestic violence, health and citizens advice.
3. T. Newburn and P. Rock, *Living in Fear: Violence and Victimisation in the Lives of Single Homeless People*, London: Crisis, 2005; B. Sanders and F. Albanese, *'It's No Life at All': Rough Sleepers' Experiences of Violence and Abuse on the Streets of England and Wales*, London: Crisis, 2016.
4. S. Ballintyne, *Unsafe Streets: Street Homelessness and Crime*, London: Institute for Public Policy Research, 1999, p. 16; Sanders amd Albanese, *'It's No Life at All'*.
5. J. Scurfield., P. Rees and P. Norman, 'Criminal victimisation of the homeless: an investigation of Big Issue vendors in Leeds', *Radical Statistics*, 99, 2005; Sanders and Albanese, *'It's No Life at All'*.
6. Newburn and Rock, *Living in Fear*, p. 13.
7. Homeless Link, *The Unhealthy State of Homelessness: Health Audit Results 2014*, London: 2014.
8. B. Thomas, *Homelessness Kills: An Analysis of the Mortality of Homeless People in Early Twenty-first Century England*, London: Crisis, 2012.

9. G. Fooks and C. Pantazis, 'The criminalisation of homelessness, begging and street living', in P. Kennett and A. Marsh (eds), *Homelessness: Exploring the New Terrain*, Bristol: Policy Press, 1999, pp. 123–59.
10. D. McCulloch, 'Analysing understandings of "rough sleeping": managing, becoming and being homeless, PhD Thesis, The Open University, Milton Keynes, 2015.
11. S. Fitzpatrick, H. Pawson, G. Bramley, S. Wilcox and B. Watts, *The Homeless Monitor: England 2016*, London: Crisis, 2016, p. xx.
12. C. Beatty, M. Foden, L. McCarthy and K. Reeve, *Benefit Sanctions and Homelessness: A Scoping Report*, London, Crisis, 2015.
13. Homeless Link, *The Unhealthy State of Homelessness*, p. 51.
14. Ibid.
15. A. Hastings, N. Bailey, G. Bramley, M. Gannon and D. Watkins, *The Cost of the Cuts: The Impact on Local Government and Poorer Communities*, York: Joseph Rowntree Foundation, 2015.
16. Data for Tables 18.1 and 18.2 are compiled from E. Schertler, *Survey of Needs and Provision 2010: Services for Homeless Single People and Couples in England*, London: Homeless Link, 2010; Homeless Link, *Support for Single Homeless People in England: Annual Review 2014*, London, 2014; and Homeless Link, *Support for Single Homeless People in England: Annual Review 2015*, London, 2015. Comparable data is not available for direct access and second-stage services and bed spaces in 2015.
17. Homeless Link, *The Unhealthy State of Homelessness*, p. 52.
18. Schertler, *Survey of Needs and Provision 2010*; Homeless Link, *The Unhealthy State of Homelessness*.
19. FEANTSA, *Impact of Anti-crisis Austerity Measures on Homeless Services Across the EU*, Brussels, 2011.

PART IV

State Control

19

Legalising the Violence of Austerity

Robert Knox

In 2015, upon learning of the election of Syriza in Greece, Jean Claude Juncker, President of the European Commission, infamously stated that '[t]here can be no democratic choice against the European treaties'.[1] Since those treaties mandated austerity, Syriza would not be allowed to implement its anti-austerity programme.

In this Juncker signals a particularly insidious aspect of austerity, namely, its tendency to remove economic policy from popular control. Such removal is usually justified by arguing that austerity is not a political choice but rather an economic and technocratic necessity. In this way, the violence documented in this book – the suicides, the evictions, the deaths from illness – is normalised in capitalist societies.

What is telling about Juncker's statement is that he does not directly appeal to economic necessity. Instead, he invokes law. This chapter demonstrates that the role of law in austerity goes beyond legitimation. It argues that modern-day austerity has been accompanied by an intensification of legal intervention into politics. The aim of these legal interventions has been to minimise popular control over the economy and oblige governments to implement austerity measures. This 'law-sterity' has occurred at the international, regional and domestic levels.

The genius of law-sterity is that pro-austerity governments are able to appeal it in order to legitimise their policies and minimise resistance against them. At the same time, the law compels governments not otherwise inclined to austerity to implement it. These austerity rules have been made effective through the use of violence. Law's violence has taken different forms at different levels. Internationally and regionally, it is by the imposition of sanctions for breaching austerity rules and – ultimately – by cutting off of vital funds, should austerity targets not be met. The loss of such funds inflicts further violence upon populations. In the UK, similar mechanisms are also in play, but they are backed by the direct coercive violence of the state. This chapter will develop an understanding of those dynamics before concluding that the aim of law's violence is to make it rational for even left-wing governments to implement 'progressive austerity'.

International financial institutions have been at the forefront of developing programmes of austerity. Although austerity is associated with economic policy in Europe following the 2008 crash, it has a longer and more geographically varied history. In particular, many of the techniques of austerity were first deployed in the 1970s, 1980s and 1990s in Latin America, Asia and Africa.

Since the 1980s, the IMF's legal mandate has been to exercise surveillance over all policies which can affect 'exchange rate stability', which potentially includes all economic policies. This is nominally limited by the fact that the IMF has a duty to 'respect the domestic social and political policies of members'. The IMF has avoided this by arguing that its legal duty can only be fulfilled through structural adjustments to the economy, involving privatising state industries, 'liberalising' labour law and reducing bureaucracy. This, the IMF argued, was not an interference in 'domestic social or economic policy' but rather a technocratic adjustment to achieve exchange rate stability.

The legal techniques pioneered by the IMF were perfected by the EU. When the precursors to the EU first came into being, European member states had all adopted Keynesian policies. In the 1970s, as the Keynesian consensus fell apart, the governments of member states looked to European institutions. Insofar as neoliberalism could be transformed into a binding legal obligation, opposition to it could be quietened.[2]

This was achieved during the 1970s and 1980s through a series of treaties which moved towards the creation of a single European market and buttressed by an activist European judiciary that extended the power of European law over domestic law and simultaneously read economic competition as the overriding objective of the treaties.[3] All members of the EU were thus bound by a European law which embedded the values of neoliberalism.

In 1992 the Maastricht Treaty on European Union was concluded. Article 104c of that treaty committed member states to avoiding 'excessive government deficits', empowering the European Commission to 'monitor' their economies. Should the Commission decide that a member state had made a 'gross error', it was to make a recommendation to the Council of Ministers that could then impose sanctions. This was supplemented by a Protocol 'On the Excessive Deficit Procedure' which set out a mathematical equation for what counted as 'excessive'. Austerity and the avoidance of the budget deficits were directly incorporated into the legal framework of the EU.[4] This is not simply an incidental part of the EU framework, but is accorded a supreme constitutional status.

The EU has also very much adopted the IMF's model of structural adjustment lending. When Greece (and thus the German banks) was threatened with default in May 2010, the EU agreed on a bailout package composed of 80 billion euros pooled from the EU and 30 billion from the IMF. In order to receive the money, Greece had to sign a 'Memorandum of Understanding' imposing strict conditions.[5] The programme's short-term objective was 'fiscal consolidation', involving 'measures that generate savings in public sector expenditure',[6] with the medium-term objectives lifted straight from the IMF's playbook, calling for:

> Reforms ... to modernize the public sector, to render product and labour markets more efficient and flexible, and create a more open and accessible business environment for domestic and foreign investors, including a reduction of the state's direct participation in domestic industries.[7]

This was coupled with a detailed timetable for the implementation of said 'reforms' and a series of quantitative targets. All of this was to be monitored by the European Commission. Such agreements have become the primary mechanism through which European institutions have dealt with the consequences of the crisis, and have been formalised in a number of 'lending facilities'.[8]

When, in 2015, this framework was challenged by the Syriza government, the creditor institutions refused to release further money to Greece unless it signed a new Memorandum embedding more austerity targets. This caused a crisis inside Syriza, with its radicals calling for a default and its moderates arguing the consequences would be worse than austerity. The radicals split, and the remaining moderates implemented a programme of austerity under protest.

At the international and EU levels, therefore, austerity has been implemented by subjecting governments to legally binding objectives. In the case of the EU specifically, this has assumed a constitutional status.

The UK has not generally been subject to externally imposed austerity. The UK is, however, guided by the constitutional imperatives of international law outlined above. Moreover, as Bickteron notes,[9] governments frequently seek to 'tie their own hands' with legal targets because this means they are able to argue that political decisions are necessary, a result of technical rules and thus neutralise resistance to those plans. This has been a common feature in UK politics.

This began most visibly in 1997 with the victory of New Labour. Then Chancellor Gordon Brown set out fiscal rules to govern Labour's economic policy. The first of these rules was 'the golden rule' that the government would maintain a balanced budget or a budget surplus. The second was the 'sustainable investment rule', requiring that government debt remain at less than 40 per cent of GDP. Both of these rules fundamentally bought into the logic of austerity.[10] This was buttressed by the Finance Act 1998, which made it the duty of the Treasury to publish a code for fiscal stability, and mandated the production of a Debt Management Report.

In the wake of the 2008 crisis, the government went even further. Echoing the EU's constitutionalisation of austerity, the Fiscal Responsibility Act 2010 imposed binding legal rules under which the Treasury had to ensure public sector borrowing decreased yearly. In effect, the Labour government attempted to use the law to create 'external' compulsions to austerity *on itself*. The Fiscal Responsibility Act was widely mocked, with George Osborne declaring it as evidence that 'either [Brown] does not trust himself to secure sound public finances, or he knows that the public do not trust him to secure them'.[11]

Despite his mockery, Osborne adopted a very similar set of techniques. In March 2011, the Coalition government passed the Budget Responsibility and National Audit Act. The Act required the Treasury to publish a Charter of Budget Responsibility outlining the Treasury's 'policy for the management of the National Debt'[12] and set out fiscal targets. Any future budgets were to conform to these targets. The Act also established the Office for Budget Responsibility, an 'independent' body whose duty was to 'objectively, transparently and impartially'[13] analyse the Charter. Famously, the Coalition set itself the target of 'public sector net debt as a percentage of GDP to be falling at a fixed date of 2015–16'.[14] Thus, the Coalition – building on New Labour policy – attempted to import the legal surveillance techniques of the IMF and EU into UK economic policy.

In 2015, in a direct reproduction of Brown's behaviour, Osborne suggested that he would enact a budget surplus law to 'legally prevent future governments from spending more than they receive in tax revenue when the economy is growing'.[15] In the end, Osborne never had a chance to enact this policy. Prime Minister Theresa May repudiated the aim of a budget surplus, but the basic framework remained in place.

UK austerity has not been applied evenly. The Conservative-led Coalition, as well as its successor Conservative government, has been loath to directly attack a number of centrally run services. Accordingly, 'a disproportionate burden' has fallen on local government (see Vickie Cooper and David Whyte's Introduction to this book).[16] These developments have created a perfect storm of austerity. Local Authorities are faced with declining budgets and a legal obligation to balance the budget. Should they fail to balance this budget, they can be subject to the full force of the law: including fines, disqualification and even possible imprisonment. At the same time, failing to balance the budget will simply mean Tory ministers deciding council spending priorities, unleashing the potential for sanctions. Any attempt to raise funding via council tax rises will be faced with a referendum, which casts them as 'excessive', and loading the dice in favour of the attempt failing.

This chapter has argued that austerity has been accompanied by the extension and intensification of legal frameworks into politics. These legal frameworks circumscribe the limits of political intervention into the economy and oblige governments to implement austerity. Should governments fail to do this, they may be in breach of their legal obligations, and so suffer the legal consequences.

These consequences can be violent in two ways. Law-sterity always involves the threat of the state imposing fines upon local government officials, which can ultimately lead to prison sentences. At the regional and international levels, fines are also held like a gun to the head of officials. As the chapters in this book collectively demonstrate, the loss of public funding inflicts a series of brutally violent policies upon populations.

By far the greatest violence that the law is able to impose is the threat of a worse alternative to austerity. Thus, in the UK, attempts by Local Authorities to resist austerity at the local level can simply mean central government stepping in to impose harsher austerity. At the international and regional levels, breaching the legal obligations to impose austerity can be met with the cutting of vital funds.

It is this latter aspect that brings us to the 'brilliance' of law-sterity. On the one hand, it enables right-wing governments to argue that austerity is not a choice but a technocratic and legal necessity. At the same time, ostensibly anti-austerity governments are faced with a huge problem. If they contest the violence of austerity, then the law demands that even greater violence be visited upon them. The choice effectively becomes gambling on a radical break with the existing order – which could overturn the legal obligations – or implementing 'progressive' austerity to avoid the more violent consequences.

In this way, law-sterity makes 'austerity-lite' the rational choice for moderate progressive governments. While a more progressive form of austerity may be implemented under protest, it is difficult to implement such a regime for any period of time without internalising its logic. This is intensified insofar as the polarising choice between 'progressive austerity' and 'radical break' tends to split the radical and moderate components of the social democratic coalition, generally leaving the latter in power. The law's violence is thus crucial in turning progressive governments into austere subjects who both implement austerity and – ultimately – internalise its logic.

It is in this light that we can read Conservative moves to decentralise local funding decisions. By maintaining the legal architecture of balanced budgets and central government oversight but combining it with the cutting of revenue, 'competition' amongst business rates and council tax referendums, the aim is to make austerity a permanent rationale for local government to act as the enforcers of a 'progressive' austerity.

In order to truly reckon with law-sterity we need to overturn a number of 'common sense' ideas about law. Rather than think of law as a set of neutral rules standing above politics, we must understand law as an expression of politics. We must reject the idea that law and violence are somehow separate. Instead, we must recognise that law's violence is an essential part of enforcing the austerity project. We must understand that it is through the extension of law into politics that austerity has been embedded and grown. This makes law in general a fundamentally hostile terrain in our struggle against austerity. Our aim cannot be to replace 'law-sterity' with a new, friendly, legalised alternative but ultimately to transcend law's violence itself.[17]

NOTES

Websites were last accessed 31 January 2017.

1. BBC News, 'Greece: the dangerous game', 1 February 2015, available at: www.bbc.com/news/world-europe-31082656
2. Chris J. Bickerton, *European Integration: From Nation-states to Member States*, Oxford: Oxford University Press, 2012, p. 125.
3. Ibid., p. 129.
4. This has been further supplemented by the Stability and Growth Pact and the European Fiscal Compact, both of which expand the austerity trends in the treaty.
5. Directorate-General for Economic and Financial Affairs, *The Economic Adjustment Programme for Greece*, European Economy Occasional Papers 6, May 2010, Brussels: European Commission, available at: http://ec.europa. eu/economy_finance/publications/occasional_paper/2010/op61_en.htm
6. Ibid., p.10.
7. Ibid.
8. In particular, the European Financial Stability Facility and the European Stability Mechanism. Importantly, in order to qualify for such, member states must already be members of the European Fiscal Compact.
9. Bickerton, *European Integration*, p. 137.
10. Robert Chote, Carl Emmerson, David Miles and Jonathan Shaw, *The IFS Green Budget: January 2009*, London: Institute for Fiscal Studies, 2009, pp. 82–97, available at: www.ifs.org.uk/publications/4417
11. The full text of the Act is available at: www.publications.parliament.uk/pa/ cm200910/cmhansrd/cm100105/debtext/100105-0012.htm
12. According to section 1(1) of the Act.
13. According to section s.5(2) of the Act.
14. HM Treasury, *Charter for Budget Responsibility: Presented to Parliament pursuant to Section 1 of the Budget Responsibility and National Audit Act 2011*, London, p.7, available at: www.gov.uk/government/publications/ charter-for-budget-responsibility
15. BBC News, 'Osborne confirms budget surplus law', 10 June 2015, available at: www.bbc.co.uk/news/business-33074500
16. Annette Hastings, Nick Bailey, Maria Gannon, Kirsten Besemer and Glen Bramley, 'Coping with the cuts? The management of the worst financial settlement in living memory', *Local Government Studies*, 41 (4), 2015, 573.
17. Robert Knox, 'Strategy and tactics', *Finnish Yearbook of International Law*, 21, 2010, 193–229.

20

The Failure to Protect Women in the Criminal Justice System

Maureen Mansfield and Vickie Cooper

The adoption of neoliberal values by most of the major political parties in the UK since the 1990s has had profound effects on vulnerable and marginalised women who come into contact with the criminal justice system (CJS). More recently, austerity-driven cuts have accelerated the neoliberal policies that have had a devastating effect on women caught up in the CJS. This chapter focuses on two effects of austerity-led policies: the privatisation of Ministry of Justice probation services and the closure of HMP Holloway women's prison to sell the land for private housing development. Without any long-term plan or strategy about the future of the prison population or provision for people in the community, those policies are generating harmful, and in some cases deadly, impacts. The chapter will demonstrate how those austerity-driven policies have resulted in the amplification of the violent and harmful conditions facing women in prison and serving community supervision orders, and have negatively affected the ability of women's organisations to advocate for women in the CJS and tackle systemic injustices.

In 2016, a total of 22 deaths of women in prison custody in women's prison estate was recorded. This is the highest number on record. Of this figure, eleven have been recorded as self-inflicted, four have been classified as not being self-inflicted and, at the time of writing this chapter, seven are awaiting classification.[1] By comparison, the second highest number of self-inflicted deaths in women's custody occurred in 2003, with a critically high number of self-inflicted deaths occurring at HMP Styal. These conditions led to the *Corston Report*,[2] which primarily involved a critical examination of the CJS for women and an inquiry into how it can better respond to women's needs.

The *Corston Report* recommended the funding of more women-led community centres and support services to provide specialist intervention for women in the CJS. The rationale for this recommendation was to reduce the risk of harm in the prison system. But recent austerity-driven cuts have led to the dismantling of these intervention strategies and the demise of specialist services set up to support women in the CJS. It is now abundantly clear that women's needs as proposed by the *Corston Report* cannot be met by the Coaltion government's 'rehabilitation revolution' which introduced a number of key reforms to the National Probation Service in England and Wales. As part of this 'rehabilitation revolution', the Offender Rehabilitation Act in 2014 legislated for the privatisation of almost all of the probation service in England and Wales. Other powers brought into effect under this Act include the extension of statutory supervision for people serving short-term *and* long-term sentences as well as the involvement of 'private providers to be responsible officers for the supervision of offenders subject to such orders'.[3] In brief, these new statutory supervision orders raise significant concern as they bring an additional 50,000 women under the statutory supervision orders, where supervisees will be held to account and potentially recalled to custody should they breach their supervision order. Even more disconcerting is that these new powers will be operated by a small number of private organisations that have little or no experience of probation supervision.

These reforms are said to 'disproportionately affect women'. Campaign groups, such as the Prison Reform Trust, have raised key concern about the disproportionate number of women now subject to these new supervision orders, primarily due to the fact that women serve short-term prison sentences. According to the Prison Reform Trust, 71 per cent of all women entering prison in 2012 were sentenced to a period of less than twelve months, compared to 57 per cent of the male prison population. What is more, the government has consistently failed to demonstrate how this Act complies with equality considerations for women's key requirements when setting community supervision conditions. The House of Commons Justice Committee even suggested that the statutory reforms were 'designed with male offenders in mind'. Thus, without sufficient regard for the particular needs of women when setting supervision conditions, 'such as caring responsibilities, domestic violence and mental illness', it is highly likely that 'women will end up in custody for breach [of a supervision order]'.[4]

Two years since the implementation of the Offender Rehabilitation Act with official statistics already showing an unusually high recall rate for women, figures released by the Ministry of Justice (MoJ) show a staggering increase of 149 per cent of adult women recalled for breaching the conditions of their licence in the period between April and June 2016 in comparison with the same period in 2015.[5] It is important to note that breaching a supervision order does not mean committing a new crime; it is a sanction for non-compliance, such as not turning up for a supervision appointment, not sticking to curfew times and/or not residing at the address stipulated in supervision terms and conditions. It is clear that women are being placed back into custody on an unprecedented scale for such breaches.

This unprecedented recall rate does not suggest a 'rehabilitation revolution' but foretells of a rehabilitation system in ruins and the demise of a public service, replaced by a private sector service. Against the backdrop of violence, and self-inflicted death and self-harm facing women in prison (see also Chapter 21 by Joe Sim), recall is the worst possible outcome for women being supervised in the community. Given the harmful and violent conditions facing those women who are sent to custody, recalling them (when most were originally sentenced on a short-term basis) generates significant upheaval in their lives and damages community relations with their families and social support networks.

When the Offender Rehabilitation Act came into effect the government outsourced the operation and management of community supervision to 21 Community Rehabilitation Companies (CRCs) in England and Wales. The main companies running these CRCs are: Sodexo Justice (led by Sodexo in partnership with Nacro); Purple Futures (led by Interserve in partnership with 3SC, Addaction, P3 and Shelter); MTCnovo; and Reducing Reoffending Partnership (led by Ingenus in partnership with St Giles Trust and Crime Reduction Initiative).

One effect of this privatisation programme has been the systematic dismantling of women's services originally set up to advocate on behalf of women in the CJS and seek alternative solutions to incarceration. Not only do these companies manage and carry out the main 'community supervision' duties but further dominate the specialist service provision 'market' where clients with identified needs (e.g. mental health, housing, education, substance misuse, counselling, domestic abuse, child care and so forth) are provided a specialist service. Currently, it is unclear whether these, often smaller, women's organisations have a place in the rehabilitation revolution. Service contracts that were awarded to specialist services have lacked clarity and/or were unsigned a year after delivery started. Smaller projects, often with more therapeutic approaches, have had resources and organisational attention removed. Ultimately, these reforms bred competition and amplified the very power dynamics that many women's organisations try to address.

Women's Breakout recently fed key data to the House of Commons Committee of Public Accounts that the development of the CRCs led to a decline in funding for women's services.[6] The result has been an increasing number of independent women's organisations pulling out of contracts. Having tried to deliver within the 'Offender Rehabilitation' model, they now recognise that it conflicts with their ethos and approach to supporting women in the CJS.

Another move that could considerably worsen service provision for women in the CJS is the closure of HMP Holloway. In 2015, Michael Gove, the former Minister of Justice, announced that closing the prison would enable women to be accommodated in 'more humane surroundings, designed to keep them out of crime',[7] thus invoking the rhetoric of 'reform' to dismantle and sell off part of the public sector. Using the language of 'reform', the government is trying to persuade the public that changes made to women's prison estate are made in the pursuit of 'progress', to support the vulnerable, while at the same time masking the extension of market forces, freeing up the land value and commodification of the suffering of its prisoners.

The government now plans to sell the North London eight-acre plot of land for private housing development. The primary rationale for the closure of HMP Holloway appears not to be the provision of more humane surroundings for women but the generation of government revenue. Looking at women's options after the closure of HMP Holloway, it is not difficult to see how this will in fact produce a more harmful environment and most likely intensify the violent conditions currently besetting women in the prison system. The closure of Holloway will see the removal of twelve beds providing specialist psychiatric care, thus resulting in some women being transferred to high security forensic hospitals. Also lost is the recently built day centre, which supported some of the most vulnerable women unable to manage in prison. Various highly skilled and established teams working within the prison were lost, including one of the most integrated psychological interventions teams, and a referral system with unusually good interdisciplinary communication. It is worth noting that prior to its closure, HMP Holloway received its best inspectorate report.[8] Moreover, a recent study on the needs for psychiatric treatment in prison recorded that HMP Holloway met the needs of prisoners at a higher level than neighbouring HMP Pentonville.[9] These positive developments and improvements in the treatment of women in the CJS were ignored as women were displaced to another prison.

The closure of HMP Holloway prison now increases the average distance that women are held away from their home communities by ten miles, from 50 to 60 miles. It geographically disperses them further from their children, families and local support networks and places an additional burden on families and support services to pay the extra cost and extra time it now takes to visit women in their new prison location.

The austerity-driven policies leading to the closure and sale of HMP Holloway undoubtedly have had a ripple effect on the wider prison estate for women, where overcrowding is a key concern. For example, the population of HMP Bronzefield in Surrey (a Sodexo Justice Service prison) is set to increase by 50 per cent[10] and women in this prison are now 'doubled-up' in their cells since the closure of HMP Holloway. HMP Downview, originally a women's prison, closed in 2012 to be converted to a men's prison. But it lay empty and was reopened in 2016, to receive women from HMP Holloway. Women reported that HMP Downview was filthy on their arrival. These conditions fail to demonstrate 'more humane surroundings' but rather indicate a decaying and untenable situation. Without a plan in place to reduce women's prison population, it is likely that the violence within the women's estate will increase.

The neoliberal ambitions underlying the closure of HMP Holloway has led to the formation of 'Reclaim Holloway', a grassroots campaign designing alternative ways on how to make use of public land for the benefit of the local community, for women who were held in the prison and for the women's organisations that served them. In this campaign we are seeing the emergence of a collaborative, cross-sector grassroots movement that is linking radical housing and anti-prison activists, with anti-carceral feminist principles at its core.

There is real hope that an effective campaign that foregrounds women's needs will emerge from Reclaim Holloway. But on its own such a campaign cannot fundamentally change a CJS that is both increasingly marketised and violent. The safety net for many women caught up in the CJS is tragically being torn apart under conditions of austerity. It took years to build up an established network of women's specialist organisations that advocated on behalf of those women in the CJS, which is now being dismantled. Women's support organisations are swimming in a perpetual state of panic, fear and anxiety, of silence, paranoia, competition and surveillance. This involves the fear of contracts being terminated or lost, or worse, money being 'clawed back' or being fined for not delivering as planned. Project funding is short, often year-on-year, as experienced staff-level organisations are being deskilled, with little time for adequate training and resourcing of staff who are themselves in financially precarious positions. This begs the question, how can these organisations continue to support women in the CJS and act as 'shock absorbers of austerity', at a time when funding has been cut and organisations are being forced to remove their services or shutdown completely?[11]

NOTES

Websites were last accessed 16 December 2016.

1. Inquest, 'Deaths of women in prison', 8 December 2016, available at: www. inquest.org.uk/statistics/deaths-of-women-in-prison
2. Home Office, *A Report by Baroness Jean Corston of a Review of Women with Particular Vulnerabilities in the Criminal Justice System*, London, 2007, available at: www.justice.gov.uk/publications/docs/corston-report-march-2007.pdf
3. Full details of the Offender Rehabilitation Act are available at: http:// researchbriefings.parliament.uk/ResearchBriefing/Summary/RP13-61
4. Prison Reform Trust, 'Prison Reform Trust briefing on the Offender Rehabilitation Bill', 11 November 2013, available at: www.prisonreformtrust. org.uk/Portals/0/Documents/Prison%20Reform%20Trust%20Briefing%20 Offender%20Rehabilitation%20Bill%20HoC%202nd%20Reading%20 11Nov13.pdf
5. Prison Reform Trust News, 'Prison numbers shoot past 85,000 as population goes up by more than 1,000 in under two months', 28 October 2016, available at: www.prisonreformtrust.org.uk/PressPolicy/News/vw/1/ItemID/375
6. Women's Breakout, 'House of Commons Committee of Public Accounts transforming rehabilitation report', 26 September 2016, available at: www.

womensbreakout.org.uk/news/house-of-commons-committee-of-public-accounts-transforming-rehabilitation-report/

7. Full speech is available at: www.gov.uk/government/speeches/prisons-announcement

8. A. Travis, 'Holloway prison given one of its best inspection reports to date', *Guardian*, 23 February 2016, available at: www.theguardian.com/society/2016/feb/23/holloway-prison-given-one-of-its-best-inspection-reports-to-date

9. Sharon Jakobowitz, Paul Bebbington, Nigel McKenzie, Rachel Iveson, Gary Duffield, Mark Kerr and Helen Killaspy, 'Assessing needs for psychiatric treatment in prisoners: 2. Met and unmet need', *Social Psychiatry and Psychiatric Epidemiology*, 2016, DOI: 10.1007/s00127-016-1313-5

10. Howard League for Penal Reform, 'Bronzefield prison: a good report but underlying concerns', 13 April 2016, available at: http://howardleague.org/news/bronzefieldinspection2016/

11. F. Bennett and M. Daly, 'Poverty through a gender lens: evidence and policy review on gender and poverty', Department of Social Policy and Intervention, Oxford University, 2014, available at: www.spi.ox.ac.uk/uploads/tx_oxford/files/Gender%20and%20poverty%20Bennett%20and%20Daly%20final%2012%205%2014%2028%205%2014_01.pdf

21

Austerity, Violence and Prisons

Joe Sim

In June 2016, the Prison Reform Trust noted that 'prisoners and staff [were] less safe than they were five years ago' as 'more prisoners were murdered, killed themselves, self-harmed and were victims of assaults'.[1] Sexual assaults had more than doubled since 2011, there were over 400 serious incidents in 2014–15 which required the intervention of the specialist National Tactical Response Group and in 2015, on average, more than 160 fires were started each month. Rates of self-harm were running at record levels with 32,313 incidents recorded in 2015, a rise of nearly 40 per cent 'in just two years'.[2]

By any standards, the prison system was in the grip of yet another incendiary crisis. It was a crisis which was reflected in the wider criminal justice system itself. For many commentators – the media, the Prison Officers Association (POA) and politicians from the main political parties – the cause both of the crisis, and the precipitous decline in the safety of prisoners and staff, were the austerity-driven cuts to the prison service budget, which between 2011 and 2015, had amounted to £900 million, or 24 per cent of the service's overall budget.[3]

There is no doubt that the impact of austerity has also been felt more widely by the most vulnerable individuals and deprived communities in the country in terms of access to, and delivery of, justice in the civil and criminal courts, and across the welfare state. The pitiless rolling back of already beleaguered welfare services has resulted in the demonisation and subsequent detention of increasing numbers of these individuals – neoliberalism's 'social junk'[4] – who have been hoovered up and violently and mortifyingly swept into the criminal justice system.

However, the dominant narrative within which the grim triad of austerity, violence and the prison has been framed is theoretically and politically problematic. This chapter provides a critical, alternative perspective to the position articulated by the POA and others: that it is austerity and public sector cuts that is the only lens through which this connection can be analysed. The key argument from this analysis is that the impact of the cuts is better understood not as determining a shift in punishment between 2010 and 2016 but as an intensification in the relentless capacity of the prison, laid down over two centuries, to inflict psychological and physical harm on to the bodies and into the minds of the poor and the powerless who comprise the vast majority of the prison population. Together with satellite institutions such as probation hostels and immigration detention centres, they constitute a network of state institutions concerned with maintaining a deeply divided, exploitative social and political 'unrighteous order'.[5]

As noted above, one of the key indicators in the dominant narrative around the crisis inside prison concerns the number of deaths. In the year to June 2016, 321 people died, an increase of 30 per cent from the previous year. Self-inflicted deaths rose by 28 per cent to 105 while 'natural' deaths rose by 26 per cent to 186.[6] Altogether, between January 2010 and December 2016, 1637 prisoners died, and 542 of those deaths were self-inflicted (data generated from the tables at www.inquest.org. uk). The deaths have been tied to the cuts during this period, in this case to the reduction in the number of prison staff. As the Prison Reform Trust note, it is

[n]o mystery that violence, self-harm and suicide rise when you overcrowd prisons, reduce staff by almost one third, cut time out of cell and purposeful activity. The backdrop is a more punitive climate, increased injustice and uncertainty which have sucked hope out of the system for prisoners and staff.[7]

However, there are three problems with assuming that this violence is principally related to the cuts. First, in focusing on the merciless nature of the cuts between 2010 and 2016, the longer history of deaths in prison have become marginalised and neglected. For example, there were nearly 2500 deaths between 1990 and 2010, 1404 of them self-inflicted. These deaths occurred before austerity measures were introduced.[8] Therefore, even if there was an increase in the rate of deaths between 2010 and 2016, notwithstanding the increase in the prison population at that time, the links between different historical periods need to be considered if a comprehensive and critical analysis of deaths in prison is to be established. Cuts and cutbacks do not cause self-inflicted deaths, they intensify already existing tendencies in the system, which underpin and give meaning to the decisions made by prisoners to take their own lives.

Second, the focus on the cuts and prison deaths has done little to challenge the binary divide which places prisoners into identity categories comprising the normal, non-vulnerable majority and the abnormal, vulnerable minority who are susceptible to self-inflicted death. In an age of austerity, establishing 'vulnerable identities'[9] is likely to generate competition for scarce resources. Concentrating resources on this minority will only legitimate the official definition of 'truth', namely, that this minority co-exists with the 'normal', non-vulnerable majority. In practice, however, it is the *fact* and *nature* of imprisonment itself, rather than this binary divide between the 'normal' and the 'abnormal', that needs to be addressed if prison deaths are to be understood and prevented. All prisoners are potentially vulnerable to self-inflicted death when faced with the degradation and mortification they endure through the corrosive exercise of penal power (see also Chapter 20 by Maureen Mansfield and Vickie Cooper).

Finally, and crucially, the dominant narrative around the cuts and prison deaths has had little to say about individual and institutional responsibility for these deaths and the lack of accountability of those who implement policies, or ignore policies, which directly results in prisoners dying. The often devastating evidence outlined in reports by the Prisons and Probation Ombudsman, the Chief Inspector of Prisons and coroners court transcripts, the recommendations for fundamental policy changes outlined in these reports and transcripts and the compelling testimonies by families of the deceased gathered by INQUEST, have been system-atically ignored year-on-year by the state, a scandal which has long preceded the period between 2010 and 2016. For INQUEST:

> The countless stories of young people who took their lives in prison show that such deaths are not isolated cases, but part of a deeply worrying pattern. Time and time again systems set up to safeguard children and young people miserably fail as revealed by a succession of investigations, reports and critical inquest outcomes. The proper protective measures and institutional culture that should protect

young people in prison from human rights abuses can no longer be left to the state to determine as they have repeatedly failed young people.[10]

The relationship between budget cuts and escalating violence has been relentlessly articulated by the POA. In evidence to the House of Commons Justice Committee, published in June 2016, the POA maintained that 'budget cuts, and resulting reductions in staffing, were intrinsically linked to the increase in violence, deaths and suicides'.[11] Like the Police Federation's self-serving interventions around cuts to the police budget, the POA's often unchallenged position, reinforced through their easy access to the mass media, has resulted in the 'truth' about prison violence being socially constructed around a binary divide between a pre- and post-cuts prison system.[12] Central to this position, has been the alleged increase in daily violence towards prison staff as a result of the cuts. However, the data on which this assertion is based is more complex and problematic than the POA recognises.

As David Scott has noted, eight prison staff have been killed in prison since 1850. The POA's position on prison officer deaths therefore, emphasises short-term historical data while ignoring long-term historical trends.[13] Furthermore, in 2014–15, there were nearly 5000 physical assaults and acts of violence against different occupational groups working inside and outside prison. This included 423 assaults and acts of violence on prison officers below the rank of principal officer. At the same time, there were 828 assaults on nursing auxiliaries and assistants, 640 on nurses, 535 on care workers and 423 on welfare and housing associate professionals not classified elsewhere.[14]

The POA's uncompromising position is clear: restoring the cuts will reduce the everyday risks and violence that staff and prisoners face and will re-establish stability and order to a system which was overwhelmingly benevolent and supportive to prisoners. This position is highly contentious, given the authoritarian nature of the majority of prison regimes, the threat and actual use of violence by the state to maintain order within them, and the view that if penal and social order is to be maintained and individual and collective deterrence is to be sustained, then the rights and liberties of prisoners should be minimal.[15] The insidious link binding the POA to the mass media, the liberal penal reform lobby, the state and politicians means the violence and bleak alienation of institutional life has been hidden behind the dominant, benevolent narrative about the need to return to pre-cuts levels of expenditure.

Additionally, institutional violence, despite some honourable and courageous exceptions within their ranks, has effectively remained unchallenged by the POA. Their public position has reduced the complex issues around prison violence to sensationalist, media soundbites which will do little, if anything, to protect staff and prisoners from the psychological and physical impact of the current wave of violence inside. Furthermore, the role of many prison officers in the victimisation of prisoners, while claiming the sanctified mantle of the respectable victim, has reinforced an individualistic and interpersonal understanding of prison violence.[16]

Restoring the prison budget to pre-cuts level will not challenge the authoritarian landing culture of prison officers, their unshackled discretion and the lack of time and resources devoted to their training, which remains amongst the lowest in Europe. More generally, it is how the budget is spent, and on what programmes and areas within the institutions that is a key issue if prisoner and staff protection is to be maintained and violence eliminated. This issue has been consistently neglected and marginalised not only by the POA but also by the succession of ministers responsible for prisons – four between 2010 and 2016 alone. In practice, expenditure is still tied to the punishment of prisoners. The pre-austerity direction of penal expenditure – £4 billion annually – was overwhelmingly orientated towards ensuring security, enforcing order and maintaining control. The harm generated by this pattern of expenditure has been marginalised in the debates about austerity and prisons. The case of prison food illustrates this point. Over the last two centuries, the quality of, and expenditure on, this food, as a political choice, has been consciously managed at a punishingly low level.[17] In 2014–15, daily expenditure on prisoners' food was £2.02 for individual prisoners, 'a rise of 3% on the previous reporting period but still below the rate of £2.20 in 2012'.[18] This expenditure graphically illustrates the deeply embedded political and cultural discourse that prisons should be places of punishment. To return to pre-austerity patterns of expenditure will neither shift, nor undermine, the punitive discourse that labels prisoners as less eligible subjects who are undeserving of a diet that will sustain them physically and psychologically.

These policies and practices dominated, and continue to dominate, every aspect of prison life to the detriment of alternative, more radical, productive responses to offending behaviour and to the health and well-being of the confined while contributing little to social integration, reducing recidivism or ensuring public protection.[19] The positive work being done with, not to, prisoners at Grendon Underwood provides a powerful example of this radical and productive response.[20] However, it is an institution which remains on the margins of penal policy due to the dominance of punitive and retributive discourses within the criminal justice system.[21]

The dominant, official narrative concerning austerity, violence and the prison conceptualises the institutional form of the post-cuts prison as a deviation from a benevolent, pre-cuts norm. However, the relentless focus on the impact of budget cuts, crucial though it is, has generated an ahistorical, reductive understanding of the brutalising nature of prison regimes whose capacity for inducing existential terror in the lives of prisoners existed long before the imposition of austerity measures. This process reflects, and is reflected by, the daily terror that the poor endure more broadly from the combined, authoritarian weight of the criminal justice and state welfare systems that lacerate and brutalise their lives, hopes and expectations, often reducing them to psychological rubble, as the data on self-inflicted deaths among welfare claimants indicates.[22] The issue around the cuts has allowed Labour Party politicians, in particular, to focus on the period between 2010 and 2016, thus avoiding critical scrutiny of their preceding 13 years in office where the gratuitous, intrusive punishment of the powerless ran parallel with an equally gratuitous lack of interest in the policing of the powerful and their insti-tutionalised, socially harmful law-breaking.[23]

This point, in turn, raises two key theoretical and political questions. First, what is the relationship between the 'iron-clad authoritarianism'[24] pursued by successive UK governments in the last four decades and the 'enduring austerity state'[25] which is emerging. Second, as neoliberalism moves on to another level of sovereign, punitive action and vengeance,[26] how can the prison, and the criminal justice system more generally, be challenged? It is important that critical scholars and activists address these questions in order to develop radical strategies which will contest the systemic violence of the prison (and the state, more generally). Developing these strategies will, in turn, not only help to reduce and eventually eliminate violence inside but also contribute to the subversion, dismantling and eventual abolition of the prison, in its present form, and the chilling role it performs in punishing the poor and the powerless.

NOTES

Websites were last accessed 2 October 2016.

1. Prison Reform Trust, *Prison: The Facts. Bromley Briefings*, London, Summer 2016, p. 1.
2. Ibid.
3. Jamie Bennett, 'Managing prisons in an age of uncertainty', *Prison Service Journal*, 222, November 2015, 16.
4. Spitzer, cited in Steven Box, *Power, Crime and Mystification*, London: Tavistock, 1983, pp. 207–8.
5. This is a phrase used by African-American left-wing activist, Marxist and member of the Black Panther Party, George Jackson.
6. Ministry of Justice, *Safety in Custody Statistical Bulletin England and Wales*, London, 2016.
7. Prison Reform Trust, 'PRT comment on HMCIP Annual Report 2014–15', Press release, 14 July 2015, available at: www.prisonreformtrust.org.uk/PressPolicy/News/vw/1/ItemID/269
8. Data generated from the tables at www.inquest.org.uk.
9. McLaughlin, cited in Kate Brown, 'Beyond protection: "the vulnerable" in the age of austerity', in Malcolm Harrison and Teela Sanders (eds), *Social Policies and Social Control: New Perspectives on the 'Not-So-Big' Society*, Bristol: Policy Press, 2016, p. 50.
10. Inquest, *Submission to Lord Harris Review: Self-inflicted Deaths of 18–24 Year Olds*, London, 2014, p. 25.
11. House of Commons Justice Committee, *Prison Safety: Sixth Report of Session 2015–16, HC 625 2016*, London, 2016, p. 22.
12. See, for example, *Guardian*, 5 May 2016; The Stephen Nolan Show, Radio 5 Live, 8 May 2016; and *Sunday Times*, 15 May 2016.
13. Cited in Joe Sim, 'Prison safety and reform: when?', Centre for Crime and Justice Studies blog, 2 December 2016, available at: www.crimeandjustice.org.uk/resources/prison-safety-and-reform-when
14. Ibid.
15. Joe Sim, *Punishment and Prisons: Power and the Carceral State*, London: Sage, 2009; David Scott, 'Ghosts beyond our realm: a neo-abolitionist analysis of prisoner human rights and prison officer occupational culture', PhD Thesis, University of Central Lancashire, 2006.
16. Joe Sim, 'The victimised state and the mystification of social harm', in Paddy Hillyard, Christina Pantazis, Steve Tombs and Dave Gordon (eds), *Beyond Criminology*, London: Pluto Press, 2004, pp. 113–32.e

17. Joe Sim, *Medical Power in Prisons*, Buckingham: Open University Press, 1990.
18. HM Chief Inspector of Prisons for England and Wales, *Annual Report 2014–15*, London: HMSO, 2015, p. 48.
19. Sim, *Punishment and Prisons*.
20. HM Chief Inspector of Prisons, *Report on an Unannounced Inspection of HMP Grendon*, London, 2014.
21. Sim, *Punishment and Prisons*.
22. Joe Sim, '"Welcome to the machine": poverty and punishment in austere times', *Prison Service Journal*, 213, May 2014.
23. Steve Tombs, *Social Protection After the Crisis*, Bristol: Policy Press, 2016.
24. Joe Sim, 'The toxic legacy of New Labour', *Criminal Justice Matters*, 102, December 2015, 31.
25. Bob Jessop, *The State: Past, Present and Future*, Cambridge: Polity, 2016, p. 233.
26. William Davies, 'The new neoliberalism', *New Left Review*, 101, September/October 2016.

22

Evicting Manchester's Street Homeless

Steven Speed

In November 2015 Manchester Metropolitan University (MMU), along with the Whitworth Gallery and Home, Manchester's new £25 million arts centre, hosted events for the Homeless Film Festival. They billed it as 'the first festival of its kind, dedicated to confronting and presenting homeless issues'.[1] Just a short walk away from the Homeless Film Festival programme, MMU and Manchester City Council (MCC) were forcibly evicting The Ark – a self-built informal settlement set up by homeless people in Manchester and home to some of the poorest people in the region.

This chapter explores how the major public sector players in Manchester have violently disrupted homeless camps behind a mask of progressive politics, exploiting the social conditions of austerity and using their control of public space to violently marginalise some of the city's most vulnerable populations for their own ends.

Between 2010 and 2015 Manchester saw a tenfold increase in street homelessness.[2] According to Shelter, the housing and homelessness charity, the structural causes of homelessness are:

> social and economic in nature, and are often outside the control of the individual or family concerned. These may include: unemployment; poverty; a lack of affordable housing; housing policies; the structure and administration of housing benefit; wider policy developments; such as the closure of long-stay psychiatric hospitals.[3]

The sharp rise of homelessness in Manchester led to a number of protests from the public and the homeless themselves. These culminated with the Homeless Action March in April 2015 against austerity and the lack of action on homelessness.[4] One outcome of the protest was the formation of a homeless camp on public land outside the Town Hall. This was a protest to raise awareness about the unprecedented rise in homelessness in Manchester, but MCC quickly gained a possession order to evict the camp despite having a duty of care to rehouse the residents.

Residents of the camp moved their tents to another area of public land in the city centre but this resulted in another possession order and threat of eviction by MCC. Again they moved their camp and again this was met with another possession order. This continued until July when MCC gained an injunction at Manchester Civil Justice Centre preventing anyone from setting up a camp on public land anywhere else in the city centre, specifically so that the homeless could not relocate to another visible site in the area of the city centre. This came after the Legal Aid Agency announced its refusal to provide legal support to the camp's residents the day before the case was due to be heard in court on the grounds that it didn't satisfy the merits test for public funding.

Following the verdict, solicitor Ben Taylor, who stood in at the last minute to represent the Manchester Homeless Camp on a *pro bono* basis, expressed his concern about MCC's policy on homelessness, noting that:

[i]t is disappointing that Manchester City Council's evidence today was that costs incurred in evicting camp sites generally was £100,000 as that money could have been properly spent providing accommodation for the homeless. If they had the situation would perhaps not be as dire as it is now.

As part of the government's austerity measures, £350 million a year has been cut from its legal aid budget. In a statement released after the injunction was granted, Carita Thomas, legal aid lawyer and Justice Alliance member, spoke in a personal capacity about the implications of the Legal Aid Agency refusing funding and asked:

[h]ow can justice be done or seen to be done if only the council has the chance to properly prepare [its case]? Homeless camp residents should have funding for a lawyer so they are on an equal footing with the council's lawyers in this complex case, especially as it raises public interest points that deserve a fair hearing for both sides.

The residents of the camp were already victims of austerity through cuts to the welfare system, high unemployment and unaffordable housing. Now they were victims of austerity cuts to legal aid. While an austerity approach to public services had caused so much pain for the residents of the camp, MCC had spent extravagant sums of money ensuring that the camp was removed from high profile public spaces.

It was after this injunction in July that a group of homeless people set up The Ark at the edge of the city centre on Oxford Road, on a patch of unused pavement that the homeless have used for shelter for many years.

It is a highly visible site and by the end of August, MMU and MCC threatened legal action against inhabitants if The Ark wasn't taken down. MMU was keen to see it removed before students returned to begin the academic year in September 2015. The precise conflict, however, was about ownership of the pavement area that The Ark was located on. The Ark had been built on property belonging to MMU, a disused stretch of land, but a small section also belonged to MCC.

Keen to remove The Ark, MMU and MCC issued a possession claim and in September they were granted possession orders for the removal of The Ark and the eviction of its residents. MCC asserted their case on the grounds that the homeless people who had set up camp were using the space to 'protest' against their policies and were in breach of the injunction from July. Court papers were issued charging two individuals with breaching the injunction that had forbidden those occupying tents to protest against MCC's homeless policies. The offence carried a maximum prison sentence of two years and/or a £5000 fine. The charge was laid despite residents of the camp repeatedly stating that the camp was there to provide a safe refuge for the street homeless of the city[5] and not as a protest.

Community Safety Manager, Justin Mundin, employed by MCC, made an affidavit[6] in support of the case against the camp. In it he pointed out that:

[v]arious messages of protest have been written on these signs regarding cuts made by the council to its homelessness budget. The signs also display a message about the injunction in place and asks people reading the signs to think about whether the injunction is, 'Wright or Wrong'. Lastly the signs display a message stating that, 'Homelessness is created by the Government and does not need to

exist in Manchester'. The signs also display messages about money the council has wasted and asks people to stop for a chat with people at the camp.

In the affidavit he made it clear that he had told residents they could potentially 'be sent to prison'. This message that *it is ok to be homeless so long as you don't complain* is reinforced when he highlighted the presence of other homeless people not resident at The Ark:

[t]here are believed to be other persons also rough sleeping on the other side of the road ... although these persons are not considered to be in breach of the injunction as they have not at any point been involved with the ongoing protest camps, or indicated any element of protest.

After numerous attempts to evict The Ark, MMU and MCC won a possession order at the fifth hearing of the case in court. The order didn't come without criticism with one judge slamming MCC, arguing that it was '[w]holly inappropriate to seek to commit people to prison in the absence of an allegation of a breach'.[7] And another dismissing MMU for 'serious failures to comply with the rules, practice directions and court orders'.[8] Indeed, the attempts made by MCC and MMU to remove The Ark became so desperate and so aggressive it became clear that their motives were not about land ownership but to ensure this visible evidence of their failure to deal with homelessness was removed from public sight.

The Ark's residents were forcibly evicted and the shelter destroyed by a security team employed by MMU. This happened despite opposition by the local community who could only watch in shock while the camp was ripped apart with Greater Manchester Police in attendance to ensure the eviction 'passed without incident'. Following the eviction, residents of The Ark released a statement[9] describing this 'unannounced act of brutal social cleansing executed by the corporate "security" forces of MMU and MCC'. The following testimony of one resident indicates the speed and force with which they were removed:

We were forced from homes and safety in the space of 30 minutes, and had our possessions and property unlawfully confiscated, damaged and destroyed ... MMU informed us of procedures to retrieve what remained of our things. We followed them, with no reply. MMU withheld tents, food, water, clothing, first aid and fire protection from us overnight. It is only by the persistent efforts of Laura, an MMU alumni, that a van arrived yesterday with the damaged remnants of the eviction. Whatever wasn't in the van had been skipped, including everything listed above. We were told to call the MMU switchboard to find out if there was any way of getting them back ... After several calls, we were informed we had to speak with MMU's solicitors.

During the eviction it was clear that the removal team was damaging property belonging to residents of The Ark. Understandably distressed by this, one resident, Ryan McPhee, was arrested as he tried to recover his property. Jackson Gadd and Rosa Methol,[10] students at MMU, witnessed the arrest and explained what happened:

MMU have come again to evict homeless people that are living on their land and they have arrested Ryan, a homeless person who made this place his home. They didn't make it clear on what grounds they arrested him. They said something about a breach of the peace. But he was just trying to get his stuff back, which they are likely to throw away.

As the team working for MMU tore down the camp with total disregard for the belongings of its residents, witnesses expressed their anger. 'Obviously The Ark was not a protest', said John Neill,[11] an MMU student. 'It was somewhere for people to feel safe and somewhere for people to live.' He added:

Alan Kane, the head of MMU security and his team were stood watching our protest yesterday and it was no surprise to see them here this morning laughing and joking whilst they were tearing down people's homes. You have to bear in mind that this is the same MMU management that is quite happy to make a fortune out of students whilst cutting their services and providing appalling standards of accommodation, and the same Manchester City Council that is cutting services and which turfed out hundreds of homeless people in April last year when they shut their refuges ... [we] are not surprised by their actions but we are disgusted by it.

Not only had the residents of The Ark suffered indirect violence of austerity through cuts to welfare, a lack of affordable housing and high unemployment. But they had also suffered direct acts of violence through court threats; physical attacks on the camp; damage to property; and ultimately the smashing of the camp for no other reason than being a reminder of the failed policies of austerity. With the number of rough sleepers in Manchester on the increase, this violent eviction seemed unnecessarily cruel to those who turned up to protest. Deyika Nzeribe,[12] a local resident, spoke about the hypocrisy of MMU and the City Council. 'This feels like the first cold day of the year and what are MMU and the City Council doing?', he asked.

It's not just that they are banning homeless people, it is them saying 'You can't gather together ... you are ok as long as you are on your own in doorways but if you try to gather together for protection, we won't let you do that' ... It's pathetic, and the City Council and MMU laud themselves for their 'corporate social responsibility'.

'I lived in the camp for two months', said Quintino Aiello,[13] a resident of The Ark:

For the first few weeks the camp really helped me. After that I stayed there to help out other homeless people. It's the second time they have kicked us out. Both times they have done it without following any procedures. They just turned up at 7am and said 'You've got half an hour to get out'. I feel frustrated because I see the police and they don't work in the middle for both sides, they just work for MMU. They don't care.

Nowhere can the violence of austerity be more tangible than this. High unemployment, a depleted welfare system and unaffordable housing left many young people in Manchester living on the streets (see also Chapter 18 by Daniel McCulloch). The camps they built to help one another and feel safe were torn down. They looked to the courts for justice and they weren't afforded legal aid due to further cuts.

George Osborne said in his 2016 budget speech, 'The British economy is growing because we didn't seek short term fixes but pursued a long term economic plan.'[14] In a 2016 BBC interview he also said, 'the UK needed to live within its means to withstand economic shocks'.[15] There is no greater economic shock than the one faced by residents of The Ark.

As The Ark was being torn down, MMU were hosting the Homeless Film Festival in Manchester's new publicly funded £25 million arts centre. And while Manchester's Labour Council were wining and dining with wealthy landowners at the MIPIM UK (property real estate exhibition),[16] telling the world about the financial incentives of their 'Northern Powerhouse' initiative and how it is a 'magnet for growth' for the region, the *Northern Poorhouse* was dismantling the homes of its most vulnerable citizens and making sure they remained hidden from view.

The inhumane hypocrisy of these extravagant yet tokenistic gestures towards solving social issues and huge vulgar demonstrations of economic progress and prosperity are all too common and merely serve the interests of those with so much to gain in sustaining the status quo. Indeed, MCC and some of their major public sector partners are set to benefit from £78 million worth of funding from central government for another arts venue due to open in 2019.[17] When the rewards being offered by the architects of austerity are so high, it is no wonder these institutions are willing to enforce austerity so violently.

NOTES

Websites were last accessed 30 November 2016.

1. Details of the Homeless Film Festival are available at: www.homeless filmfestival.org
2. Alex Hibbert, 'Charity boss blasts council figures saying there are just 70 homeless people living in Manchester', *Manchester Evening News*, 7 December 2015, available at: www.manchestereveningnews.co.uk/news/ greater-manchester-news/charity-boss-blasts-council-figures-10564361
3. Shelter's position is outlined on its website and available at: http://england. shelter.org.uk/campaigns_/why_we_campaign/tackling_homelessness/ What_causes_homelessness
4. *Salford Star*, 15 April 2015, available at: www.salfordstar.com/article.asp?id= 2698
5. See details on The Ark's Facebook page, available at: www.facebook.com/ thearkmcr
6. A copy of the affidavit is available at: https://drive.google.com/file/d/oB6Sa WooJhopVam81RkhMMThDcFE/view?pref=2&pli=1
7. *Salford Star*, 30 September 2015, available at: www.salfordstar.com/article. asp?id=2938
8. Ibid.

9. End Homelessness Manchester, Statement from The Ark Manchester, 22 October 2015, available at: www.facebook.com/endhomelessnessmcr/posts/170723183272722
10. Interview with author, 20 October 2015, outside The Ark.
11. Ibid.
12. Ibid.
13. Ibid.
14. George Osborne's speech in full is available at: www.gov.uk/government/speeches/budget-2016-george-osbornes-speech
15. BBC News, 'Budget 2016: George Osborne warns of cuts of 50p per £100', 13 March 2016, available at: www.bbc.co.uk/news/uk-politics-35796861
16. See the report on website run by the property development company, CoStar, available at: www.costar.co.uk/en/assets/news/2015/March/MIPIM-2015-Northern-Powerhouse-is-once-in-a-generation-chance/
17. BBC News, 'Manchester to get new £78m theatre named The Factory', 3 December 2014, available at: www.bbc.co.uk/news/entertainment-arts-30314737

23

Policing Anti-Austerity through the 'War on Terror'

Rizwaan Sabir

Many of the counter-terrorism policies introduced in the UK since the middle of the twentieth century have gradually been expanded and directed towards activists, dissidents and campaigners involved in direct acts of political action, protest and trade unionism. It is now well known that police and MI5, for example, used an infrastructure largely created to tackle armed groups in the North of Ireland to keep anti-nuclear campaigners, anti-racism and environmental activists as well as MPs under surveillance.[1] Revelations on the 'spy cop scandal' in which undercover police systematically infiltrated left-wing protest groups from the 1980s until, at least, 2010 are still coming to light.[2] So are reports that 'troublesome' construction workers who were active within the trade union movement were 'blacklisted' and prevented from securing employment.[3] The policing of activists and protest groups – who are generically and pejoratively labelled as 'domestic extremists' in current policy parlance – through a highly coercive and politicised policing infrastructure is therefore neither new nor without precedent.[4]

This chapter uses information acquired under the Freedom of Information Act 2000[5] to show how the non-violent and peaceful anti-austerity protest groups UK-UNCUT and Occupy London are policed through a counter-terrorism infrastructure. The chapter argues that any approach which conflates peaceful protest with terrorism enables violent and coercive policing practices to be normalised and employed against those democratically and legitimately working to resist austerity and neoliberalism. Such practices challenge the claims that the UK government is committed to human rights processes and that the UK is a 'liberal democracy'.

There are countless definitions of 'terrorism' but in UK law the term very broadly describes violence employed by non-state actors as a way of furthering a political, racial, religious or ideological goal.[6] Other than being defined in an extremely broad way, the term is a pejorative and propagandistic one that is used to delegitimise opponents of state power and obscure 'state terrorism'.[7] While the state has not officially labelled anti-austerity activists, protest movements or those who challenge neoliberalism as 'terrorists', there has been a tendency to police 'domestic extremists', especially on matters relating to intelligence and surveillance, through a 'War on Terror' infrastructure.[8] Protestors, as a result, are increasingly viewed as 'terrorist-like'. Such a category combines and collapses acts of civil disobedience, protest activity and low-level criminal behaviour such as trespassing and property damage with the politically charged category of 'terrorism'. This process of collapsing categories has very significant consequences in practice. It shapes and feeds stereotypical ideas and imagery which associates protestors and movements with a violent minority that has to be policed through a highly militarised counter-terrorism infrastructure. At the same time, it helps manufacture consent and sustain indifference amongst the general public in relation to the state's use of coercion and violence against such groups. I now demonstrate how two peaceful and non-violent protest groups who challenge austerity and neoliberalism came to labelled as 'terrorists'.

In 2011, a one-page document nebulously titled 'Terrorism/extremism communiqué' began circulating on the internet.[9] The document, which had the City of London Police emblem, comprised information relating to armed attacks conducted by the likes of al-Qaida and the Revolutionary Armed Forces of Colombia (FARC).[10] Included in the communiqué, however, were the non-violent and peaceful protest groups Occupy and UK-UNCUT. Both of these groups seek to resist unfair economic policies and challenge austerity, amongst other things. After verifying the authenticity of the communiqué, and working in partnership with the *Independent*,[11] I obtained full details of this 'Terrorism/extremism communiqué' through a Freedom of Information Act request to the City of London Police. The information obtained comprised seven individual 'Terrorism/extremism communiqus'. All seven of them mentioned and included information on the activities of Occupy, UK-UNCUT and other peaceful groups.

One communiqué, for example, states that a 'Yoga and meditation flash mob' is planned by the group Wake Up London. Another communiqué notes how 'UK-UNCUT are planning to attend a conference regarding NHS Reforms and the dismantling of the NHS'. In another, there is talk about 'reconnaissance' being undertaken by Occupy activists within the City of London. In all the communiqués, businesses are instructed to confidentially report suspicious activity to the 'anti-terrorism hotline'. The issue here is not only that such groups have been included in the same category as terrorism but police and counter-terrorism officers in conjunction with businesses and corporations are surveilling and policing non-violent and peaceful protestors through an infrastructure that is fundamentally set up to confront terrorism.

After exchanges of correspondence with me and others who were concerned about those practices, City of London Police released a statement explaining why these two groups had been included in the 'Terrorism/extremism communiqués' (Figure 23.1). The statement notes that the information included in the communiqués was collected by Special Branch and the Counter-Terrorism Department situated within the City of London Police. The statement accepted that the title of the communiqué was inaccurate in that it did not reflect the non-violent nature of the protest movements. This was, however, claimed to be the result of a 'mistake' and an 'error'. Moreover, '[i]t was never our intention to suggest that we view the Occupy movement as being terrorist or extremist in nature', City of London Police claimed.

While the 'error' claim may have seemed initially plausible, on scrutiny, it is unconvincing. First, it is worth emphasising that any act that is undertaken on seven separate occasions looks less like an 'error' and more like a habit; in this case, the habit of not distinguishing between peaceful protest and terrorism. Second, those responsible for collecting information and producing the communiqués are Special Branch and the Counter-Terrorism Department; a fact which means we might reasonably expect that peaceful protestors will be viewed through a terrorist-like gaze. Third, there is still talk about City of London police undertaking activity to counter 'hostile reconnaissance' through a project codenamed (at the time of writing) 'Servator'. Here, we see, yet again, 'criminals, whether extreme protest groups, organised crime groups or terrorists' being referred to in the same sentence.[12]

Figure 23.1 City of London Police press release

Incorporating the policing of peaceful political protestors challenging austerity into a counter-terrorism infrastructure is not without real consequences. Such consequences were clearly visible in the policing of the 2009 G20 London protests. It was during the policing of these protests that the newspaper vendor Ian Tomlinson was killed by a police officer from the anti-riot Territorial Support Group (TSG) unit. Militarised policing tactics were also employed in the policing of Climate Camp's 2008 protest at Kingsnorth power station in Kent, where 1500 public order police officers were deployed to police 1000 protestors.[13] Here, they were subject to unlawful anti-terror stops and searches.[14] As reported to a Parliamentary Select Committee, not only by protestors but journalists too, the police, rather than facilitating protest were using those anti-terrorism powers to 'intimidate' and 'harass' protestors as a way of dissuading them from organising and protesting in the future.[15] Violence and threats of violence, in other words, were being used to discipline, control and prevent peaceful and democratic protest (see also Chapter 16 by Will Jackson, Helen Monk and Joanna Gilmore).

While unlawful police activity and violence is usually presented as undertaken by overzealous 'bad-apple' officers, these officers are not operating in a vacuum. They are operating within the context of a narrative set by politically charged policing institutions. Just take Her Majesty's Inspectorate of Constabulary's (HMIC) language selection when describing environmental activists: they operate 'in *cell like* structures in a *quasi-terrorist* mode to keep secret their movements and intentions'.[16] When one also takes into consideration that the various units dedicated to dealing with 'domestic extremism' have all been placed under the control of the Counter-Terrorism division within the Metropolitan Police,[17] again, the concrete practices of policing are evidence of how the boundaries between terrorism and peaceful protest have been collapsed. More importantly, such practices are evidence of the processes through which the criminalisation of, and use of coercion and violence against, peaceful and non-violent protestors is institutionally guided from the top down.

The targeted use of coercive policies and practices against activists and campaigners through a counter-terrorism infrastructure is neither new nor unique. What the above examples relating to UK-UNCUT and Occupy London demonstrate is that the state and police *continue* to view non-violent political protest through the gaze of 'terrorism' and therefore feel justified in using violence and coercion against them. Though the opponent and nature of the conflict may have changed in the so-called 'War on Terror', the boundaries remain blurred between peaceful protest and 'terrorism' in practice. This blurring is not without consequence. It generates and perpetuates the public's indifference to the criminalisation of peaceful protestors and legitimises the continued use of militarised, violent and coercive police policy and tactics against them. Such policing practices undermine the UK's purported commitment to human rights processes and its claim that it upholds principles of liberal democracy.

NOTES

1. Seamus Milne, *The Enemy Within: Thatcher's Secret War Against the Miners*, London: Verso, 2004; Rob Evans and Paul Lewis, *Undercover: The True Story of Britain's Secret Police*, London: Faber and Faber, 2013.

2. Evans and Lewis, *Undercover*; Evaline Lubbers, *Secret Manoeuvres in the Dark: Corporate and Police Spying on Activists*, London: Pluto Press, 2012.
3. David Whyte, 'Policing for Whom?', *The Howard Journal of Crime and Justice*, 54 (1), February 2015, 73–90.
4. Tony Bunyan, *The History and Practice of the Political Police in Britain*, London: Quartet Books, 1980.
5. Information released by City of London Police to Rizwaan Sabir under Freedom of Information Subject Access Request, 4 January 2012, Ref: COL/11/625, available at: www.scribd.com/document/77329771/City-of-London-Police-OccupyLSX-FOI-Disclosure (accessed 17 November 2016).
6. HM Government Terrorism Act 2000, Section 1, Part 1, full text available at: www.legislation.gov.uk/ukpga/2000/11/pdfs/ukpga_20000011_en.pdf (accessed 24 November 2016).
7. Scott Poynting and David Whyte (eds), *Counter-terrorism and State Political Violence: The 'War on Terror' as Terror*, London: Routledge, 2012, pp. 1–11.
8. Joanna Gilmore, 'This is not a riot!': regulation of public protest and the impact of the Human Rights Act 1998', PhD Thesis, School of Law, University of Manchester, 2013, chapter 8.
9. Rizwaan Sabir, 'How police branded OccupyLSX and UKUNCUT as "terrorists"', *Ceasefire*, 7 January 2012, available at: https://ceasefiremagazine.co.uk/police-branded-occupylsx-ukuncut-terrorists/ (accessed 24 November 2016).
10. Ibid.
11. Kevin Rawlinson, 'Police face new questions over approach to protest groups', *Independent*, 6 January 2012, available at: www.independent.co.uk/news/uk/home-news/police-face-new-questions-over-approach-to-protest-groups-6285707.html (accessed 24 November 2016).
12. Details of the City of London Police's Project Servator are available at: www.cityoflondon.police.uk/community-policing/project-servator/Pages/Project-Servator.aspx (accessed 17 November 2016).
13. House of Commons, *Demonstrating Respect for Rights? A Human Rights Approach to Policing Protest*, Joint Committee on Human Rights, Seventh Report, Session 2008–09, 23 March 2009, London: The Stationary Office, available at: www.publications.parliament.uk/pa/jt200809/jtselect/jtrights/47/47i.pdf (accessed 24 November 2016).
14. Afua Hirsch, 'Police accused of misusing terror laws against peaceful protests', *Guardian*, 23 March 2009, available at: www.theguardian.com/uk/2009/mar/23/police-terrorism-protest-g20-law (accessed 24 November 2016).
15. House of Commons, *Demonstrating Respect for Rights?*, p. 13.
16. My emphasis, cited in Gilmore, 'This is not a riot!', p. 183.
17. Ibid., p. 188.

24

Austerity and the Production of Hate

Jon Burnett

This chapter is about the ways that two forms of institutionally produced hatred – hatred targeted at migrants and hatred targeted at welfare claimants – have become closely interlinked by 'austerity politics'. This chilling symbiosis has become apparent in a relentless barrage of headlines about migrant hordes, supposedly exploiting public services and undercutting wages, and the British benefit 'cheats' supposedly too idle to work and abusing the welfare state. As the *Daily Express* condemns the 'millions' of migrants grabbing 'our jobs',[1] it celebrates the latest 'blitz' on British 'benefit cheats'.[2] As the *Sun* launches a war on benefits culture ('leading the charge to rid Britain of a generation of scroungers'),[3] it simultaneously issues a 'red-line' demand to the prime minister to 'halt immigration from the EU', claiming that 'this is not racism ... [i]t is a simple question of numbers'.[4]

Such campaigns are organised separately. But they feed off and into each other. And they are replicated day after day to the point where they have become a routine aspect of popular culture. Both are voyeuristically treated in television programmes like *Benefits Street* and *Immigration Street*. Those programmes stem from the same ideological enterprise: to reduce their subjects to objects of ridicule and contempt, turning human struggles into a sneering form of entertainment.

The chapter shows how this tabloid barrage is sustained by an aggressively violent politics that is being orchestrated from the centre of government. It further shows how the conditions that fuel this violence have been intensified by 'austerity politics'. The chapter therefore argues that hate is produced in a context where the blame for an economic crisis is placed on its victims, and in the process generates further victims of hate (see also Chapter 3 by John Pring). The violent effects of this politics make their targets more vulnerable to racist attacks and hate crimes. While the institutional orchestrators of this hate will never be held accountable, they are, as this chapter will show, clearly identifiable.

When David Cameron gave his first major speech on immigration as prime minister in 2011 he was lauded by a coterie of right-wing commentators for insinuating that migration 'threatens our way of life'.[5] In a speech that was described by the British National Party (BNP) as 'advocating [our] policy',[6] Cameron claimed that immigration had 'created a kind of discomfort and disjointedness', and that 'controlling immigration and bringing it down [was] of vital importance to the future of our country'.[7]

Despite being peppered with criticisms of the previous government's immigration policies, much of what Cameron proposed built upon what had gone before. His demand for 'good immigration', not 'mass immigration',[8] for example, echoed the managed migration strategy that New Labour had already put in place, in which migration was to be managed as a means of meeting labour and skills shortages. At the same time, the notion that migrants' access to the welfare state had to be restricted was of paramount importance. For Cameron, the link between immigration and welfare was explicit:

Migrants are filling gaps in the labour market left wide open by a welfare system that for years has paid British people not to work. That's where the blame lies – at the door of our woeful welfare system, and the last government who comprehensively failed to reform it ... So immigration and welfare reform are two sides of the same coin. Put simply, we will never control immigration properly unless we tackle welfare dependency.[9]

Five years later, and against the backdrop of the EU referendum which proved fatal to Cameron's premiership, these claims had become Conservative political orthodoxy. And at their core reside two of the folk-devils that have been elevated to the forefront of narratives of austerity: the migrant and the home-grown 'scrounger'. When the government invokes its 'skivers' versus 'strivers' rhetoric, its bankrupt 'shirkers' versus 'workers' discourse, it is migrants and welfare claimants who are frequently the targets. And the relentless procession of policy experiments they are subjected to are linked, ideologically, through a framework central to the politics of austerity. For if one of the aims of successive layers of immigration policy has been to reduce migrants to units of labour, denied access to social rights as much as the law will allow, another aim of successive layers of welfare 'reform' and social policies is also to create an expendable workforce from British citizens within, who are rapidly being stripped of their right to access welfare provision. The mechanisms put in place to achieve these aims are not the same. But one goal they have in common is to satisfy an unquenchable demand for exploitable labour, and the government recognises that presenting them as symbiotic legitimises the long-standing assault on and transformation of the welfare state.

It is in this context that measures such as the creation of a 'hostile environment' for refused asylum seekers and undocumented migrants, the ramping up of deportations and workplace raids, and the attack on migrants' welfare are linked to a more general escalated attack on social security and an assault on workplace protections. These things, of course, have their own roots and histories. They cannot be reduced simply to their relationship with each other, and they are certainly not the sole responsibility of the current Conservative administration. But, together, they make up part of an ongoing attempt to restructure the composition of Britain's labour force through the appeasement of nationalist demands to 'manage' and ultimately reduce migration to the UK. They are two flanks – in other words – of the same political project.

And when resentment to welfare and free movement is legitimised, hate becomes normalised. As campaign groups, support centres and self-organised networks have repeatedly shown, certain forms of violence have intensified under the rubric of austerity. But they are rarely given official recognition. In a survey published by the Disability Hate Crime Network in 2015, 'scrounger rhetoric' was highlighted in the testimonies of around one in six of 61 disabled people who described being verbally or physically assaulted in disability hate crimes.[10] Six charities in 2012 stated that a narrative of 'benefit scrounging' or 'faking' was fuelling hostility.[11] Discussing an increase in disability hate crimes coming before the Crown Prosecution Service (CPS) between 2008/09 and 2013/14, one of the co-founders of the activist group Disabled People Against the Cuts (DPAC) remarked that the figures were 'no doubt fuelled by the constant media-fuelled campaign against benefit claimants'.[12] There were around 62,000 disability-related hate crimes each year in 2012/13 and 2013/14, according to the Crime Survey for England and Wales

(CSEW). In 2014/15, the last year for which figures are available, 2508 offences were recorded by the police – an increase of 15 per cent from two years earlier.[13]

It took only a few days after the outcome of the EU referendum to find an outlet in abuse and attacks, including: Eastern Europeans told to 'go home'; cards with 'no more Polish vermin' posted through letterboxes; racist graffiti daubed on community centres; people stabbed; and Muslim-owned businesses firebombed.[14] But while the violence has been given a new sense of acceptability, it is a continuation of what has been a long feature of the UK, and has intensified under conditions of austerity. Nobody listened in 2014 when charities such as Flowers of Human Hearts, which provides support and advice to Polish people, warned that hate crimes against Eastern Europeans were rising and that this was related to the narratives spun around the recession.[15] Nobody listened when groups such as the Alliance Against Romanian and Bulgarian Dis-crimination warned in the same year that a climate was being created where physical attacks could be carried out with impunity.[16]

Of the 106,000 racist incidents recorded in the CSEW on average a year,[17] not all, of course, are targeted at migrants. But of those that were, and of those that continue to be carried out, there appears to be a special ferocity reserved for those people who have lost or, it is assumed, are not in employment. In Peterborough a few years ago, homeless migrants living in tents were subjected to arson attacks after a local MP, lauding a scheme by the authorities to have them removed from the country, called them 'vagrants' and a 'drain' on his constituents, telling a national newspaper, '[i]f they are not going to contribute to this country, then, as citizens of their home country, they should return there'.[18] In Hull some years ago, a homeless Polish man was left with shattered collar bones, broken ribs and cracked vertebrae after being run over (and reversed over for good measure) while looking for food in some bins by a man who shouted at him to 'get a job'.[19] In the run-up to the EU referendum, far-right groups took it upon themselves to begin roaming around, looking for homeless migrants so that they could be filmed, humiliated and presumably later identified for punishment.[20] They have continued to do so.[21]

Of course, the surges of violence against migrants and disabled people can neither solely be reduced to the politics of austerity nor are the only forms of violence linked to austerity. As the academics Sylvia Walby,

Jude Towers and Brian Francis have shown, for example, 'violent crime against women and by domestic perpetrators is increasing', and this increase is linked to an economic crisis that has 'reduced income levels and increased inequalities and thereby reduced the propensity of victims to escape violence, including exiting violent relationships or enabling conflicted households to split up'.[22] The intensifications of homophobic violence, meanwhile, cannot be separated from the ongoing evisceration of LBGT specialist support services.[23]

But as particular forms of individual violence escalate under the rubric of austerity, they increasingly mirror the institutional violence that is being implemented by the government. And in this context they serve the interest of the UK's political elites. When disabled people are assaulted as 'scroungers' who ought to be forced into any form of employment, when there are attempts to hound migrants out of country through physical force and intimidation if they are no longer deemed to be of economic value, this violence echoes – whether unwittingly or not – the stated aims of government policy. They are ideologically connected to the policies which express these same things as desired outcomes, albeit in different ways, and inflict serious social harms in order to achieve them.

This is manifested, for example, in the intensification of workfare policies and benefit sanctions, in conjunction with other methods of welfare 'reform', which, in their attempts to force people into deregulated, flexible labour markets, routinely lead to death (see Chapter 4 by Jon Burnett and David Whyte). According to some estimates, 80 people per month die shortly after being declared 'fit for work'.[24] It is manifested in the immigration policies which, well before the EU referendum, had already successfully managed to reduce people to units of labour (with EU citizens initially denied access to things like housing benefit and losing the right to reside if out of employment after certain periods, and non-EU nationals subjected to other forms of conditionality), and are utilised to remove those who no longer fulfil their 'role' (see also Chapter 5 by Victoria Canning).

A climate of hate crimes in contemporary Britain is therefore supported and sustained by austerity politics in a context where the blame for an economic crisis is deliberately targeted against the most vulnerable groups. Thus, the targeting of benefit claimants can merge with certain forms of racism and ultimately be mobilised to render the most precarious sections of the workforce more compliant and 'flexible'.

The individualised hate that is given increased legitimacy under the context of austerity cannot be divorced from the institutional violence that is accelerating in the name of austerity.

NOTES

Websites were last accessed 2 December 2016.

1. Macer Hall, 'MILLIONS of EU migrants grab our jobs: time for Brexit to FINALLY take control of our borders', *Daily Express*, 18 February 2016, available at: www.express.co.uk/news/politics/645052/2m-EU-migrants-grab-jobs-Brexit-take-control-of-our-borders

2. Giles Sheldrick, 'New blitz on benefit cheats', *Daily Express*, 6 April 2013, available at: www.express.co.uk/news/uk/389780/New-blitz-on-benefit-cheats

3. 'Help us stop £1.5bn benefits scroungers', *Sun*, 12 August 2010, available at: www.thesun.co.uk/sol/homepage/features/3091717/The-Sun-declares-war-on-Britains-benefits-culture.html

4. 'Brits tell Cameron: draw a red line on immigration or else', *Sun*, 18 December 2013, available at: www.thesun.co.uk/sol/homepage/news/politics/5331413/sun-yougov-poll-reveals-brits-want-halt-to-immigration-from-eu.html

5. Andrew Porter, 'David Cameron: migration threatens our way of life', *Daily Telegraph*, 13 April 2011, available at: www.telegraph.co.uk/news/uknews/immigration/8449324/David-Cameron-migration-threatens-our-way-of-life.html

6. In reference to the speech, the BNP's Simon Darby suggested that 'if we had copyright on our manifesto we'd have lawyers round his office within hours'. See 'Tories advocate BNP policy', *East London Advertiser*, 15 April 2011, available at: http://eastlondonnews.co.uk/tories-advocate-bnp-policy/

7. David Cameron, *Prime minister's Address to Conservative Party Members on the Government's Immigration Policy*, 14 April 2011, available at: www.guardian.co.uk/politics/2011/apr/14/david-cameron-immigration-speech-full-text

8. Ibid.

9. Ibid.

10. This online survey was of 100 people, of whom 87.2 per cent had experienced a hate crime. 'DHCN survey created by Katherine Quarmby', Disability Hate Crime Network, 27 July 2015, available at: http://dhcn.info/dhcn/category/articles-and-reports/

11. Diana Pilkington, 'Scroungers' rhetoric over benefits fuels abuse says charities', *Independent*, 6 February 2012, available at: www.independent.co.uk/news/uk/politics/scroungers-rhetoric-over-benefits-fuels-abuse-say-charities-6579630.html

12. '213% increase in disability hate crime "fuelled" by propaganda, say campaigners', *Welfare Weekly*, 12 January 2015, available at: www.welfare weekly.com/disability-hate-crime-fuelled-by-propaganda/

13. Hannah Corcoran, Deborah Lader and Kevin Smith, *Hate Crime, England and Wales 2014/15*, Home Office Statistical Bulletin, London, May 2015.

14. Matt Payton, 'Racist hate crimes increase five-fold in week after Brexit vote', *Independent*, 1 July 2016, available at: www.independent.co.uk/news/uk/ crime/racism-hate-crimes-increase-brexit-eu-referendum-a7113091.html

15. Johnny McDevitt, 'New figures reveals dramatic increase in hate crimes against Polish people', *Guardian*, 11 June 2014, available at: www.theguardian. com/society/2014/jun/11/polish-people-rise-in-attacks-blame-recession-politicians-media

16. 'Xenophobic violent attacks of European Union citizens in UK', Alliance Against Romanian and Bulgarian Discrimination in UK, 20 March 2014, available at: www.aarbd.org/open-letter.html

17. Corcoran, Lader and Smith, *Hate Crime*.

18. Jon Burnett, *The New Geographies of Racism: Peterborough*, London: Institute of Race Relations, 2012.

19. 'Truck driver mowed down stranger at KFC takeaway in random attack', *Hull Daily Mail*, 26 June 2010, available at: www.hulldailymail.co.uk/truck-driver-mowed-stranger-kfc-takeaway-random-attack/story-11972119-detail/story. html

20. Nick Charity, 'Britain First video of Mansfield homeless found "profane" and "evil"', *Mansfield Chad*, 20 June 2016, available at: www.chad.co.uk/ news/local/britain-first-video-of-mansfield-homeless-found-profane-and-evil-1-7972941

21. At the end of June 2016, for example, Britain First launched a 'campaign' to rid Sherwood Forest of migrants who were sleeping there.

22. Sylvia Walby, Jude Towers and Brian Francis, 'Is violent crime increasing or decreasing? A new methodology to measure repeat attacks making visible the significance of gender and domestic relations', *British Journal of Criminology*, 31 December 2015) 26, available at: http://bjc.oxfordjournals. org/content/early/2015/12/31/bjc.azv131.full.pdf+html

23. See, for example, Tamsin Rutter, 'Out in the cold: LGBT housing services devastated by housing cuts', *Guardian*, 20 May 2015, available at: www. theguardian.com/housing-network/2015/may/20/lgbt-housing-devastated-austerity-cuts-homeless

24. Frances Ryan, 'Death has become a part of Britain's benefit system', *Guardian*, 27 August 2015, available at: www.theguardian.com/commentisfree/2015/ aug/27/death-britains-benefits-system-fit-for-work-safety-net

Notes on Contributors

Leah Bassel is Associate Professor in Sociology at the University of Leicester. She is author of *Refugee Women: Beyond Gender versus Culture* (2012), *The Politics of Listening: Possibilities and Challenges for Democratic Life* (forthcoming) and *Minority Women and Austerity: Survival and Resistance in France and Britain* (with Akwugo Emejulu, forthcoming).

Emma Bond is Associate Professor at the University of Suffolk, where she is Director of Faculty Research. Emma has led research projects funded by the Home Office and the European Commission on online risk, domestic abuse and youth unemployment.

Jon Burnett is a Lecturer in Criminology at the University of Swansea. He has published widely on issues relating to forced labour, racism and neoliberalism, hate crime and medical power. He is a member of the Council of the Institute of Race Relations.

Charlotte Burns is Senior Lecturer in Environmental Politics and Policy at the University of York, where she researches environmental policy and politics. She is currently engaged in a project funded by the Leverhulme Trust investigating the impact of austerity upon environmental politics and policy in Europe.

Victoria Canning is a feminist campaigner, asylum rights activist and Lecturer in Criminology at the Open University. She is currently researching the gendered harms in seeking asylum in Britain, Denmark and Sweden and works with various organisations including Merseyside Women's Movement and Migrant Artists Mutual Aid.

Vickie Cooper is a Lecturer in Criminology at the Open University where she is Co-Director of HERC (Harm and Evidence Research Collaborative) and researches issues related to homelessness, criminal justice system, housing and eviction.

Danny Dorling is Halford Mackinder Professor of Geography at the University of Oxford. His work concerns issues of housing, health, employment, education, inequality and poverty.

David Ellis is Postdoctoral Research Associate at the University of Liverpool, where he researches issues around personal indebtedness in the UK and its historical growth in relation to welfare reform. David has collaborated in major research projects with organisations including Democratic Audit and the Law Commission.

Akwugo Emejulu is Professor of Sociology at the University of Warwick. Her research interests include the political sociology of race, gender and the grassroots activism of women of colour in Europe and America. She is author of *Community Development as Micropolitics: Comparing Theories, Policies and Politics in America and Britain* (2015) and *Minority Women and Austerity: Survival and Resistance in France and Britain* (with Leah Bassel, forthcoming).

Joanna Gilmore is Lecturer in Law at the University of York researching public order policing and community-based responses to police misconduct. She is a founding member of the Northern Police Monitoring Project, a community initiative established to monitor policing practices and provide support, advocacy and advice to the victims of police violence.

Simon Hallsworth is Professor of Sociology and a Pro-Vice-Chancellor at the University of Suffolk. He has written extensively on issues around urban violence, imprisonment and contemporary state development. His most recent book is *The Gang and Beyond; Interpreting Violent Street Worlds* (2014).

Laura Hamilton is a PhD student and researcher at the Thomas Coram Research Unit, University College London. Her research focuses on inequality, food and young people. She is also involved in a European Research Council-funded study on Families and Food in Hard Times.

Daniel Holder is currently Deputy Director of Belfast-based human rights non-governmental organisation (NGO), the Committee on the Administration of Justice (CAJ). In this role he is also Co-Convener of the Equality Coalition, the umbrella network of equality NGOs and trade unions convened by CAJ and UNISON.

Will Jackson is Lecturer in Criminology at Liverpool John Moores University. His research focuses on policing, security and protest. His current work, in collaboration with the Network for Police Monitoring, is on the policing of anti-fracking protests. He is co-editor of *Destroy, Build, Secure: Readings on Pacification* (2017).

Robert Knox is Lecturer in Law at the University of Liverpool. He is also editor of the journal *Historical Materialism* and a member of the Isaac and Tamara Deutscher Memorial Prize Committee. His primary interest are in the fields of Marxist and critical legal theory.

Ruth London spent four decades in the Global Women's Strike, Women Against Rape and then Climate Camp. Ruth helped found Fuel Poverty Action in 2011 to confront the energy giants and government policies which kill thousands in cold homes while destroying the planet.

Joanna Mack is Honorary Senior Research Fellow at the University of Bristol and the Open University. She was a member of the 2010–15 research team Poverty and Social Exclusion in the UK and runs the website www.poverty.ac.uk. She is co-author (with Stewart Lansley) of *Breadline Britain – the Rise of Mass Poverty* (2015).

Maureen Mansfield principally works in the voluntary sector, specifically women's organisations such as Women in Prison and currently with the Women's Resource Centre. Maureen is a steering group member of the Reclaim Justice Network, she is involved with Reclaim Holloway campaign and a founding member of Holloway United Therapies and Holloway Prison Stories.

Daniel McCulloch is Lecturer in Criminology and Social Policy at the Open University, where he researches issues on homelessness, poverty and the experiences of deaf and hard of hearing prisoners.

Helen Monk is Lecturer in Criminology at Liverpool John Moores University, where she is Co-Director of the Centre for the Study of Crime, Criminalisation and Social Exclusion (CCSE). Her research interests include the policing of women, women's involvement in social movements, women's experiences of sexual coercion and violence, and the formation of identity and subjectivity. She is co-editor of *Women, Crime and Criminology: A Celebration* (2017).

Rebecca O'Connell is Senior Research Officer at the Thomas Coram Research Unit, University College London. Her research focuses on food, children and families. She is co-author, with Julia Brannen, of *Food, Families and Work* (2016) and Principal Investigator of a European Research Council-funded study on Families and Food in Hard Times.

Mary O'Hara is an award-winning journalist, author and media consultant specialising in social affairs and social justice. She freelances across a number of publications and platforms in the UK and the USA, including the *Guardian*. She is author of the book *Austerity Bites* (2015) and a Fulbright Scholar.

Hilda Palmer is Acting Chair of the UK Hazards Campaign. She has worked at Greater Manchester Hazards Centre since 1987.

Kirsteen Paton is Lecturer in Sociology at the University of Liverpool teaching about class and urban sociology. She is the author of *Gentrification: A Working-class Perspective* (2014). Her recent research explores regeneration, stigma and evictions in relation to welfare reform in the UK.

John Pring is editor of Disability News Service in the UK. He is author of *Longcare Survivors: The Biography of a Care Scandal* (2011) which investigates the horrific abuse of adults with learning difficulties that took place at two residential homes.

Rizwaan Sabir is Lecturer in Criminology at Liverpool John Moores University, where he researches counter-terrorism, counter-insurgency and the 'War on Terror' in the UK. Rizwaan is a regular contributor to the media and frequently works with lawyers and advocacy groups in the UK and overseas on issues involving his subject specialism.

Joe Sim is Professor of Criminology at Liverpool John Moores University. He is the author of a number of books on prisons including *Punishment and Prisons* (2009). He is a trustee of the charity Inquest, which campaigns around the issue of deaths in custody.

Steven Speed is Lecturer at Staffordshire University and works as a writer, photographer and digital media artist. He researches social movements and is a director of Mary Burns Publishing and the co-founder of *Salford Star*.

Paul Tobin is Lecturer in Politics at the University of Manchester, specialising in European and environmental politics. His postdoctoral research was at the University of York, working on Charlotte Burns' investigation into the impact of austerity on environmental politics in Europe, funded by the Leverhulme Trust.

Steve Tombs is Professor of Criminology at the Open University with research interests in corporate and state crime and harm. He has a long-standing relationship with the Hazards movement and is a trustee and board member of Inquest.

David Whyte is Professor of Socio-Legal Studies at the University of Liverpool where he teaches and researches corporate violence and corporate corruption. He is the editor of *How Corrupt is Britain?* (Pluto Press, 2015).

Index